Library of
Davidson College

**Managing the
German Economy**

Managing the German Economy

Budgetary Politics in a Federal State

Jack H. Knott
Michigan State University

LexingtonBooks
D.C. Heath and Company
Lexington, Massachusetts
Toronto

Library of Congress Cataloging in Publication Data

Knott, Jack H., 1947–
  Managing the German economy.

  Bibliography: p.
  Includes index.
  1. Fiscal policy—Germany (West) 2. Germany (West)—Economic policy.
  3. Budget—Germany (West) I. Title.
  HJ1120.K59   332.5′23′0943   80-8888
  ISBN 0-669-04401-6   AACR2

Copyright © 1981 by D.C. Heath and Company

All rights reserved. No part of this publication may be reproduced or transmitted in any form or by any means, electronic or mechanical, including photocopy, recording, or any information storage or retrieval system, without permission in writing from the publisher.

Published simultaneously in Canada

Printed in the United States of America

International Standard Book Number: 0-669-04401-6

Library of Congress Catalog Card Number: 80-8888

To Michael and Lisa

Contents

	List of Figures	xi
	List of Tables	xiii
	Preface	xv
	Acknowledgments	xvii
Chapter 1	**The Politics of Economic Stabilization**	1
	From Economics to Politics	3
	Partisanship and Electoral Competition	5
	Political Decision Making	6
	Plan of the Book	10
Chapter 2	**German Political Economy**	15
	Sources of Economic Tradition	15
	Current Economic Controversy	22
	Partisan Conflict	25
	Federal-Political Relations	28
	Bureaucratic Politics	31
Chapter 3	**Conflicting Criteria and Loose Coupling: Planning the Federal Budget Policy**	39
	Conflicting Budget Criteria	40
	Economic Measures of Budgetary Impact	43
	Econometric Models and the Decision Process	45
	The Goal Projection and Incremental Budgeting	48
	A Fixation with the Nominal Growth in GNP	51
	Loose Coupling	54
Chapter 4	**Planning and Flexibility: Sharing Uncertainty among Organizational Goals**	61
	Planning for Contingencies	63
	Predicting the Future	64
	Extending the Conflict	66
	Providing a Special Checking Account	68
	Deciding the Macroamounts	69
	Planning and Flexibility	73

	Uncertainty, Organizational Goals, and Economic Management	74
Chapter 5	**Meeting Social Needs: Economic Management and State Budgeting**	**83**
	Fiscal Policy and State Budgets	84
	Formulating the Macrobudget Figures	89
	The Execution Stage of the Budget Cycle	93
	Summary and Conclusions	95
Chapter 6	**Federal Politics and Macroeconomic Policy Guidelines**	**103**
	The Macrobudget as a Public Good	103
	Collective Action and Federal Competition	106
	An Attempt at Joint Economic and Budgetary Guidelines	108
	From Boom to Recession	113
	Policy Preferences and Goal Projections	115
	Public Needs and Selective Interests	119
Chapter 7	**Curing Local Fiscal Pathologies through Grants in Aid**	**127**
	Evaluating Institutions and Policy Instruments	129
	Canceling Federal Policy: 1966 to 1967	131
	Individual State Differences	134
	Avoiding Reliance on Grants in Aid	140
Chapter 8	**Resisting Macroeconomic Objectives: The Regular Grant-in-Aid Programs**	**145**
	Bureaucratic Autonomy versus Executive Leadership	146
	Stabilization versus Programmatic Purposes for Grants	147
	Conflicting Budget Criteria Revisited	149
	Organizational Strategies and Interests	152
	Financial Uncertainty and State-Local Grants	155
	Organizational Processes and State Differences	158
Chapter 9	**Imposing Macroeconomic Objectives: The Antirecession Grant-in-Aid Programs**	**165**
	Two Tenets of Public Finance	165
	Budgetary Control and Fiscal Federalism	167

	Stabilization and Allocation Objectives	168
	Who Decides the Programs?	170
	The Distribution of Antirecession Funds	172
	Allocation among Expenditure Areas	175
	Uncertainty and Federal Relations	177
Chapter 10	**Bureaucratic Politics and Macroeconomic Policy**	183
	Sources of Incompatibility	184
	Accommodating Purposes	187
	Turbulence and Federal-Fiscal Relations	194
	Analysis and Interactive Politics	197
	Bibliography	203
	Index	211
	About the Author	216

List of Figures

2–1	Real Percentage Annual Changes in Prices and GNP	16
2–2	The Federal Financial System in West Germany	29
2–3	Organization of the Macrobudget and Economics Sections of the Finance Ministry	34
2–4	Organization of the Budget and Macroeconomic Sections of the Economics Ministry	35
3–1	The *Kreislauf System*	47
3–2	Gross National Product, Actual and Projected (Percentage Annual Change)	50
4–1	The Anticyclical Bias of Federal Expenditures, 1965–1979	75
4–2	Bureaucratic Structuring of the Trade-Off between Inflation and Unemployment	76
4–3	Demand and Supply of Fiscal-Policy Programs	79
5–1	Total Governmental Personnel Costs (Percentage Annual Change)	86
5–2	The Mandatory Character of Baden-Württemberg's Budget, 1976	87
5–3	Percentage Annual Change in Debt Assumption	88
7–1	Local Government Capital Investments and Personnel Expenditures (Percentage Annual Change)	132
7–2	Categorical Investment Grants of Group 1 and Group 2 States in Extraordinary Budget, 1962–1971 (Percentage Annual Change)	137

List of Tables

1–1	Political and Cognitive Uncertainties	10
2–1	Vertical Tax Distribution after Finance Reform, 1969	30
2–2	The Yearly Budget Cycle and Major Institutional Participants	36
6–1	Detailed Macroeconomic and Budgetary Guidelines	110
6–2	Economic and Budgetary Projections for the Levels of Government, 1974–1979	111
7–1	The Participation of the Federal Government, States, and Municipalities in Low-Cost Housing, 1966–1967	134
7–2	Federal-State Expenditure on Categorical Grants for Investment to Local Governments, 1966–1967 and 1969–1971	136
7–3	State Categorical Grants for Investment and Total Local Public Investment, 1966–1967 and 1969–1971	138
7–4	Categorical Investment Grants and Total Local Public Investment in Extraordinary Budget, 1966–1967	139
8–1	Financial Aid of the Federal Government to the States, 1970–1975	150
8–2	Effect of Antirecession Programs on Federal Financial Aid, 1974–1975	150
8–3	Federal Financial Aid to the States, 1974–1979	151
8–4	Unemployment Rates and Antirecession Programs, Distribution Shares, by State, 1967	159
9–1	Chronological List of Antirecession Programs	169
9–2	Share of the Antirecession Programs Going to Municipal Infrastructure	169
9–3	Federal Share of the September 1974 and 1975 Antirecession Programs Going to Each State	172
9–4	The Anticyclical Reserves of the States, August 1975	174

Preface

Macroeconomics has become an everyday feature of government budgeting. Forecasting models, economic indicators, and budget concepts, such as the full-employment surplus, occupy decision makers and animate the political debate about the budget. Whereas using the public budget to stimulate or slow down the economy used to be viewed as suspect, these practices now are taken for granted. Keynesian economics has become conventional politics.

My aim in this book is to examine the impact of economic management on budgeting. Normally this issue would be viewed the other way around. In discussions with economists, for example, most preferred to approach the subject in terms of the failings of the budget as an instrument of macroeconomic policy. From their point of view, the budget is a cumbersome instrument with which to achieve the policy goal, the content and timing of which is their main concern. The public-finance branch of economics comes closer to worrying about budgeting. A finance problem is the trade-off between the economic stabilization, allocation, and distribution purposes of the budget. The advice, however, is to keep the purposes separate with very little effort put into discovering whether this approach is desirable or feasible in practice. Understandably the general emphasis has been on policy outputs rather than on decision processes.

Political scientists, on the other hand, have extensively studied decision processes, especially in particular policy areas, but have paid less attention to macroeconomic-policy outputs. Hence we have learned a good deal about the political relations between legislative committees and executive agencies, the incremental ways of thinking about the budget, and the influence of fair shares and power configurations on resource allocations and budget change. But the impact of macroeconomic criteria has hovered in the shadows.

My interest is in the influence of these criteria: on how budgets are made, on whether and to what extent they introduce conflict into budgeting, and how these conflicts are resolved politically. In addition, policy must not be ignored: Do macroeconomic criteria change budget totals? In what ways? By studying more thoroughly the impact of macroeconomics on budgeting, we may also gain a better understanding of how budgeting influences macroeconomic policy.

An emphasis is placed on formal economic models and their application in budgetary decisions. Another ingredient is the extent to which macroeconomic priorities and timing determine budget planning and debate. The layout of the institutional responsibilities for budget policy is a third consideration. How has the growing influence of the Economics Ministry, for example, affected the traditional roles and practices of the Finance Ministry? Finally, do bureaucrats present the options and data, while political executives choose the particular mix of preferences? At what stage in the process do economic criteria enter and do they remain intact through later stages?

But as I began the study, certain elements of German political economy greatly changed my thinking on the relation between macroeconomic policy and budgeting. Since macroeconomic policy is usually the preserve of the central government, I had given little thought to federal relations, including state and local budgeting. Yet the evidence soon became overwhelming that federal political relations played an integral part in determining budget policy. Increasing capital expenditures, changing tax rates, or subsidizing industries could not be accomplished without the cooperation of other levels of government. Especially grant-in-aid strategies constitute a formidable part of the efforts at discretionary fiscal policy. The beginning of wisdom about practical macroeconomic policy in the Federal Republic is the realization that budget totals are not set solely by the Bonn government.

My analysis, then, is more than an account of political economy in West Germany or even of macroeconomic policy and budgeting. Rather the study examines the relation between analytical criteria and political decision making, investigates the effects of prediction uncertainty on long-range budget planning, analyses the influence of scarcity of resources on organizational autonomy, judges the effects of technical forecasting difficulties on goal conflict, and traces the influence of economic uncertainty on federal political relations. Organizational decision-making theory is the cement that binds these diverse elements together.

A word should also be added about the interview methodology used in the analysis. The study is based on a series of over fifty interviews conducted during 1974 to 1976 with officials in the Finance and Economics Ministries, in the Chancellor's Office, and in the Bundestag. In addition, interviews were conducted in all the German *Länder* (state governments), primarily with the budget directors but also with various finance officials in the Finance Ministries. When possible, a member of the Bundesrat, Finance Planning Council, or National Municipal Association was also contacted. All interviews were conducted in German.

The technique employed was an open-ended questionnaire that usually lasted for approximately two hours. The types of questions that were asked probed what the official does in his work, what kinds of proposals he makes, where he gets and sends information, and what special problems he has and how he deals with them. For the most part, taxes were not considered as part of the interview schedule because the decision process that determines them is independent of budgeting and would require a separate investigation.

Most of the interviews were not tape-recorded; instead I wrote out each interview immediately after its completion. The quotations in the text, therefore, are not exact translations but paraphrased versions of actual responses. In general I felt that the tape recorder prevented some respondents from providing free and open answers to the questions. To protect their anonymity further, the respondents' identities are not revealed in the text. Yet without their insights and information, this book could not have been completed.

Acknowledgments

Generous funding from the International Institute of Management in West Berlin enabled me to initiate the study of macroeconomic policy and budgeting in West Germany and carry out field research in all the German *Länder* and in the federal government in Bonn. The institute provided me with much-needed and appreciated intellectual and collegial support for my work, even during the months when I did little except study the German language and it looked as if I had made no progress at all on the work itself. I especially want to thank Fritz Scharpf, the institute's director, for critically reading my work and stimulating me to undertake the federal relations aspects of the study. His critical thinking and encouragement were invaluable for improving and carrying out the research design. I also owe a debt of gratitude to Bernd Reissert who constantly and with admirable patience corrected my factual errors and set me straight in the statistical analyses. Without his help, chapters 7 through 9 would have been less readable and accurate. In addition, I must thank Karl-Heinz Bentele for his insightful aid in interpreting the data presented in chapters 7 and 8 and for graciously allowing me to use his apartment in Bonn during my numerous trips there in 1974 and 1975.

My sincere appreciation is also given to the many civil servants in Bonn and the various *Länder* who provided the main empirical basis for the study. Their general willingness and, at times, enthusiasm in discussing the issues presented to them made my work very enjoyable and contributed immeasurably to the result.

This study, in addition, was supported by a university scholarship from the University of California, Berkeley. While at Berkeley, George Break, Guiseppi DiPalma, and Ernst Haas encouraged me at various stages of my work and made useful comments on earlier drafts of the manuscript. Their general support has meant a great deal to me. Thomas Hammond and Jonathan Bendor, at that time graduate students at Berkeley, also contributed considerably to my intellectual development and offered constant advice and evaluation of ideas. The eighth floor of Barrows Hall did not provide much in physical appearance but as a place for learning and collegiality, I have known no better.

To Aaron Wildavsky I owe the most because he more than anyone else has taught me about government and how to study it. He bolstered me at every step of the way, helped me see when I made mistakes, and showed me why when I made progress. His graduate seminar in budgeting introduced me to the politics of the budgetary process and to the centrality of organization theory in the study of public administration. Without his shared intellect and personality, the study would not have been undertaken at all.

Major revisions in the manuscript were done at Michigan State University. The Political Science Department was very kind to grant me time off from teaching, as well as secretarial support. In this respect, I especially want to thank Jerry Zemper and Karen Parry for their extraordinary efforts in handling my constant stream of material. Two colleagues at Michigan State University, Gary Miller and Terry Moe, helped me think about these issues, although they may not have realized the application to this book at the time. While I acknowledge with deep gratitude all the people who have made this book better, the burden of responsibility for any errors or omissions lies with me.

My dearest thanks are reserved for Vicki, Michael, and Lisa, the other people in my life, who missed their husband and father when he was away and made his work take longer than it otherwise would have when he was home. I complained too much, but they know I did not mean it.

1
The Politics of Economic Stabilization

If the advent of Keynesian economics and the erosion of laissez faire have created the intellectual conditions requisite for the formulation of over-all government policy, they do not by any means guarantee the political conditions necessary for its implementation.[1] —Norton E. Long

Managing the economy ceases to dazzle us with its magic. Many policymakers are impatiently awaiting an economic Einstein's deeper magic for the spell to be broken. Yet managing the economy seems to require more than further improvements in economic theory. Policy decisions too frequently fail to reflect textbook prescriptions; and policies that in retrospect do look like sound economic choices often were carried out for other reasons. The interests of policymakers do not always square with the goals of balanced economic growth. Currently policymakers seem more intent on balancing government accounts than on balancing the economy. Perhaps we are learning that to improve the management of the economy is a matter of how the government works not only a concern of how the economy operates.

Managing the economy is aimed at the goals of economic prosperity: price stability, steady growth, foreign balance, and full employment. But in practice economic management invokes fundamental political conflicts that go beyond economic preferences. One conflict is between due process and timely intervention; another is between anticyclical moves, including deficit spending, and traditionally sound financial management. If spending is to be varied in the short run to balance the economy, longer-term programmatic plans may also be jeopardized. Sometimes, however, certainty of results, for example, spending on energy sufficiently or health care, takes precedence over the economic contingency of the moment. Policymakers thus face choices between economic trade-offs and other goals of due process, equity, financial solvency, and the like, each of which has an institutional and political advocate in government and the society.

But the dimming of economic management's glimmer is not solely a matter of politics. Predicting economic events in the 1970s proved to be a difficult undertaking. The oil embargo of 1973 plus growing world-economic interdependencies have sent forecasters time and again back to adjust their models. Confidence that refined econometric models can fine-tune the economy, however, seems increasingly questionable. We have also plunged headfirst into an era of concurrent inflation and recession. The past comfort of knowing the interconnections between the major economic variables is replaced with the current frustration over *stagflation*. Knowing that only one or the other malady could occur at one time used to allow policymakers to adjust policy instruments accordingly; now a form of indecision rules, whereby inflation and recession are attacked alternatively.

These issues of the political economy of macroeconomic policy command a growing attention in the Western world, including the Federal Republic of Germany. Although the Federal Republic has fared rather well in economic performance, it has not escaped the economic uncertainties or political conflicts found elsewhere. The past decade has brought severe economic recession and periods of uncommonly high inflation by German standards. At present the country is again experiencing a flare-up of inflation and the dampening effects of the recession in the United States.

As in other western countries, these issues have also highlighted the political tension between macroeconomic-policy goals and the other priorities of budgeting. Macroeconomic policy and budgeting collide in decisions on budget totals, the public debt, and the allocation of scarce resources to specific government activities. Accommodating the goals of economic management—growth, price stability, jobs—with other significant objectives of the budgetary process—paying for programs, management control, financial solvency—is thus a main dilemma confronting policymakers. Resolving these competing budget purposes, it will be argued, makes macroeconomic policy less the product of an economic "science" of budgeting and more the result of political constraints impinging on the central government, including the complex functional federalism that characterizes the West German system.

Yet while managing the German economy must contend with the politics of budgeting, a second argument is that the budget process must also grapple with the uncertainties of macroeconomics. During certain periods, German policymakers had to rely on economic forecasts that remained reliable for only a few months. Institutional conflicts also broke out between the supporters of reducing inflation and those who placed more weight on employment. Uncertainty in economic policy thus altered aspects of the budget process in ways that affected decisions on substantive programs, financing, and federal fiscal relations.

The central focus of this book, therefore, is on the interactions between the uncertainties of economic management and the politics of budgeting, two issues that premise the decisions that produce fiscal policy for the German economy. Before proceeding to the analysis of these decisions directly, however, the theories underpinning the study of the political economy of economic management must be introduced. A comparison will be made between the theory of government found in macroeconomics and the political-party and electoral-competition theories in political science. The argument is put forward that while both approaches are invaluable for political economy, there is also a need for a closer examination of economic management from an organizational, decision-making perspective.

From Economics to Politics

Like the shift in philosophical position that often accompanies scientific breakthroughs, on a more modest scale, Keynesian economics changed many peoples' understanding of government and its relation to society. Keynes ushered in an era in which society no longer reacts passively to economic forces beyond its control. He demonstrated that through the taxing and spending powers of government, society has the potential to influence directly those economic factors that produce national income. Since a growing, stable economy presumably benefits most other societal goals as well, only a small leap of faith is required to transform government policy into the caretaker of economic well-being.

Fiscal policy, as these actions are called, is the management of the economy through the public budget. It is the transformation of government taxing and spending decisions into economic actions that affect the national product. The logic is straightforward: government taxing and spending decisions either add to or detract from the total demand for goods and services in the society, which in turn affects how much is spent of them, and hence what is earned in national income. The implications for policy are understood by even busy decision makers. To stimulate demand, the government either lowers taxes, increases expenditures, or both; to dampen demand, it does the opposite. Fiscal policy is also powerful medicine. An increase in government spending, for example, generates income for the country two to three times larger than the initial government outlay. Three decades of economic growth in most western countries, moreover, attest to fiscal policy's influence.

But the Keynesian understanding of the economy proved to be deficient in various ways. Keynesian theory, for example, does not satisfactorily deal with the monetary aspect of the economy nor with the supply side, especially productive capacity and investment.[2] The theory also makes overly optimistic assumptions about the relation between employment and prices and about the impact of world economic events on domestic demand management.[3] Although the road that Keynes paved is still trodden, its travelers must endure the inevitable discomfiture of telltale cracks and potholes.

Some economists continue to spell out Keynesian theory in great detail through the ever more elaborate construction of econometric models of the economy. Effort is put into more accurate predictions, more precise measurements, and refinements of the relations between variables.[4] Fine-tuning of the economy is the goal. But even in the height of the Keynesian Camelot, the monetarist school of thought, primarily identified with the work of Milton Friedman,[5] criticized Keynes's reliance on discretionary fiscal policy to manage the economy. More recently, the onslaught of stagflation and the dramatic rise in energy costs have brought a wider range of economists into the debate.[6]

A further serious problem with Keynes has developed over his notions of how the government operates. Embedded in his approach is an implicit theory of the state. Since the needs of the economy are supposed to drive the decisions of government, the problem of the state is subsumed under the problem of the economy. Appropriate policy responses derive not from the ebb and flow of political activity but from an analysis of the impact of government economic activity on the determinants of national income. Hence government is conceived as an important sector of the national economy in much the same way that a worker is defined as a factor of production in microeconomics. Each is a unidimensional actor that exists to serve the economy or the firm.

Viewing government as an economic sector allows economic analysis to solve the problem of prosperity in its own terms without regard for other consequences. Other noneconomic goals remain outside the framework of the problem. Goals of the analysis are postulated in advance and restricted to the overall objective of economic equilibrium. It is assumed that decision makers possess enough understanding of the relationships between the goals to place them in an ordinal utility function, represented by a series of indifference curves. Second, these goals, and the trade-offs between them, are related to each other in an integrated fashion and placed in a simultaneous system of equations. The series of equations constitute a closed system that is deductively determined by the original assumptions in the utility ordering. Finally, the task is to manipulate the variables in the equation system in order to maximize the stated goals. The purpose is to achieve the best policy mix to reach the objectives, given the constraints of the system.

A conception of government as an economic sector, however, restricts the range of values that enter into policy decisions. One value—economic equilibrium—sets the parameters of conflict. Other political values, to borrow from the language of statistics, are held constant in order to see more clearly the effects on the economy of varying taxing and spending. Politics plays a role only to the extent that disagreements arise over the major economic objectives, thereby confining conflict to the theoretical issues within macroeconomics. Left untouched by this view of government as an economic instrument are conflicts between macroeconomic objectives and other political goals, the ways these broader conflicts are resolved politically, and the effects of these processes on policy outputs.

The consequence is a divergence between economic theory and fiscal-policy practice. Since fiscal policy's domain of applicability ranges over virtually all activities of government, the application of fiscal-policy criteria affects the goals and procedures of a cross section of government organizations. Institutions responsible for making budgetary and fiscal decisions, however, must accommodate interests whose adherents will not necessarily be able or willing to adopt the best solutions for the economy; political costs and benefits may dictate otherwise. They are more likely to combine fiscal-policy objectives with other priorities to produce programs that do not conform to economic ideals but which do represent rational decisions in a give-and-take institutional and political environment. Since fiscal policy is not the only game in town (nor always the most rewarding), policymakers may refuse to play or prefer to change the rules.

Partisanship and Electoral Competition

Political influences on the practice of fiscal policy are as varied as the purposes of government. In the growing literature on the subject, the dominant emphasis is on electoral and partisan competition. Edward Tufte, for example, has shown that government efforts to increase disposable income in society tend to peak just prior to major elections.[7] Even the government's handling of stagflation is noticeably better in periods that precede elections. The political party in power also makes a difference. Douglas Hibbs works with the assumption that socialist-ruled countries tolerate more inflation and less unemployment than conservative governments and finds some support for these propositions.[8] Even choice of economic instrument depends to some extent on the political party that dominates the government. Andrew Cowart's studies demonstrate that a conservative orientation in government circles is directly related to a preference for monetary instruments to manage the economy.[9] He also finds that left-oriented regimes are more active with either monetary or fiscal policy than are conservative governments.

Although these studies are invaluable for understanding political influences on economic policy, they remain distant from the decision maker, leaving open questions of interpretation. Whereas electoral studies stress the relation of elections to changes in disposable income, managing the economy is not only done every four years but continuously. The month-by-month economic analyses, the production of forecasts, and the promotion of options come from the organizational units in the government ministries. The upper echelons of the federal bureaucracy, their interactions with the top political leadership, and their relations to important external groups concerned with economic policy form the contexts for actual stabilization and antirecession programs. These same organizational settings also have considerable influence on the implementation of what is passed.

Electoral studies also focus on the general electorate and political parties as the entities that have the most important political impact on economic management. Policymakers, however, see electoral competition as only one influence among others that determine their choices. They must not only contend with the general public but also with organized groups such as union and employer associations, the central bank, special interest groups, and so forth. A further crucial influence on the German federal government's fiscal choices is state and local government. Most budgetary fiscal policies have little impact without the cooperation of other governmental levels. Not unlike the United States, German *Länder* (state governments) and cities constitute a formidable lobby for certain subsidy and revenue-sharing practices that effect directly budgetary efforts to influence the economy.

Electoral and partisanship studies, finally, do not address the issue already alluded to of fiscal policy's impact on institutional processes and goals. What may appear as short-term measures to obtain electoral gain may instead represent real uncertainties concerning the prediction and assessment of trends in the economy. An organizational analysis, in contrast, takes into account these cognitive limitations on decision making and is centrally concerned with the effect of uncertainty on political strategies and agreement processes.

Political Decision Making

To understand fiscal policy as a political decision-making process requires a different approach from that found in macroeconomics or electoral studies. Political decision-making processes are particularly influenced by two types of factors. The first factor is a problem of cognition. The issues that policymakers face are extremely complex, yet policymakers have only limited time, money, and other resources with which to make choices.[10] Policymakers, rather than employ formal analytical–problem solving to cope with complex issues, instead adopt simplified decision rules that rely heavily on tradition, rules of thumb, analogy, and other common traits of everyday problem solving. Decision making under cognitive uncertainty is fragmented, simplified, sequential, and historical.

Fiscal policy is an example of a complex problem that is approached in this manner. To begin with, the magnitude of the figures that policymakers must comprehend are beyond the normal calculational abilities of decision units. Programs to stimulate the economy are denominated in the billions of dollars. Only through a detailed simulation can it tentatively be determined what the effects of these expenditures will be on the economy. Policymakers generally do not have the time to wait for the calculations, the inclination to pay the costs, or the confidence to trust the results. Consequently policymakers rely on simplifying norms to aid them in deciding what to do. Policymakers employ analogies to familiar situations and especially to the recent past; they also divide the decision into more manageable fragments; and they rely on judgments that reflect less a thorough assessment of economic need than an accepted and traditional approach to the problem.

Fiscal policy is also a complex problem because predictions of trends in the economy, on which fiscal policy actions must rest, often cannot be made very far in advance. During particularly unstable periods, a two- to three-month lead time is common, with forecasts adjusted several times throughout the year. So as not to overcommit themselves too soon, policymakers take a sequential approach to the problem by spending (or not spending, as the case may be) a little at the beginning of the period, waiting to see what happens, and then adjusting further responses to the updated information. Continual adjustment produces an emphasis on the direction of policy changes rather than on their magnitude. If going in one direction seems to bring good results, further moves will be undertaken. In this way, goals are not fixed in advance but gradually emerge out of an inductive process of adjusting efforts to results.

To add insult to injury, major relationships between fiscal policy variables are not well understood. That marvelous trade-off device known as the Phillips curve, which plots the relation between employment and prices, no longer works as it once did. Ambiguity in economic theory has led in turn to confusion over appropriate policy instruments. Sometimes policy has taken the form of stop-go lurches; at other times, protracted indecision. Doing the best one can under the circumstances, especially when they are unfavorable, does not guarantee a smooth ride. Yet ambiguity also serves the purpose of achieving agreement and in some ways actually facilitates the planning of the budget policy by not highlighting contradictions or inconsistencies.

Even with sufficient knowledge, however, decision makers may lack the requisite power to implement the chosen alternative that is supposed to maximize utility. Efforts to bring others into agreement with the chosen alternative adds another dimension of uncertainty to the decision problem. Policymakers must calculate the strengths and weaknesses of others and what kind of coalition is needed to achieve success. Of crucial importance is the impact of the chosen policy on political and institutional relations and preferences. Determining who opposes a proposal with what intensity and for which reasons is a complex problem in its own right. Hence the second major factor facing decision makers is a political uncertainty over who opposes and who supports a given course of action.

Fiscal policy challenges other goals and interests inside and outside the government. Not everyone in the government or the society is concerned primarily with the effects of government-policy actions on economic equilibrium. Each interest can jeopardize or facilitate a chosen course of action. Discussion, bargaining, and compromise between the most relevant interests precede final decisions. A policy option is "good" not only because it is the best choice to solve the problem; it must also generate sufficient support and agreement.

The concern for agreement prevents political decision makers from approaching a problem on its own terms as though other things were equal. They cannot afford to restrict the relevant range of values to economic goals but must also consider other important objectives. By expanding the goal domain the problem of knowing the trade-off between them or even agreeing on what some of the goals consist of becomes more difficult. As Aaron Wildavsky says, goals in politics are "multiple, contradictory, and vague."[11] While a local maximization of goals may be feasible under certain conditions, a more global maximization of goals remains out of reach. Consequently policies emerge as the results of political interactions among the major, relevant interests.

In sum, decision makers respond to cognitive uncertainty by simplifying problem-solving modes of everyday life; they react to political uncertainty by various forms of interaction—bargaining, compromise, and other forms of exchange. The best schematic representation of decision making under these different forms of uncertainty has been developed by Thompson and Tuden,[12] and later elaborated by Landau.[13] Their concern was to fit decision-making styles to different problem situations. Relying on the decision-premises approach employed by Herbert Simon, they postulate that making and executing policy decisions depend on two conditions: (1) the level of knowledge concerning cause-effect relations within a problem area; and (2) the level of agreement over goals within the problem area.

Policymakers generally do not have complete knowledge about cause-effect relations because of inadequate data and underdeveloped social theory. If they do X, they do not know that Y will follow with a known probability. But even when the requisite knowledge is available, they still are likely to disagree over the desirability of the results. They may know, for example, that A produces B and that C produces D, but they cannot agree on whether B or D is the more preferred outcome. Consequently they will exchange values until an agreed solution is reached, if at all.

The relatively rare situations of complete knowledge about and agreement on objectives, in contrast, are reserved for the stable aspects of an organization's core technology, according to Thompson. The other extreme—complete disagreement on goals and means—is also not the usual type of decision situation. It connotes a breakdown in the decision-making apparatus and calls for "crisis" measures to avert disaster to the organization. A dictator, "strong man," solution emerges that achieves agreement through coercive measures.

What are the implications of the political decision-making model of budgeting for macroeconomic policy? The most basic implication is that the decision to impose macroeconomic criteria on budget choices is based on political costs and benefits. Under relatively normal economic conditions, imposing macroeconomic criteria brings marginal benefits for the economy but high costs in other budget purposes. On political grounds, then, it is to be expected that most budget choices are judged on other than macroeconomic criteria. Yet if ignoring the economy becomes a large enough issue with heavy political costs, policymakers then should become more willing to impose macroeconomic criteria, despite the consequent disruptions in other budget purposes. Certain budget interests, however, can be expected to resist macroeconomic criteria, especially once the economy is in less danger. Moreover, ignoring other budget interests entirely is likely to lead to a strong opposition coalition against macroeconomic criteria even in the midst of economic difficulties.

When macroeconomic criteria are imposed, we should expect that they do not replace other criteria but get combined with them to produce budget policies that reflect an ambiguous mixture of interests. This means that if antirecession programs, for example, were drawn up solely on macroeconomic grounds, they would be quite different from actual antirecession policies in size, composition, and duration. Since the mixture of criteria is ambiguous, no formal trade-off device can be used effectively to determine them. Rather the particular combination that emerges is more likely to be the product of negotiations among the affected interests. Ambiguous criteria may aid in the process of reaching agreement, although the effect of ambiguity, as we shall see, is dependent on the particular decision-making context.

When macroeconomic criteria are adopted, there are costs in other budget purposes. It follows, then, that political pressures will develop to shift the undesirable budget consequences to other actors in the system. In other words, political pressures can force policymakers both to impose macroeconomic criteria and try to avoid the budget effects that are viewed as undesirable by many interests inside and outside the government. One primary avenue for shifting budgetary costs is the federal system. The federal government can try to place the burden on the states *(Länder)* which may attempt to shift it to the local governments. Trying to shift the burden internationally is also a viable strategy but probably a less successful one. These strategies, if followed, lead to tighter financial control on macroeconomic aid than is desirable in theory. They also can lead to efforts to promote individual policymaker benefits at the expense of the collective benefit—a form of "prisoner's dilemma."[14] Having one's cake and eating it too, as the old saying goes, is as rare in public policy as it is in life.

When macroeconomic criteria are imposed on budgeting, in addition, the complexity of the issues facing policymakers is likely to force the adoption of informal norms to guide policy choices. The political impetus to adopt these norms derives from time pressure to act, the importance of image and rhetoric in the policy process, and the many interests involved. But, even given more time and a less politically charged atmosphere, real uncertainties over prediction and diagnosis still remain. As a result, the various types of uncertainty can be expected to determine the tempo and substance of the political debate as much as the other way around. We will see that uncertainty, for example, shortens the time frame for budget planning and can lead to indecision over a chosen course of action. Small programs are adopted at sequential intervals that attack specific problems rather than the overall issues of the economy.

Finally, political decision making has implications for the use of formal economic models in the planning of the budget policy. The key differences between the budgetary process and economic theories are contained in the utilization of these models. The decision process is loosely connected, tends to combine priorities rather than rank them, and depends on compromise solutions. The economic models, in contrast, make mutually exclusive categories for analysis, construct tight interconnections among components of the problem, and view the economy as the highest budget priority. To accommodate their analytical needs with their decision-making needs, therefore, policymakers are willing to sacrifice some accuracy for flexibility. Paying attention to the exact form of analysis employed is crucial for understanding the relation of economic models to the particular decision-making context.[15]

Plan of the Book

West German fiscal policy reflects the interaction of a composite of conflicting interests; actions are the products of how these interests are accommodated. There are two conflict threads that make up the policy fabric. These are derived from the dichotomy between cognitive and political uncertainty contained in the political decision-making model. The first thread represents institutional and political conflict between effected groups and their support for or opposition to a chosen course of action. The second thread is based on controversies in macroeconomic theory over the understanding and prediction of cause-effect relationships in fiscal policy. How these conflict threads intertwine in the making and executing of policy is the subject of this book (see table 1–1).

Chapter 2 provides necessary historical and descriptive background. It outlines four sources of economic tradition in the Federal Republic that contribute to how economic problems are perceived and what government actions are considered legitimate and appropriate to deal with these problems. The chapter

**Table 1–1
Political and Cognitive Uncertainties**

Political Uncertainty: disagreements over political support for or opposition to fiscal-policy actions.

1. Parliamentary and regime partisan debate over the proper role of the state in the economy;
2. Government organizational conflict between the Economics and Finance Ministries, the Central Bank (Bundesbank), and the spending ministries;
3. Federalism, which provokes conflict over revenue sharing, subsidies, local autonomy, and party politics; and
4. Interest groups that fight for programmatic goals without regard to overall economic policy effects.

Cognitive Uncertainty: disagreements in macroeconomic theory over the cause-effect relationship in fiscal policy.

1. Uncertainty over the prediction of trends in the economy; and
2. Uncertainty over the diagnosis of what the trends mean for fiscal policy actions and instruments.

also describes the major economic-policy issues facing the Federal Republic and relates these issues to partisan conflict, federal relations, and bureaucratic politics.

Chapters 3 through 6 comprise the main body of the book. Chapter 3 focuses on the application of formal economic analyses in a political organization setting during the planning of the budget policy. The analysis employs Herbert Simon's concept of "tight or loose coupling" to explain the difference between decision making and analytical structures and their interaction. Chapter 4 is concerned with the implementation of budget policy. It examines the problem of predicting economic trends and shows how prediction uncertainties affect decision making and organizational relations. The hypothesis is that prediction uncertainties are distributed politically among the organizational actors.

Chapter 5 shifts the focus of the analysis from the central government to federal political relations. The chapter contrasts the state governments' conception of economic management with that of the federal government. Chapter 6 then discusses joint budget and fiscal policy planning between the states and the central government and explains the changing organizational interests of each side with varying economic conditions.

Chapters 7 through 9 are concerned with the use of intergovernmental grants in aid to manage the economy. Chapter 7 examines the hypothesis that demographic factors—size, wealth, population—might determine the variable success of grants as an economic-policy instrument. Chapters 8 and 9, however, develop an alternative political explanation for grant policies based on the political costs and benefits of imposing macroeconomic criteria on grant decisions.

Finally, chapter 10 presents a summary and conclusion of the practice of economic management in the Federal Republic and offers some recommendations for accommodating budgetary, political, and economic goals.

Notes

1. Norton E. Long, "Power and Administration," *Public Administration Review* 9 (Autumn 1949):257-264.

2. Paul Craig Roberts, "The Breakdown of the Keynesian Model," *The Public Interest* 52(Summer 1978):20-33.

3. Jude Wanniski, "The Mundell-Laffer Hypothesis—A New View of the World Economy," *The Public Interest* 39(Spring 1975):31-52.

4. Otto Eckstein, President of Data Resources, Inc., notes that econometric models do not only have a Keynesian base. "Today's models," he says, "draw eclectically on many sources, on Kuznets-Keynes-Timbergen for the income expenditure approach, on Frisch for the role of shocks in the cycle, on Hawtrey-Hayek for the effects of error on capital structure and finance, on the labors of the 1960s for better dynamic equation structures and numerous other technical

refinements." See his letter to the editor of the *Wall Street Journal*, "Value of Econometric Models," 27 August 1979, p. 13.

5. Milton Friedman and Walter Heller, *Monetary Versus Fiscal Policy* (New York: Norton Books, 1969).

6. See, for example, the article in *Time*, "To Set the Economy Right," (27 August 1979):24ff. I report these controversies, of course, not to refute or support one approach or another but merely to indicate in journalistic fashion that serious disagreements in macroeconomic theory do exist and that they add an element of uncertainty to economic policy.

7. Edward Tufte, *Political Control of the Economy* (Princeton, New Jersey: Princeton University Press, 1978).

8. Douglas Hibbs, "Political Parties and Macroeconomic Policy," *American Political Science Review* 71, no. 4 (December 1977):1467-1487.

9. Andrew Cowart, "Economic Policies of European Governments I: Monetary Policy," *British Journal of Political Science* 8(July 1978):285-311 and "Economic Policies of European Governments II: Fiscal Policy," *British Journal of Political Science* 8(October 1978):425-439.

10. David Braybrooke and Charles Lindblom, *A Strategy of Decision* (New York: The Free Press, 1970); Charles Lindblom, *The Intelligence of Democracy* (New York: The Free Press, 1965) and "The Science of Muddling Through," *Public Administration Review* 19(Spring 1959):79-88; Herbert Simon, *Administrative Behavior* (New York: The Free Press, 1965); James Thompson, *Organizations in Action* (New York: McGraw-Hill, 1967); and John Steinbrunner, *The Cybernetic Theory of Decision* (Princeton, New Jersey: Princeton University Press, 1974), especially ch. 2-5.

11. For Aaron Wildavsky's understanding of goals in the policy process, see his *The Politics of the Budgetary Process* (Boston: Little, Brown and Co., 1964); "The Political Economy of Efficiency: Cost Benefit Analysis, Systems Analysis and Program Budgeting," *Public Administration Review* 26, no. 4 (December 1966):292-310; "Rescuing Policy Analysis from PPBS," *Public Administration Review* 29(March/April, 1969):189-202; and "Policy Analysis Is What Information Systems Are Not," *New York Affairs* 4(Spring 1977):10-23.

12. James Thompson and Arthur Tuden, "Strategies, Structures and Processes of Organizational Decision," in James Thompson et al., eds., *Comparative Studies in Administration* (Pittsburgh: University of Pittsburgh Press, 1959).

13. Martin Landau, "Decision Theory and Comparative Public Administration," *Comparative Political Studies* 1, no. 2 (July 1968):175-195.

14. Albert O. Hirschman, *Development Projects Observed* (Washington, D.C.: The Brookings Institution, 1967) and *Exit, Voice and Loyalty* (Cambridge, Massachusetts: Harvard University Press, 1970); Wallace Oates, *Fiscal Federalism* (New York: Harcourt, Brace Jovanovich, 1972); and Mancur Olsen, *The Logic of Collective Action* (Cambridge, Massachusetts: Harvard University Press, 1970).

15. Charles E. Lindblom, "Still Muddling, Not Yet Through," *Public Administration Review* 39(November/December, 1979):517–526; and Charles E. Lindblom and David K. Cohen, *Usable Knowledge: Social Science and Social Problem Solving* (New Haven: Yale University Press, 1979).

2   German Political Economy

In their economic and budgetary policies, the federal and state governments must take into account the requirements of macroeconomic equilibrium. Within the boundaries of the free enterprise system, these policies must contribute equally to a stable price level, full-employment, and foreign balance with steady, moderate economic growth.[1]

—Law to Promote Stability and Growth in the Economy

The 1970s offer a unique opportunity to analyze the vicissitudes of managing the German economy with the public budget. The seemingly unending years of strong economic expansion in the 1950s and 1960s (interrupted only by a minor recession in 1966 to 1967) came to an abrupt halt in 1974. In 1975 gross national product (GNP) fell by 3 percent; unemployment reached over the 1 million mark; and some very prominent West German companies were operating at 60 to 70 percent capacity. At the same time, inflation grew worse, as yearly rates of 6 to 7 percent became common. Near the end of 1978, the country still had not recovered completely, as economic growth rates continued to lag behind those of the 1950s and 1960s, although after 1977 the inflation rate did fall to low levels by western standards (see figure 2-1)

To stimulate the lagging economy, the German federal government passed four special budget programs during 1974 to 1975. But by 1976, due to opposition from many sides, the Federal Government Coalition had retreated from using the budget for stabilization policy. It cut investment grants to the Länder, passed no additional stimulus programs (despite continued high unemployment), and turned instead to the tax and monetary instruments. This cautious policy in Bonn generated heated debate in the country. It also led to a strict monetary policy to defend the value of the mark despite a current-account deficit in 1979 and a shrinking trade surplus.

Understanding the German response to these conditions requires a more detailed investigation of the issues and the fiscal traditions in the postwar era. The traditions differ from those in the United States, adding certain dimensions to the economic debate not found elsewhere. West Germany also has a federal structure unlike other federal systems that gives the government special problems and opportunities in managing the economy.

Sources of Economic Tradition

The economic controversy and attendant political uncertainty over the inflation and recession in the 1970s are deeply embedded in the German political economy

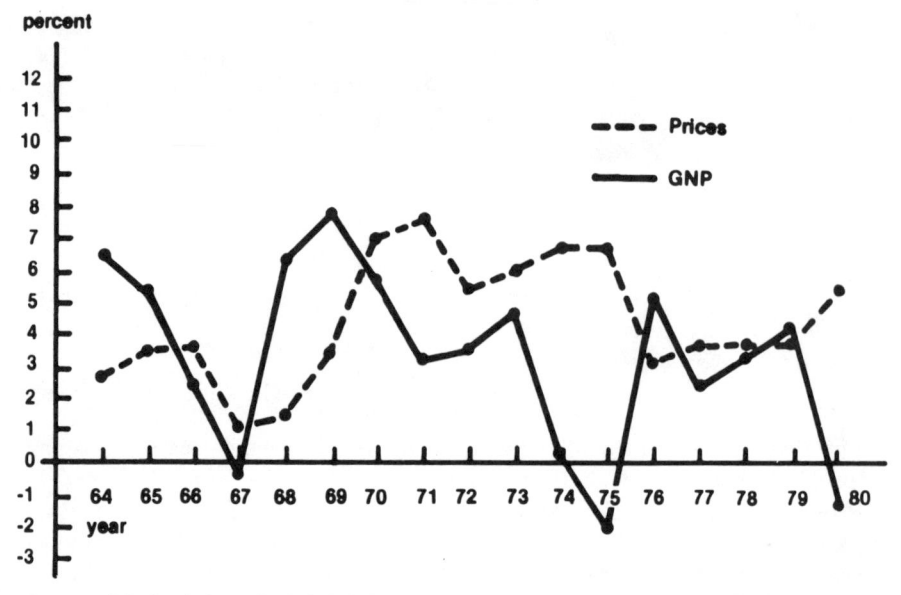

Source: Calculated from Statistisches Bundesamt, *Jahrbuch der Bundesrepublik Deutschland, 1970–1980* (Stuttgart: W. Kohlhammer Verlag).
Note: Changes of 1964 to 1970 are in 1962 prices and 1971 to 1980 are in 1970 prices. The 1980 change is an estimate.

Figure 2–1. Real Percentage Annual Changes in Prices and GNP

in the postwar period. There are four traditions in economic theory and practice that are particularly noteworthy in this respect: the corporatist tradition in which the state actively intervenes to influence investment policy in specific economic sectors; the tradition of separating policy from administration whereby the central government acts as a large analysis staff whose policy recommendations are carried out and administered by lower government levels and private industry; the conservative fiscal tradition that fears inflation, "loose" monetary policy, and deficit spending; and the more recent tradition that has developed which emphasizes macroeconomic management and business-cycle policy. Each of these traditions, moreover, finds expression in and support from the contemporary political and institutional structure.

The economic philosophy that dominated the reconstruction period was neither Marxist nor laissez-faire liberal. Marxist doctrine held little appeal because of the centralized "command" features of the East European systems, which reminded many leaders of the centralized, planned economy of the Nazis. Official government policy took the opposite course through attempts to dismantle the influence of the state in the management of the economy.

Neither was government policy based on pure free enterprise, despite the rhetoric of the first economics minister, Ludwig Erhard, who preached the virtues of private property and the superiority of the price mechanism to allocate scarcity. Actual price cartels were discouraged, but bigness and industrial concentration per se did not come under policy opprobrium. By the early 1950s, in fact, the old prewar banking and industrial conglomerates had reappeared in astonishingly similar guise.

The economic philosophy of the role of the state that emerged, known as the Social Market Doctrine *(Sozialmarkt Doktrin),* was decidedly interventionist but from a microeconomic viewpoint.[2] The neoliberal philosophy contained elements of social justice, whereby the "losers" in the market were to be compensated by the state, and elements of government regulation, in which the state would intervene to control the direction of economic activity. The emphasis was not on macroeconomic aggregates, however, but on specific targets in particular industries; and not on consumer demand, but on investment supply. Concern for full employment received less attention than the substantive needs in energy, infrastructure, and export industries. The popular phrase of today—structural, long-term adjustment—had achieved common currency already in the early fifties and meant then what it still does now: government efforts to promote investment and break bottlenecks to production in certain key industries. At that time the targets were iron, coal, and steel; today the policy is centered on nuclear power and other energy forms, high computer communications technology, and environmental protection.

The intervention of the state in the economy was not based on a formal plan, even at the microlevel. The central government would do the basic analysis of the problem and provide the overall framework for the policy, including certain incentives for relevant participants to move in the desired direction. The actual choice of projects, however, was left primarily in the hands of outsiders. With regional development loans, for example, the central government would decide the overall amount available for each state and the general loan categories, but the state governments and the private banks would do the processing of the applications and the allocation of funds. Similarly, government loans relied heavily on advice from the major banks, whose top executives occupy key positions on the boards of most major firms.[3]

The advantage of separating policy from its administration has been that the central government uses the varied resources of the private sector and local government to greatly bolster its own calculating and implementing capacity. The disadvantage has been the tendency for the administrators to make policy and not just implement it and for the policymakers to get involved in administration in order to protect their interests. The shift from budgetary to monetary policy in the 1970s, in part reflects the frustration of the central government with this policy-administration dichotomy.

The third economic tradition, that of a strict, conservative fiscal philosophy, was practiced by the postwar finance minister, Fritz Schäffer. The legacy of the Nazi regime ingrained in the public philosophy the belief that Hitler's rise to power had been precipitated by the hyperinflation and economic collapse of the 1920s. The neoliberal economic school also assumed that a successful competitive market depends on the maintenance of a stable monetary system. Perhaps not so surprisingly, the original constitution of the Federal Republic, or Basic Law as it is called *(Grundgesetz)*, stipulated that the central government must balance its accounts each year. The conservative fiscal philosophy of the postwar regime also prompted the government to take actions to balance the budget and pay for its programs without regard for their effects on national income. The consequence was a large budget surplus generated by booming German industry.

With the departure of Schäffer and the installation in office of Fritz Etzel in 1958, the "social" part of the Social Market philosophy took on greater importance. Social spending had languished due to the enormous needs of the industrial reconstruction and the conservative fiscal emphasis. Rather than lower taxes to diminish the budget surplus, known as the Julius Tower, government policy kept tax rates high, unlike the British and the Americans who passed tax cuts during this period. Increased spending occurred most notably in the old-age-pension scheme adopted in 1957 and in the large expansion of agricultural subsidies, known as the Green Plan. These forms of intervention in the economy, both the corporatist-sector development and the subsidization of various groups, social classes and regions led Hans Arndt to conclude that "economic policy can no longer be differentiated from social policy."[4]

German corporatist and fiscal traditions influenced the government's handling of the inflation and recession in the 1970s. The corporate emphasis intimately tied fiscal policy to budget policy; or in other words, joined economic management with decisions regarding allocation. Government stimulus programs in 1967 and 1974 to 1976 were not across the board but were concentrated on certain industries and regions. In 1967 it was the coal industry in North Rhine-Westphalia; in 1975 government largess fell on the construction industry, on border areas, especially with East Germany, and on automobiles, in particular Volkswagon. The German economic tradition is thus a form of fine-tuning, not in the Keynesian mode of public sector adjustments to disequilibrium in economic aggregates but in the microeconomic mold of intervention in specific sectors. Conservative financial management also shaped fiscal policy, especially during the 1974 to 1975 period when inflation remained at abnormally high levels. Again, the retreat from a stimulative budget policy in 1977 partially represented the government's intention to hold down the size of the budget deficit and work toward balance by 1980 (a goal apparently as difficult to achieve in Germany as in the United States).

Aggregate-demand management Keynesian style, to turn to the fourth tradition, came to the Federal Republic fairly late in the economic recovery. Throughout the 1950s and into the next decade, according to Andrew Shonfield, "There was no attempt . . . to make the timing of public investment fit the broader needs of economic policy for controlling the business-cycle."[5] Official government policy during this period did not focus on the usual targets of full employment, aggregate demand, or economic equilibrium. The concept of the state as a stopgap for the economy *(Der Staat als Lückenbüser der Wirtschaft)* never guided Adenaur's fiscal policy.

By 1964, however, the government became bold enough to use the phrase *deficit spending* for the first time. That year the Council of Economic Experts was also given responsibility for preparing an annual economic report and completing other analyses of trends in the economy. But unlike the American body of the same title, the German Economic Council remains aloof from the politics of fiscal policy and does not consider itself tied to the policy preferences and political fortunes of the chief of state. The yearly economic report of the council, though taken seriously by the government as an appraisal of the economy by highly respected experts, has often been criticized in its policy recommendations as too removed from political reality in Bonn. Yet its pronouncements, which often criticize government behavior, are used as important ammunition in the broader economic debate, either by the opposition party or the regime, depending on the position the council has taken.

A similar function is performed by certain prominent, independent economic-research institutes, such as the German Economic Research Institute in West Berlin. (Other prominent economic-research organizations include the Allensbach Institute for Public Opinion Research, the Ifo Institute for Economic Research in Munich, and the Institute of World Economics in Kiel.) These institutes provide yearly assessments of the economy as well as do contract work for the government. Like the Economic Council, however, the government can often ignore their advice, although they do offer crucial outside information for the parliament, which has little research capacity of its own. In addition, official regime projections and forecasts must compete with outside information generated by the state governments, labor unions, and industrial associations. Each of these bodies brings a certain perspective to its outputs, and especially in the case of the state governments and business and labor entities, the projections are made with an eye on collective-bargaining and revenue-sharing agreements. As the other partner to these negotiations, the central government must also treat its projections as bargaining tools to attain certain goals, not merely as supportive data for economic management.

The separation of the council and the research institutes from the government has had the further consequence that government analyses and projections tend to be closed from outside input and discussion until they are officially adopted as policy. By worrying that expert economic analysis would be co-opted (and therefore biased) if it were too closely associated with the government, the designers of the system reinforced the opposite effect; namely, the isolation of the government from possibly desirable outside participation. Hence, while multiple analyses and projections compete in a broader political context, actual government policy is formulated by a relatively restricted group of in-house, career civil servants. Neutrality is nice, but there is a fine line between co-optation and contributory input.

The turning point in the development of the public budget as a macroeconomic instrument was 1967. In that year, the government passed the Stability and Growth Law for the Economy. The law laid the legal foundation for a discretionary, anticyclical-budget policy and served as the basis for the changes in the Basic Law and the Finance Reform which took place in 1969. The latter two changes contained important action-forcing mechanisms to reorient the budget to economic management.[6]

The Stability and Growth Law and the constitutional and budgetary changes that followed affected economic policy in four areas: they established a mechanism for the creation of monetary reserves to counteract swings in the business cycle; abolished the old legal restrictions on borrowing by the federal government; created new institutions for joint federal financial planning; and led to the legal basis for using intergovernmental grants in aid as discretionary fiscal-policy instruments.[7]

The anticyclical-reserve funds *(Konjunkturausgleichsrücklage)* were the centerpiece of the new policy. The reserves enabled the government to freeze a certain percentage of its tax yield at the Bundesbank, drawing these funds out of market circulation. The effect, when the amount is great enough, reduces disposable income and slows down economic growth. The mechanism works as follows: The federal government with the approval of the Bundesrat (the Upper House of Parliament) can issue an executive order to declare that it and the state governments must contribute up to 3 percent of last year's tax yield to the anticyclical reserves. The federal government also has the right to raise (or lower) the income-tax rates by 10 percent (sections 26 and 27 of the Stability Law) and place the added revenue in the special-reserve fund. The accumulated reserves may only be spent in recession periods to cover spending programs designed to stimulate the economy *(Konjunkturprogramme)*. During the 1974 to 1975 recession, for example, the existence of the reserves proved invaluable for coaxing nervous state governments into participating in joint federal-state antirecession budget measures. Since these funds cannot be released without the concurrent approval of the federal government, the states do not get the money unless they go along with the federal government's fiscal-policy programs—an effective carrot-and-stick arrangement.

Political pressures, on the other hand, have inhibited the intended functioning of the reserve mechanism. The federal government passed a special law *(Das Stabilitätszuschlaggesetz)* in 1972, for instance, that released the accumulated reserves at a time when the economy was growing rapidly and consumer demand was strong. The federal government then used the funds not for business-cycle spending programs but for rebates to the taxpayers, a move to ease the political situation. The federal government also attempted to raise tax rates 10 percent and use the proceeds for its own purposes without the approval or participation of the states.

The stability law further mandated a change in article 115 of the Basic Law that placed restrictions on borrowing by the federal government. The old provision gave the federal government no legal basis for a deficit. The implementation of the Finance Reform, in constrast, allowed credit financing up to the officially designated level of investment expenditures, or beyond in the event of economic necessity, effectively removing any legal challenge to deficit spending. As a result, the change in the constitution made the definition of legitimate borrowing a political judgment in the economic debate.

Further consequences of the 1967 to 1969 reforms concerned federal-political relations. Two new intergovernmental institutions were established, the Finance Planning Council and the Business-Cycle Council. The purpose was to improve the coordination of financial and debt planning between the various levels of government and especially to bring the lower levels into the management of the economy. Since anticyclical spending and borrowing by the federal government could in principle be offset (and often was offset) by budgetary priorities of the state and local governments, planning a joint–budget policy was seen as essential for a sound fiscal policy.

The Finance Planning Council is composed of the various finance ministers of the state and federal governments along with representatives from the national municipal associations. Its task is to meet at specified intervals throughout the year in order to make yearly and multiyear budget plans and overall economic projections. The Business Cycle Council, on the other hand, consists of the respective economics ministers and deals primarily with short-term impacts of government fiscal activities on the economy. But because of the finance ministries' domination of budgeting, especially on the state level, this aspect of even short-term budget activity has increasingly resided with the Finance Planning Council. Consequently the council has gradually found itself torn between longer-term budgetary planning and short-term economic management.

The economic and budgetary reforms, finally, brought intergovernmental grants in aid into the fold of economic-policy instruments. Although the states and the federal government possess independent budget authority (article 109, Basic Law), throughout the postwar period the federal government's categorical investment grants programs to the states continued to grow. (It is forbidden to give federal grants directly to the municipalities.) The 1969 Finance Reform legitimized these extraconstitutional–cofinancing schemes in a program called Joint Tasks *(Gemeinschaftsaufgaben)*. Of greater import for fiscal policy, however, was the creation of special Financial Aid Programs *(Finanzhilfen,* article 104a4) for the express purpose of countercyclical–economic policy. Since the more traditional Joint Tasks are heavily regulated and governed by joint federal-state, semi-independent commissions, they lack the flexibility and short-term perspective required for fiscal policy. The 1974 to 1976 stimulus-investment packages placed heavy emphasis, therefore, on the newly established Financial Aid Programs.

In sum, aggregate-demand management with its focus on full employment arrived relatively late in West German economic practice; but rather than replace older philosophies entirely, it came to represent an additional value, albeit an important one, existing in tension with other preferences. These tensions in turn are reinforced by institutional divisions at the federal and state government levels and between the finance and economics ministries and the spending ministries. While the government no longer faces a legal constitutional requirement to balance its budget, a political interest still persists in a conservative fiscal and monetary policy. The peculiarly corporatist tradition of the Federal Republic, which emphasizes state intervention into the market economy on the microlevel, also ties fiscal policy to allocation preferences. Substantive planners, therefore, view unkindly short-term aggregate measures that jeopardize their special allocation priorities.

Modern, aggregate-demand management has also raised questions about the Federal Republic's traditional structure, which consists of a large, concentrated private sector and a relatively smaller, decentralized public sector. The federal government, especially, has a smaller budget and limited powers compared to other western countries. Fiscal policy thus adds another impetus to the argument for enlarging the geographic size of the state governments (by reducing the number of states) and centralizing fiscal authority in Bonn. Resultant tensions in federal-political relations cause local authorities to view federal macroeconomic pronouncements as wolves in sheeps clothing, fearing that the economic proposals conceal federal-government intrusions into their autonomy. Advocates of centralization, on the other hand, see the federal system as an anachronistic artifact of western-power occupation that goes against German tradition but, more importantly, hinders the macroeconomic-policy functions of the modern state.

Current Economic Controversy

The optimism generated by the 1967 to 1969 economic and budgetary reforms dissipated in the 1970s. Macroeconomic management proved to be more difficult than anticipated and the newly created instruments less efficacious.[8] Three developments were particularly disturbing to a leadership and populace that had grown accustomed to steady economic growth with no inflation. Economic growth came to a halt in 1974, pushing the economy into the worst postwar recession. Much of the loss was centered on the export market, which comprises over 20 percent of gross national product. Of equal concern was the persistent increase in prices between 1970 to 1976, spurred by the sharp rise in the cost of energy. And finally, the resultant economic argument that broke out over the causes and cures for the inflation and recession left leaders with little confidence that policy measures would succeed in the short run.

The fundamental economic dispute centered on the causes of the recession and the appropriate means for responding to it. If the best economic theories were to be believed, inflation and recession were simply not supposed to occur simultaneously. But in 1973 the impact of the oil–price rise reverberated throughout the European economies, pushing up prices and pulling down production.

Although West Germany experienced a rather mild inflation compared to other prominent European countries, the rates (which hovered around 6 to 7 percent) were high enough to raise real fears in a population that remembered (or had been taught) the collapse and hyperinflation of the 1920s.

The government thus found itself in a serious political dilemma. If it followed the standard Keynesian doctrine of deficit spending its way out of the slump, inflation would surely increase beyond the politically acceptable limit. Following a restrictive course offered no better prospects. Unemployment had surpassed the 1 million mark in 1974, a political threshold in its own right beyond which few leaders felt very comfortable.

Confusion over stagflation was coupled to a deeper worry about the competitiveness and vitality of the German economy. Many policymakers and economists believed that the recession came about because of structural deficiencies in the economy rather than through the normal fluctuations in the business cycle. These prophets of doom saw the 1974 downturn as merely the beginning of a much longer period of slow, uneven growth. The party was over, they thought; people must adjust from the economic miracles of the fifties and sixties to the necessities for economic survival in the seventies and eighties. Short-term economic stimulus of the traditional variety, far from aiding the economy, might actually cause harm.

There were two main components to the structuralist argument. The first was that the West German market had become saturated with everyday industrial products, such as automobiles, appliances, televisions, and so on. Further rapid expansion in production would outpace consumer demand; only fickle shifts in product tastes would provide movement in the market. The second component was the fear of cheap competition. The strength of the German mark plus the relatively high pay of German workers meant that several standard industrial products could be produced cheaper and more efficiently in less developed countries. This foreign competition was expected to intensify in coming years.[9]

The structuralists opposed the injection of short-term stimuli into the economy. What they wanted was a major long-term restructuring from medium-technology products to high-technology ones. The West German economy should produce fewer cars, machine parts, and appliances, they believed, and more computers, telecommunications systems, nuclear reactors, and other sophisticated products. Short-term stimulus measures only hindered the necessary structural changes that inevitably would take place. No less prominent institutions than the Ministry of Science and Technology and the Redevelopment Bank *(Kreditanstalt für Wiederaufbau)* beat the structuralist drum.

Was the recession foreign caused or domestically produced? This argument enervated the political parties. The drop-off in production was centered in export sales, especially to the United States. If the recession was foreign based, many government officials and economists reasoned, further government stimulus would only exacerbate domestic excess capacity, thereby worsening inflation.

A policy of stimulating exports also had its drawbacks. Despite the export decline, West Germany still maintained a surplus on the trade account. In 1980 this surplus had even turned to a slight deficit. The slowdown had not put pressure on the German mark but had taken pressure off the American dollar. A resurgence of exports could conceivably introduce renewed strains into the international monetary system, forcing further revaluations of the German mark against the dollar thus threatening worse slowdowns in the future.

The controversy over the recession's causes inevitably led to sharp disagreements over the proper cure. Each option—lowering taxes, increasing the volume of money, increasing expenditures—had its detractors and its supporters. For many, monetary policy did not receive much higher marks. The culprit was the European capital market. West Germany is not a large country that can insulate itself from world economic trends or from the monetary policies of its neighbors. Previous experience with monetary policy had demonstrated that actions taken abroad frequently have offset domestic-policy measures. Not until 1976, therefore, following two years of heated dispute over the use of the public budget for fiscal policy, did the government turn reluctantly to monetary policy as the primary instrument for dealing with the economy.

The economic dispute also leveled its sights at public spending. If the government were to follow the Keynesian preference for stimulating demand, the short-run pressure on prices would increase. Besides, the automatic stabilizers built into the modern public budget already primed the demand pump. Unemployment compensation in particular jumped dramatically during this period, forcing the Labor Ministry to seek a supplemental appropriation late in 1975. Public-works projects were contemplated, too, but they especially raised the inflation spectre. Discretionary spending, therefore, was concentrated on the supply side. The so-called business-cycle programs *(Konjunkturprogramme)* heavily emphasized public investment in construction and private investment in new equipment and plants.

The inevitable counterargument ran: subsidies to private firms do not increase employment; by rationalizing production procedures, the labor component actually is reduced, thus worsening employment in the short run by the very means designed to improve it. A corollary antisupply side argument was also heard: investment is defined too narrowly as the purchase of things: equipment, plants, machinery, buildings. Investment in people—better teachers, administrators, police officers, and so forth—is just as important but is neglected because of the difficulty of measuring the immediate returns. These people costs, so this argument runs, are viewed by investment mongers as mere consumption expenditures, when in fact they are important investments.

The fundamental disagreements over the diagnosis of and cures for the problems of the economy were coupled with a severe inability to predict economic trends with any accuracy more than a few months in advance. Policymakers knew that economic production was headed down once it occurred, but they did not know how far down it would go or for how long. Policymakers also had trouble predicting changes in price levels. Would prices continue to rise, or level off and begin to decline? No one knew for sure.

These issues—foreign competitiveness, inflation, the deficit, uncertainty, and unemployment—persist to the present, despite medium good growth years in 1976 to 1979. The 1973 oil-price increase that led to the recession of 1974 to 1975 is being repeated in the oil-price rise of 1979. In both instances, the monetary authorities have taken a strong defensive position on the mark and have allowed unemployment to ease upward. For 1980 German economic growth once again is estimated to be negative, at -1.0 percent, while prices increased 5.5 percent over last year, an unacceptably high level for German politics. The currently shrinking German trade surplus also intensifies the structuralist and business-cycle debate and poses even greater difficulties for economic management. In 1980 the trade surplus was estimated to amount to only $6 billion, while the current account deficit is $-15 billion. The prospect of increased public borrowing to deal with the 1980 to 1981 slowdown in turn raises fears in the long-term capital markets, since the federal deficit in 1979 was still estimated at a hefty 29.5 billion DM. Thus while the figures are not as bad as some other countries, the stagflation issue figures prominently in the policy debate and partisan politics.

Partisan Conflict

Conflict over economic policy divided the major political parties throughout the postwar period. Two large parties and one smaller party have held regular positions in the federal cabinet.[10] The largest party grouping is the Christian Democratic Union (CDU) in alliance with the Christian Social Union (CSU) of Bavaria. The CDU/CSU presided over the building of the successful free-enterprise, market economy after the devastations of World War II; in periodic coalition with the much smaller Free Democratic Party (FDP), it held power in Bonn continuously from the end of the war until 1966. It then joined the other large party, The Socialist Party of Germany (SPD) to form the "Grand Coalition," which lasted for three years until 1969, when the SPD gained enough strength to govern alone in coalition with the smaller FDP. This SPD/FDP coalition has remained in power in Bonn to the present, winning the 1980 election by the widest margin ever.

The CDU is largely identified with the social-market philosophy of the fifties and sixties. The party is a friend of big business and big banking, enjoying considerable support in the Federation of German Industry, an association dominated by the larger industrial and financial conglomerates. It also maintains a strong tradition of fiscal conservatism, despite the gradual acceptance of Keynesian thinking under Ludwig Erhard and later under Kurt Kiesinger during the

Grand Coalition. The party places heavy emphasis on capital investment, states rights, and price stability. It accepts economic management but not at the expense of these other more fundamental goals.

Inflation and the subsequent recession in 1974 and 1975 prompted the opposition party, CDU/CSU, to attack the Bonn government for economic mismanagement. From 1969 to 1973, the German economy had grown at a rapid 10 to 12 percent per year. Bonn's economic-policy response sought to hold down government spending, especially on the capital expenditure side. But several factors militated against holding down total expenditures. In 1965 through 1969 public–investment spending had grown dramatically, partly because of the antirecession-investment programs of 1967 but also due to increasing tax revenues and strong demand. These investments, however, led directly to sharp increases in labor and maintenance costs that became regular features of the public budget. Consequently the SPD/FDP inherited strong expenditure growth which it could do little about.

The SDP/FDP was not entirely blameless for the magnitude of budget growth. Once in office, it embarked on a program to raise salaries and wage benefits to public employees along with efforts to expand the social-welfare system. As a result, investment expenditures as a percent of total government outlays declined noticeably during this period, whereas consumption expenditures, and particularly personnel expenditures, increased significantly.

The 1974 to 1975 recession also smattered the federal government's budget plan for the first time with red ink, a situation that has persisted to the present. (The deficit for 1979 was 29.5 billion DM.) Like the earlier large increase in personnel costs, the SPD/FDP did not entirely control this development nor foresee its full extent. A Tax Reform bill passed the Bundestag in 1974 aimed at removing some of the worst inequities in the tax code. In accomplishing its purpose, the bill also lowered tax rates to yield savings of approximately 11 billion DM and initially was criticized on all sides as inflationary. Once the recession set in, however, the tax cut, now viewed more favorably, contributed to the deficit, along with the surge in spending for unemployment compensation. The main discretionary contribution by the regime was the passage of periodic stimulus-investment programs, referred to earlier.

From the perspective of the CDU/CSU, these policies contributed greatly to the current economic problem. The government's failure to adequately maintain investment was viewed as partially responsible for the economic slowdown and served as an important element in the CDU/CSU's argument that the recession was "home grown." The increases in wage settlements and overall personnel costs coupled with additional social expenditures was also seen as a key cause of the inflationary pressure afflicting the economy.

With these attacks, the opposition sought (unsuccessfully) to woo the FDP away from the government coalition. The courting of the FDP, however, gave the smaller partner in the coalition more independence than it otherwise would have had and put pressure on the SPD to keep the coalition together by adhering to the middle road in economic policy—an uncomfortable position for large segments of the party.

The SPD had a long tradition of leftist opposition to CDU/CSU economic policy. The SPD's opposition to the CDU/CSU directed market economy derived from the military division of Germany after the war. In the interwar period, the SDP had been the largest single party but lost much of its old constituency to the German Democratic Republic (GDR) in the east. The SPD thus opposed the remilitarization of West Germany as well as the reconstruction of a separate market economy oriented toward Western Europe and the United States. The SPD also espoused a Marxist economic philosophy that favored central planning and the nationalization of basic industries.

But developments made it clear to the SPD that it would have to modify its hostile opposition to the free-enterprise–economic system, if it ever hoped to come to power in Bonn. Beginning with the currency reform of June 1948, the brainchild of the CDU Finance Minister Ludwig Erhard, the economy had shown remarkable vitality, and citizens turned their energies to the emerging "economic miracle" instead of preoccupying themselves with the division of the country. The result was the Godesberger Program, adopted by the SPD leadership in 1959, which moved the party from a leftist, worker orientation to a broader, popular political base. From a position of constant criticism of the CDU/CSU, the party gradually moved toward compromise and cooperation. It began working with the CDU/CSU in the Bundestag and voted for bills which it favored, even if they had been sponsored by the government. In response, the CDU/CSU modified its opposition toward the SPD, paving the way for the Grand Coalition in 1967.

The effects on economic policy came slowly but were perceptible. The mild recession of 1967 was fought with two large government-expenditure programs; budget deficits began to appear, and economic and financial planning procedures were introduced in the Finance Reform of 1969. With the subsequent formation of the SPD/FDP coalition, economic policy moved further away from the conservative, fiscal tradition. Under the SPD Finance Minister, Karl Schiller, public–wage settlements became larger and social spending increased.

Greater government spending and the retreat from fiscal restraint created tensions in the government coalition. As the 1974 recession set in, the FDP began to advocate a policy of tax incentives for private business as a way to promote investment. For those in the FDP who favored the structuralist interpretation of the recession, the private market was preferred to active government intervention. The FDP also tended to see inflation as a greater enemy than unemployment, calling on its liberal, free-enterprise traditions to support its opposition to big government. The only area of economic policy in which the SPD and the FDP found agreement was in the contention that the recession had not been caused by government policies but had been imported from abroad.

Yet the SPD was not only pressured from the right of the political spectrum. The party's younger members, active in the Young Socialist Movement, became more and more vocal in their criticism that the exercise of power by the party's leadership had compromised the party's fundamental socialist traditions. This attack from the "new left" gained momentum when Helmut Schmidt, a practical government manager and former finance minister, replaced Willy Brandt as chancellor, who had been and still remained the intellectual leader of the party. Chancellor Schmidt thus faced a sizable minority in his party that opposed any compromise with the FDP on economic-policy issues. Because the SPD did not have enough votes in the Bundestag to govern alone, however, a hard-line policy that did not take into account FDP preferences meant political suicide in the short run. It thus has been Schmidt's successful balancing act on economic-policy issues that has taken him and his party through the 1976 and 1980 elections triumphantly.

Federal-Political Relations

The management of the economy with the public budget inevitably involves federal-political relations—the major uncertainty in the organizational environment of the federal ministries.[11] Two facts stand out: three-quarters of total public spending, including 85 percent of total public investment, are spent by the state and local governments; and five out of eight of the major state governments (excluding the two city-states, Bremen and Hamburg) are dominated by the opposition party, the CDU/CSU. If the federal government intends to increase or decrease public spending to offset trends in the economy, aside from a few areas in which it has prominence such as the military, it must obtain the co-operation of the states and municipalities. But since the majority of these are governed by the opposition party, the usual central-local institutional barriers to agreement are overladen with political-party conflicts. Less favorable conditions for the exercise of macroeconomic policy would be hard to find.

West Germany has a functional federal system in contrast to the United States which has geographic federalism. In practical terms, this means that the federal government is primarily concerned with the formulation of policy. Most federal ministries in West Germany, with a few important exceptions, have no field offices, familiar to regional capitals in the United States. Consequently the federal budget is relatively small in comparison to state and local budgets. Most federal policies also have financial implications for the state governments.

The means by which the federal government can influence state and local spending are limited. One option is the joint budget planning carried on in the Finance Planning Council. As a vehicle for imposing federal fiscal-policy priorities on lower levels of government, however, the council lacks the necessary clout. Its recommendations have no binding character and have frequently been violated by the members. But achieving agreement through consultation and persuasion, as chapter 6 demonstrates, depends on many factors beyond the control of the federal government.

The other major avenue at the federal government's disposal is grants in aid. These can be broken down into categorical investment grants and general purpose, revenue-sharing grants (see figure 2–2). The latter are regulated by the Financial Equalization Laws *(Finanzausgleichsgesetze)* based on standard-distribution formulas. The revenue-sharing system comprises the vast bulk of intergovernmental transfers. Taxes are collected by the central administration and distributed to the states, which in turn disburse a share of their income-tax revenue to the municipalities (see table 2–1). But since these transfers are regulated by law and based on standard formulas, varying amounts for fiscal-policy purposes, (see chapter 7), poses grave political and constitutional difficulties for the federal government.

Categorical grants offer the most likely mechanism to impose fiscal-policy priorities on the local governments but, in this instance also, various restrictions prevent their full use for this purpose. To begin with, the federal government

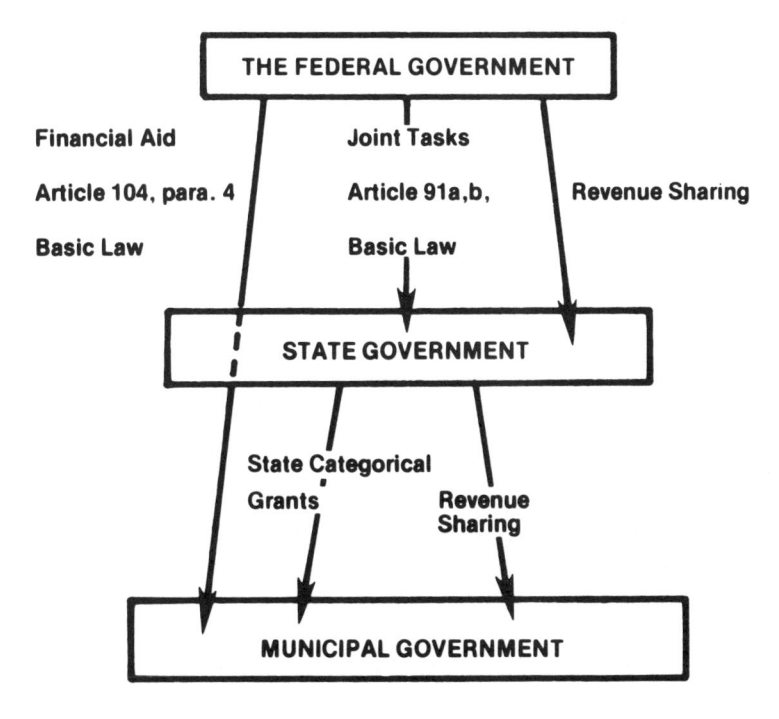

Figure 2–2. The Federal Financial System in West Germany

Table 2–1
Vertical Tax Distribution after Finance Reform, 1969

Major Types of Taxes	Federal	State	Local
Income tax	X	X	X
Sales tax	X	X	
Business tax	X	X	X
Customs tax	X		
Property tax		X	X
Consumption tax	X		
Fiscal monopolies	X		
Motor-vehicle tax		X	X

may only give subsidies to the states, not to the municipalities. Most of these are contained in the Joint Tasks, which do not easily suit fiscal-policy needs, as indicated already. Only through the special Financial Aid Programs does the federal government possess an instrument capable of influencing local government procyclical spending behavior.

The implications of the federal system for the practice of fiscal policy go beyond grants in aid. Because tax revenues are shared according to the expenditure needs and requirements of each government level, each level, and especially the state and federal levels, compete over tax income. Slowing down the growth of state spending to dampen a boom may mean an unfavorable shift in the tax distribution away from the states. Federal-government investment subsidies that push up state and local spending may boomerang in lowering tax receipts at the federal level. Consequently the distribution and type of expenditure, which are normally allocation issues, are intimately tied up with macroeconomic management.

There are also important partisan, political considerations that animate the federal financial system and which have led to a deterioration in federal relations. The SPD came to power in Bonn in 1969, but the state governments remained dominated by the CDU/CSU. This turn of events, plus the 1969 Finance Reform, have given the states an important avenue for political opposition to federal fiscal policy. The Finance Reform stipulated that any measure passed by the Bundestag (the Lower House of Parliament) which has financial implications for the states requires the approval of the Bundesrat. But unlike the U.S. Senate, whose members are elected by popular vote, the Bundesrat membership is appointed by the state administrations. Membership in the Bundesrat is also not based on a fixed number of representatives from each state but is determined by a type of proportional system based on certain population thresholds. Traditionally the Bundesrat is supposed to be primarily a technical body to advise the federal government in the formulation and especially the implementation of policy, but the party split strengthened the Bundesrat as a source of political opposition.

Thus barriers to federal cooperation are formidable. The fact that the states administer policy gives them a very different institutional orientation than that of the federal government. The political-party split reinforced the institutional conflict. There is also considerable competition between the levels of government over tax revenue and in particular over the sales-tax distribution, whose formula is determined every two years by statutory laws. Hence, the wonder is not that the federal government does not always pursue policy according to the strict guidelines of macroeconomics but rather that it has pursued fiscal-policy goals to the extent that it has.

Bureaucratic Politics

The federal government must work with the states and municipalities to manage the economy with the public budget, but it alone is responsible for the formulation and promotion of actual policy measures. Before worrying about the states, therefore, fiscal policymakers must contend with the relevant organizational units in the federal ministries. There are two organizational factors that determine the process of gaining support for a chosen course of action: the decentralized federal organizational structure; and the small size of the federal bureaucracy.

Agreement on policy is not centrally planned nor mandated by directive from the chancellor's office.[12] The Federal Republic's cabinet form of government disperses power over policy formulation among various ministries. Unlike the United States, the chancellor, as head of the cabinet, does not preside over a large executive-office staff that serves as the main center for new legislation, policy planning, and management control of the bureaucracy. Instead key ministries take over these functions, forcing the chancellor to ally with them to govern successfully. Financial control over the federal bureaucracy, for example, is exercised by the Finance Ministry, whose head, the finance minister, plays a dominant role in the cabinet and is often a political figure of only slightly lesser eminence than the chancellor himself. Likewise, agricultural policy, economic policy, environmental policy, and so on are planned, supported, and promoted by these respective ministries.

Dispersion of power over policy does not mean that the cabinet operates according to the theoretical norm of a collegial committee of ministers with the chancellor as the chair of the meetings. Certain policies and ministries are more important politically than are others, and positions of power in these areas are given to key political leaders in the coalition. These leaders thus form a subgroup in the cabinet, which takes responsibility for major policy decisions. Prior to the 1976 election, this inner group consisted of Helmut Schmidt and Hans Apel (the chancellor and finance minister respectively, both members of the SPD) and Hans Friedrichs and Hans Dietrich Genscher (the economics and foreign ministers, both members of the FDP leadership). After the election, Apel became minister of defense, while Hans Matthoefer took over the finance job. Otto Graf Lambsdorff also replaced Friedrichs as economics minister. In addition, this inner circle also includes key party and parliamentary leaders, such as Herbert Wehner, the chairman of the SPD party faction in the Bundestag, and Willy Brandt, the chairman of the SPD. These leaders meet regularly in formal sessions and informally and comprise the nucleus of top government policymaking.

The cabinet's organizational structure also works against full cabinet decision making. Each general policy area, such as economic or social policy, is organized into interministerial cabinet subcommittees that prepare proposals and meet independently of the whole body. In the economic-policy area, the members of the economic cabinet might include the finance minister, the economics minister, the chancellor, and the labor minister. Achieving success in the cabinet involves first and foremost the support of the relevant members of these particular subcommittees. If the subcommittee has the backing of the inner circle, the full cabinet is unlikely to overturn its proposals.

Ministerial government affords to the senior–civil servants a central role in public policy. The ministries are relatively small in comparison with cabinet departments of other countries, with the Finance Ministry being the largest; it had only 1800 personnel in 1976. Each ministry is organized hierarchically into divisions *(Abteilungen)* which are divided into subdivisions *(Unterabteilungen)*. These subdivisions in turn are comprised of several sections, known as *Referate*. An average ministry will have five to ten divisions with ten to twenty subdivisions, each containing approximately five to seven sections. The sections are small working groups that rarely have more than five to ten members and sometimes fewer. While the structure is hierarchical, it is not excessively so, for the various sections exist on the same plane, and the members (with the exception of the section head) relate to each other on a collegial division of labor basis.

Civil servants as a rule spend their entire career in one ministry and often within one division. Lateral entry is less common than in the United States, except for political appointees, but the number of appointees is far below what is available to the incoming U.S. president. The federal government, therefore, relies heavily on its in-house technical expertize with very little turnover or movement among ministries. Inevitably strong institutional loyalties and perspectives develop even within a single ministry, while at the same time colleagues in other divisions and ministries are familiar figures to each other.

Stretching the point a bit, these ministries may be conceived as large policy-analysis staffs in contrast to the giant administrative departments, with their numerous field offices and thousands of personnel, common in the United States. To create a roughly analogous organizational structure in an American context would require the retention and enlargement of the White House staff, the executive-office staff, and the staffs of the department secretaries; and the dispersion of the remaining departmental functions, with the exceptions of the post office and the military, to the state governments. Hence the familiar policy-administration conflict fought in the United States between the presidency and the cabinet departments, in the Federal Republic is carried out between the federal government and the states.

Conflict over budget policy is centered on institutional and policy issues. The policy conflict derives from the multiple purposes of budgeting and the efforts by the adherents of each purpose to achieve their goals. The institutional conflict is based on the contrary political interests that develop around the institutional roles and organizational structures that embody these different purposes. These conflicts are resolved for the most part by back-and-forth interaction through discussion, consultation, and argument between the various ministries, divisions, and subdivisions involved in economic and budgetary policy formation. Eventually an acceptable policy is forged. No single organization has complete jurisdiction over all the purposes of the budget taken together; rather each adjusts its own interests to the preferences of the other organizations involved in making budget policy.

Finance Ministry budget examiners, for example, are steeped in detailed allocation issues. They work in subdivision B of the Budget Division which contains numerous sections that reflect the various activities of government: defense, social welfare, education, and so forth. Section leaders in this subdivision hold meetings with their counterparts in the spending ministries to determine how much should be spent on what in each policy area. Officials who work in subdivision A, in contrast, are concerned with macrobudget policy, financial-control issues, and the broader allocations of the total budget. And more recently, division I, which deals with longer-term financial planning, has added economic-analysis and forecasting sections as a counterweight to analyses done by the Economics Ministry (see figure 2–3).

The size and composition of the budget also has important implications for federal-political relations and monetary and debt policy. Officials who work in these areas (divisions V and VII) care less about detailed allocation issues and more about the impact of the budget on revenue-sharing and debt management. One works closely with the state governments, and the other with the Bundesbank, thus bringing somewhat different perspectives to the discussions than those of the Budget Division and the Financial Planning Division. Reaching agreement on a budget plan initially entails accommodations among these various Finance Ministry interests.

The Finance Ministry looks at the budget first and other concerns second; the Economics Ministry reverses the order: it looks at the economy foremost and considers the budget only to the extent that it influences economic policy. For Economics Ministry officials who work in division I, which deals with macroeconomic and business-cycle policy, the composition of the budget is less important than the budget totals. Their contacts with the Finance Ministry, therefore, are mostly centered on the macrobudget and forecasting units and hardly at all with the program-oriented allocation sections. Officials in one subdivision (sub-

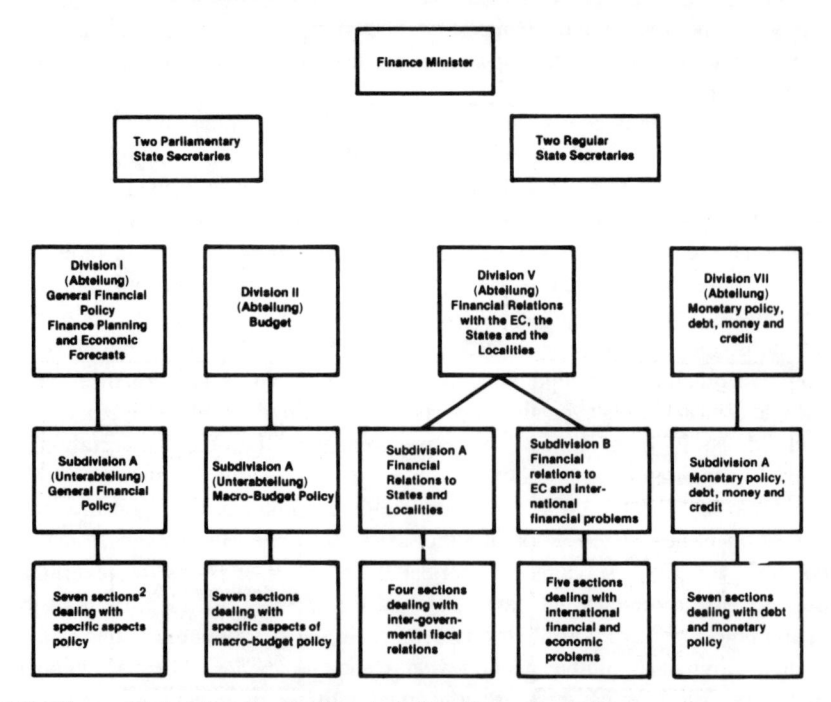

```
                    ┌─────────────────┐
                    │ Finance Minister │
                    └─────────────────┘
          ┌──────────────────┐   ┌──────────────────┐
          │ Two Parliamentary │   │   Two Regular    │
          │ State Secretaries │   │ State Secretaries│
          └──────────────────┘   └──────────────────┘
```

Division I (Abteilung) General Financial Policy Finance Planning and Economic Forecasts	Division II (Abteilung) Budget	Division V (Abteilung) Financial Relations with the EC, the States and the Localities	Division VII (Abteilung) Monetary policy, debt, money and credit
Subdivision A (Unterabteilung) General Financial Policy	Subdivision A (Unterabteilung) Macro-Budget Policy	Subdivision A Financial Relations to States and Localities / Subdivision B Financial relations to EC and international financial problems	Subdivision A Monetary policy, debt, money and credit
Seven sections[2] dealing with specific aspects policy	Seven sections dealing with specific aspects of macro-budget policy	Four sections dealing with inter-governmental fiscal relations / Five sections dealing with international financial and economic problems	Seven sections dealing with debt and monetary policy

[1] The Finance Ministry has nine divisions, including twenty-two subdivisions.
[2] Each section *(Referat)* has a section leader and assistants.

Figure 2-3. Organization of the Macrobudget and Economics Sections of the Finance Ministry

division A) are responsible for the development of specific policy instruments and specific business-cycle programs, while the other officials concerned with macroeconomic management (subdivision D) carry out the forecasts, statistical analyses, and goal projections (see figure 2-4).

Similar to the Economics Ministry, officials in the chancellor's office work mostly with budget totals and not with the details of particular budget areas. The office has two divisions that deal with economic and budget policy. Division IV contains economic and budgetary experts, some of whom used to work in the Economics and Finance Ministries. Division V of the chancellor's office, on the other hand, houses planning and political advisors whose main task is to worry about the political fortunes of the SPD regime and the application of SPD programs to government policy. Consequently the chancellor's office adds still another perspective to budget policy: partisan ideology and electoral politics.

Interministerial committees attempt to give some coherence to this bundle of interests.[13] The Interministerial Working Group on Macroeconomic Fore-

German Political Economy

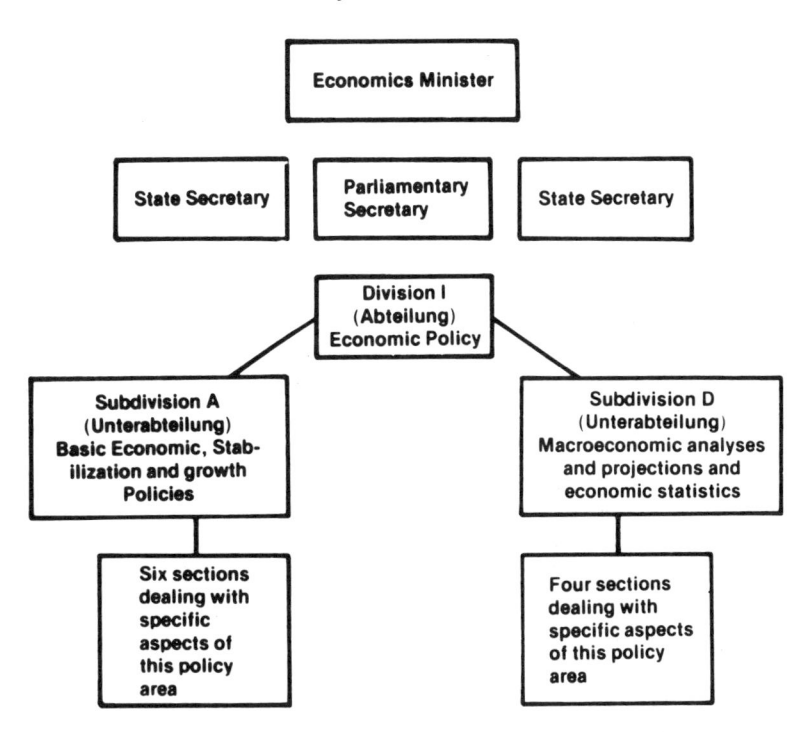

```
                    ┌─────────────────────┐
                    │ Economics Minister  │
                    └─────────────────────┘

┌────────────────┐  ┌────────────────┐  ┌────────────────┐
│ State Secretary│  │  Parliamentary │  │ State Secretary│
│                │  │    Secretary   │  │                │
└────────────────┘  └────────────────┘  └────────────────┘
                    ┌─────────────────────┐
                    │     Division I      │
                    │    (Abteilung)      │
                    │   Economic Policy   │
                    └─────────────────────┘
┌────────────────────┐              ┌────────────────────┐
│   Subdivision A    │              │   Subdivision D    │
│  (Unterabteilung)  │              │  (Unterabteilung)  │
│ Basic Economic,    │              │ Macroeconomic      │
│ Stabilization and  │              │ analyses and       │
│ growth Policies    │              │ projections and    │
│                    │              │ economic statistics│
└────────────────────┘              └────────────────────┘
┌────────────────────┐              ┌────────────────────┐
│ Six sections       │              │ Four sections      │
│ dealing with       │              │ dealing with       │
│ specific aspects   │              │ specific aspects   │
│ of this policy     │              │ of this policy     │
│ area               │              │ area               │
└────────────────────┘              └────────────────────┘
```

Notes: The economics Ministry contains a total of six divisions including twenty-one subdivisions. Each section contains approximately four to ten persons including a section leader *(Referent)* and assistants. The section is known as a *Referat*.

Figure 2–4. Organization of the Budget and Macroeconomic Sections of the Economics Ministry

casts and Short-term Prognoses *(Arbeitskreis Gesamtwirtschaftliche Vorausschätzungen)*, which meets at the beginning of December, oversees the preparation of the short-term economic projection for the following year produced by the Economics Ministry. Then the Tax Estimate Committee *(Arbeitskreis Steuerschätzung)* adopts these projection results for its first estimate in December to February but finds that it regularly has to reexamine these estimates throughout the coming year (see table 2–2).

The general outlines of the budget are known once the Finance Ministry negotiations with the spending ministries are completed, usually in late spring or early summer. These prospective budget amounts must then be reexamined in light of the updated economic projections. The most important analytical exercise for this purpose is the yearly goal projection, which usually takes initial form in late May or early June. In addition, the general outlines of the budget that are emerging from the negotiations must now be reviewed in light of the updated estimate of tax yields.

Table 2-2
The Yearly Budget Cycle and Major Institutional Participants

Month	Ministries	Finance Ministry	Finance Cabinet to Full Cabinet	Economics Ministry	Other
Formulation phase November	lower ministry officials begin budget planning; last updating of the Finance Plan				
December to February	formulation of the ministries budget proposals; transfer of the proposals to the Finance Ministry	budget recommendations sent to top ministry officials; development of the basic economic and budget guidelines (*Grundannahmen*)	passage of the yearly economic report (*Jahreswirtschaftsbericht*)	preparation of the yearly economic report; formulation of short- and middle-term economic forecasts and projections	Interministerial Working Group on Macroeconomic Forecasts and Short-Term Prognoses; Interministerial Working Group on the Tax and Income Estimates
Negotiation phase March to May		examination of the budget proposals; discussions with the ministries; settlement of disputed issues	consultations and discussions of economic and budget policy	improvement and review of the projections throughout the year	
June to July		review of economic data and guidelines; preparation of the macrofigures of the budget proposal; updating of the Finance Plan	final report and recommendations of the Finance Cabinet presented to the full Cabinet		both working groups review estimates and prognoses
Decision phase August to November		presentation of the budget proposal and the Finance Plan to the Cabinet	Discussion and passage of the government's budget proposal; presentation of the government's budget proposal to the Bundesrat		

The tax-yield estimate is not the end of the adjustment process but rather the beginning of further adjustments. If the actual budget that is emerging does not fit the economic projections, changes may have to be made by the Economics Ministry and then renegotiated with the Finance Ministry. The budget must also be accommodated to the debt policy and federal-political relations as well as possible electoral or partisan developments. The budget policy that results is not planned in advance but represents numerous compromises and adjustments to the interests and goals of the participants.

These are the organizational structures and general decision processes for managing the economy with the public budget. The question is: What kind of fiscal policy do they produce?

Notes

1. Law to Promote Stability and Growth in the Economy. Passed by the Bundestag with the concurrence of the Bundesrat on 8 June 1967, first paragraph (Gesetz zur Förderung der Stabilität und des Wachstums der Wirtschaft).

2. Hans-Joachim Arndt, *West Germany: The Politics of Non-Planning* (Syracuse, New York: Syracuse University Press, 1966), especially chapter 3. See also Frederick Reuss, *Fiscal Policy for Growth Without Inflation* (Baltimore: Johns Hopkins University Press, 1963) for an analysis of the discriminatory nature of tax policy in the recovery.

3. Andrew Shonfield, *Modern Capitalism: The Changing Balance of Public and Private Power* (London: Oxford University Press, 1965), especially chapter 11 on West Germany.

4. Arndt, *West Germany*, p. 46.

5. Shonfield, *Modern Capitalism*, p. 267.

6. See, for example, *Das neue Haushaltsrecht* (Bonn: Bundesministerium der Finanzen, 1969); T. Maunz, G. Duerig, and R. Herzog, *Grundgesetz Kommentar* (Munich: C.H. Beck'scher Verlag, 1973); Kommission für die Finanzreform, *Gutachten über die Finanzreform in der Bundesrepublik*, 2nd ed. (Stuttgart: W. Kohlhammer Verlag, 1966); and Fritz Naschold, "Untersuchung zur Mehrjährigen Finanzplanung des Bundes," *Gutachten* (Bonn: Projektgruppe Regierungs-und Verwaltungsreform, 1971).

7. Two valuable studies of the budgetary process are: Hans Clausen Korff, *Haushaltspolitik: Instrument Oeffentlicher Macht* (Stuttgart: W. Kohlhammer Verlag, 1975); and Albrecht Zunker, *Finanzplanung und Bundeshaushalt: Zur Koordinierung und Kontrolle durch den Bundesfinanzminister* (Frankfurt am Main: Alfred Metzner Verlag, 1972).

8. Heinz Markmann and Diethard B. Simmert, eds., *Krise der Wirtschaftspolitik* (Cologne: Bund-Verlag, 1978).

9. American Enterprise Institute for Public Policy Research, *A discussion with Herbert Giersch: Current Problems of the West German Economy 1976-77* (Washington D.C., 1977); and Joachim Starbatty, *Stabilitätspolitik in der freiheitlich-sozialstaatlichen Demokratie* (Baden-Baden: Nomos, 1977).

10. See Heino and Ursula Kaack, *Parteien Jahrbuch, 1973-74: Dokumentation und Analyse der Entwicklung des Parteisystems der BRD* (Meisenheim am Glan: Anton Hein Verlag, 1978).

11. David P. Conradt, *The German Polity* (New York: Longman, 1978); and Nevil Johnson, *Government in the Federal Republic of Germany: The Executive at Work* (Oxford: Pergamon Press, 1973).

12. Renate Mayntz and Fritz Scharpf, *Policy Making in the German Federal Bureaucracy* (New York: Elsevier, 1975).

13. Heribert Schatz, "Auf der Suche nach politischen Problemlosüngsstrategien: Die Entwicklung der politischen Planung auf Bundesebene," in *Planungsorganization: Die Diskussion um die Reform von Regierung und Verwaltung des Bundes,* Renate Mayntz and Fritz Scharpf (Munich: R. Piper, 1973), pp. 22-28. The Committee for Macroeconomic Forecasts is composed of representatives from the Federal Statistical Office, the Economics Ministry, the Finance Ministry, and the Central Bank. The president of the Statistical Office is the chairman, but the actual operations are run by the Economics Ministry. The Working Group makes forecasts twice yearly. The Tax Estimate Committee is headed by the Finance Ministry and has the following membership: Economics Ministry, Federal Statistical Office, Central Bank, representatives of the state governments, the leading economic-research institutes, the National Municipal Association, and the Council of Economic Experts.

3

Conflicting Criteria and Loose Coupling: Planning the Federal Budget Policy

We tend to choose the middle way. . . . If we set 2 percent as a goal (for the GNP growth rate), we may believe 4 to 6 percent is possible; if we set zero growth, it could be a 2 percent decline.[1] —Official in Chancellor's Office

Applying macroeconomic criteria to the public budget is a two-sided problem. On the one side, macroeconomic managers must determine the proper spending totals in the budget in view of the requirements of the economy. These decisions occur during the planning stage of the budget process. The policy problem consists of adjusting forecasts of trends in the economy to predictions of what macrobudget figures are expected to look like. Since both budget and economic estimates vary and can be altered by actions of the government, the problem is to set realistic and politically acceptable targets for each sector. In the Federal Republic, judgments about these targets are combined in the yearly *Goal Projection (Jahresprojektion),* a document that fuses political preferences and economic analyses. The *Goal Projection* is the economic guide to the upcoming budget and is produced six to nine months before the budget goes into effect.

The other side of the fiscal-policy problem is *fine-tuning:* adjusting the macrobudget to shorter-term changes in economic trends. Suppose that in the later phases of the planning process (which lasts approximately twelve to eighteen months) or in the execution phase, the economic trends change, calling for budget responses from the government. The policy concern at this point is not with the total figures in the coming budget, for these amounts are pretty well fixed. Instead the need is to adjust spending around the planned amounts through the passage of supplementary budget programs or budgetary cuts.

This chapter deals with the problem of applying macroeconomic criteria to judge the budget during the planning phase. The subject is the impact of the political decision-making process on the use of formal economic analyses to make fiscal-policy judgments. Chapter 4 then looks at fine-tuning during the implementation phases of the budget process. Here the issue is reversed: How do the uncertainties of analysis affect decisions concerning the budget? And since the state governments spend and administer most of the federal-budget programs that are agreed upon, chapter 5 analyses the effects of fiscal-policy–decision making on state budgeting.

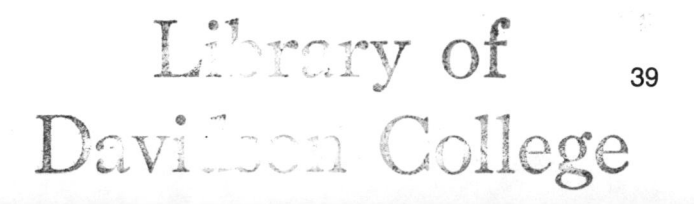

Conflicting Budget Criteria

Analysis is a major input into economic management. To make judgments about fiscal policy, policymakers must have information on economic trends and the impact of the public budget, including tax changes, spending shifts, debt, and borrowing. These analyses are carried out in the respective organizational units in the Economics and Finance Ministries responsible for fiscal-policy decisions. They are then brought together in the interministerial committees concerned with tax and income estimates and macroeconomic forecasts. Without these analyses, policymakers have no estimate of what economic problems exist, much less what actions might be taken to deal with them.

But analysis, because it is used for government fiscal policy, must compete in the complex and conflict-ridden arena of budgeting. Although Keynesian economics defines the public domain as a sector of the economy and the public budget as an economic document, budgeting serves many other purposes, many of which are highly political in nature. Budgets are used to fund programs, force ministries into line with government policy, and allocate scarce resources among competing interests.[2] Thus budgets serve as plans, as records of the past, as conflict-resolution mechanisms, and much more. Unfortunately the multiple purposes of budgets do not all complement each other. Emphasis on one budget purpose in fact jeopardizes the achievement of the others.[3]

Budget purposes compete because judgments about the budget are based on conflicting criteria. What is a "good" budget for the budget examiner in the Finance Ministry may represent a "bad" result for the budget officer in the spending ministry. Typically, the Finance Ministry acts to guard the public purse by applying financial and management-control criteria to budget judgments.[4] Spending ministries, in contrast, are advocates of doing more to solve the policy problems in their task areas and employ substantive criteria to assess budgets. There are also political and planning criteria. For the political executives, who gets funded is always of paramount importance. Planners, on the other hand, look to the longer term and feel uncomfortable with either temporary efficiency measures or political posturing. Budgetary–decision making, therefore, is a matter of accommodating conflicting criteria that are embodied in contrary political and organizational roles.

Not recognizing this political uncertainty inherent in budgetary–decision making makes budget behavior difficult to comprehend. The most familiar manifestation of this behavior is the practice of *padding*. Spending ministries are inclined to ask for more than they expect to get, knowing that the Finance Ministry will cut their requests. The Finance Ministry in turn proposes a budget below what it is willing to fund, suspecting that the spending ministries have padded their requests. Thus while budget behaviors have the manifest goal of funding government activities, they also serve the latent political purpose of accommodating conflicting criteria.

Managing the economy adds another criterion that conflicts with the more traditional views of the budget. If spending is cut back to dampen demand in the economy, the reductions may threaten worthwhile programs. If spending is speeded up to "pump prime" the economy, the increases may overturn recently adopted financial-control measures. Similarly trying to gear spending to the business cycle gives an economic–time referent to budget planning. Moreover, political pressures compress time horizons to a few months, especially during a recession—citizens want actions now to reduce unemployment and stimulate consumer demand. Yet these short-term measures often have longer-term lasting effects. Finally economic management places emphasis on budget totals (the macrobudget) rather than on the detailed composition of budgets. And just as guardian and advocate roles develop in the budgetary process, so economic-management roles evolve that have their own institutional and political adherents.

Macroeconomic and budgetary roles in the German system are centered in the Economic and Finance Ministries. Until the 1967 to 1969 reforms, the Budget Division in the Finance Ministry had exclusive jurisdiction over federal-budget policy; it played the guardian role. By the late 1960s, however, two new interests emerged. One was multiyear financial planning and the other was economic management. Division I (the Planning Division) in the Economic Ministry was assigned economic-management functions including economic aspects of budget policy.[5] The Finance Ministry, perceiving a threat to its traditional role, established its own Division I to deal with budget policy and the economy. Not to be left out, the chancellor's office also created an economic management unit in Division IV, the Budget Division.

Conflicting criteria and multiple goals are accommodated in the German bureaucracy through back-and-forth discussion and negotiation. Most policies originate at the section level. Each section has only four to six members, including a section head *(Referatleiter)*. Schmid and Treiber provide the following description of the Bonn bureaucracy: "Often the policy areas of individual ministries overlap each other to a considerable extent. . . . The overlapping may be quite functional because in this way the consideration of varying perspectives is guaranteed institutionally."[6] An organizational structure of small–decision units and overlapping jurisdictions raises the problem of agreement. Schmid and Treiber also describe the decision phases of program development in the federal bureaucracy "as (an) iterative, political process . . . (whereby) program development oscillates from one phase to another and in which single phases are often repeated."[7] Not unlike the United States, policymaking and budgeting in the Federal Republic involves iterative, sequential, and fragmented decision processes.[8]

The importance of analysis for making fiscal-policy decisions raises the question of the relation between analysis and the political and institutional features of the budget process. One way of approaching this question is to look at the literature on the use of analysis to make budgetary-allocation decisions. In the United States, this literature is mostly focused on such decision-making reforms as program budgeting and program evaluation. In both instances the impact of the decision process on the use of analysis has been considerable.[9]

Two main themes of these investigations into decision-making reform are the incompatability between analysis and politics and the general superiority of analysis as a mode of problem solving. Reflecting the first theme, Paul Diesing argues, for example, that analytical decision making evaluates a proposal on its own terms, according to how well it solves a problem.[10] Political decisions, in contrast, are not based on the substantive merits of a proposal but on who stands to win or lose by it. Similarly Harold Garfinkel maintains that scientific and political decisions do not fit well together without fundamental sacrifice to each other's logic and purpose.[11] A scientific procedure demands single-minded pursuit of factual accuracy and theoretical clarity, while politics involves compromise and ambiguity. E.S. Quade, who is supportive of the second theme, maintains further that "analysis offers an alternative to 'muddling through' or to settling national problems by yielding to the strongest pressure group."[12] From this view, politics makes only a negligible contribution to sound problem solving and may even hinder the best solutions.

But the general belief in the incompatability between analysis and politics is slowly giving way to a more integrated view that politics and analysis each make a unique contribution to problem solving. For politics, this contribution in many respects is like the contribution that the market makes in economics.[13] Both markets and political decision making are forms of social interaction that operate through numerous independent actions to coordinate and simplify complex problems. Interaction in simple form is very close to unthinking action, such as the tossing of a coin to decide a situation. But voting or bargaining rules in politics and free-market competition in captalist economies are also forms of interaction. While these actions occur among social groups, they are far from devoid of analysis.

The value of this distinction is the recognition that both analysis and interaction work in tandem. They can be used together for solving problems. In other words, analysis and politics are not just contradictory rationalities but also complementary problem solving modes:

> Our argument [is] that analysis and interaction are both competitive with and complementary to each other . . . analysis is not simply to be undertaken against a background of political and social processes. Analysis and the other social processes both carry the burden of problem solving for society, and society chooses among various combinations of the two.[14]

Certain types of analysis may not fit well with certain types of interaction; the two must be appropriate for each other. But one does not necessarily need to replace the other. In many circumstances interaction may be preferred to analysis, while in other instances analysis may supplement interaction.

How different combinations emerge is still an open question. Efforts to choose different combinations, according to Wildavsky, are constrained by limitations on knowledge and power.[15] Without the political power to act, analysis cannot be applied. Likewise, an uncertain knowledge base leads to unintended consequences. Hence without sufficient knowledge to make the necessary calculations and constrained by contrary political interests, management-analysis systems, such as PPBS and MBO, have failed to achieve the impact on decision making anticipated by their founders.

To answer this question of the relation between analysis and politics in macroeconomic policy, the issue of power is addressed first: What is the impact of political decision making on the use of analysis? Three types of analyses are examined—formal measures of budgetary impact; econometric models of the national economy; and economic goal projections—each of which is relevant to one or more aspects of macroeconomic policy. The approach will be to see how budgeters and economic forecasters perceive the use of these economic analyses to assess budget policy. The investigation, however, will lead us to examine other important forms of information beyond these formal models.

Economic Measures of Budgetary Impact

An enlarged number of participants in the budgetary process complicates the problem of finding satisfactory criteria for planning the macrobudget policy. Indicative of the problem has been the readiness of the spending ministries to take advantage of the fact that macroeconomics offers them a counterargument to cuts in their budgets during times of recession. In the 1975 recession, for example, some ministries publicly opposed cuts in their budgets and even advocated significantly greater spending, thereby undermining the financial and administrative control of the Finance Ministry.[16]

The Finance Ministry's difficulty derived from the fact that available methods for calculating the proper economic impact of the public budget on the private economy do not agree with one another. In the United States, the most commonly employed measure of economic impact is known as the full-employment-surplus-budget, a concept that has not achieved much use in the Federal Republic. A measure developed by the Council of Economic Experts, known as the neutral budget, enjoys much greater attention. This measure works in the following way. In a base year the share that public expenditures comprise of the total production potential in the economy is determined. If in subsequent years expenditures grow at the same rate as the production potential, the development is considered to have a neutral effect on the economy. The income side of the public budget is considered to have no effect on the economy if the income grows subsequent to the base year at the same rate as the growth in GNP. The rules do not imply, however, that a constant share of GNP is a prerequisite for fiscal neutrality. As long as increases in expenditure and income are balanced with each other according to the criteria given, an increasing state share of GNP will have no effect on the business cycle.[17]

But, according to West German policymakers, the full-employment-surplus budget or the neutral budget only give the proper direction for expenditure growth—either expansionary or contractionary.[18] A Finance Ministry economic forecaster explained: "These concepts do not tell you how large the deficit should be in absolute terms. Whether it should be 25 or 35 billion cannot be determined."

An official in the Economics Ministry supported his colleague: "A difference between 30 to 40 billion is not easily distinguishable. Basically, the purpose of these concepts is to indicate the direction, either expansionary or contractionary."

The imprecision of economic criteria caused budgeters to express concern about using economic measurement as a basis for the budget policy. "As yet economic science has not developed a correct measure or criterion for the effect of the public budget on the economy," said one official, "when uncertainty exists in the scientific area, it is difficult to introduce these concepts into the political–decision process."

Some officials seemed confused by the existence of more than one measurement concept. "When we calculate these concepts for the Federal Republic, we come to different results," one official commented. "Under one concept it seems that we must do something, and with another concept, we don't."

Another budgeter argued that, "for every measure we must have a model and a computer. . . . Two billion less taxes. What should we do? The computer must spew out what changes and policy measures are economically right. So it would be if we had a model. But in any event this is not so."

But the failing of economic measures of budgetary impact to gain decision makers' acceptance is not merely their imprecision. Most of the budget officials felt that even if a precise measure were developed, it still would not fit well with the political-decision process. The reason is that none of these measures take into account nor explain how the macroeconomic purpose of the budget should accommodate the other purposes of the budget. For the most part these measures are based on fairly complicated formulas that produce a single correct figure for the size of the public-budget deficit—a figure which often does not appear reasonable on simpler, noneconomic grounds.

A central criticism of these concepts is that the information they produce is both not useful and little understood by decision makers. An economic forecaster in the Finance Ministry expressed succinctly the commonly held opinion that, "the use of these [formal economic] concepts has a certain negative psychological effect. By this I mean that many people simply do not understand them well enough to use them in their work. This coupled with their imprecision makes them difficult to use in the formation of the public budget."

Another budget official worried "whether with such a complicated criterion one can present the budget convincingly to the public and the politicians."

"It is fully absurd to assume" exclaimed another budgeter, "that a political decision body calculates its decisions according to [an economic] formula."

A formula was not helpful in convincing spending ministries to employ an economic-management perspective in determining substantive budget priorities. Budgeters complained, in fact, that the cabinet found it easier to agree on economic goals as long as specific budget measures were not mentioned. But at a later point in time, when specific budgetary items must be decided, then difficulties arise: "To have a beautiful budget—no deficit, marginal growth rate, the right impact on the economy—one must eventually make hard decisions about what is to be changed. This can be very difficult and lead to not enough money for schools or not enough money for road construction or not enough money for something else." The budget amounts the formal concepts recommended were considered too undifferentiated and based on reasoning that did not fit with the decision premises of individual officials or politicians.

These premises do not separate the financial and programmatic policy effects of expenditure change from the overall macroeconomic effects. Formal economic measures of the budget, explained a finance official, do not motivate decisions because "the measures leave a lot out of consideration. . . . The type of financing, for example, is left out of the question. The long or short-term nature of loans is also left out. Many of these features cannot be quantified in any model. What types of investment are left out. The foreign sector is not adequately considered. . . ." For macrobudgeters, questions of types of investment (in what sectors and regions and of what form) as well as policy priorities (in energy, education, or internal security) comprise the main parameters of choice.

Formal economic measures of the deficit, therefore, have only limited influence on the setting of the budget policy because they tend to produce insufficient information in imprecise form. The imprecision arises because the measures indicate direction of expenditure change but not absolute amounts. Insufficient information is produced due to the inability of the models to tell decision makers where to cut the budget or where to expand it; what kinds of investments are needed; how many policy areas should be cut and by what amounts; in what ways the composition of the debt affects the capital market; and how stabilization requirements fit with other policy priorities of the government. A formula cannot resolve most of these issues. Instead bargaining and compromise are required among the major participants. "These are only measures that are used to show that they support our conception of what the deficit should be . . ." declared a macrobudgeter. The implication was that if the information does not support their conception of what to do, they do it anyway.

Econometric Models and the Decision Process

The German Federal Government also does not employ an econometric model of the national economy. Such a model would relate variables to each other through precisely measured coefficients in a recursive system. Models of this type have the ability to measure multiplier effects from one variable onto another by taking the most common, average development in the recent past and extrapolating it onto the immediate future. They also estimate separately only the exogenous variables (mainly the foreign sector), while the rest of the values, known as endogenous, are determined within the framework of the model itself by empirically estimated coefficients that are connected to each other through a series of mathematical equations. Both the IFO Institute in Munich and the German Institute for Economic Research (DIW) in Berlin, for example, have developed econometric models for the whole economy of the Federal Republic. Despite the existence of these models, however, the federal Economics Ministry has not developed one of its own nor does it use one of the existing models for its in-house analyses. Why not? The answer is found not in what they do not do but in what they actually do.

The federal Economics Ministry utilizes a type of National Accounts Model *(volkswirtschaftliche Gesamtrechnung)* that serves as a basis for a general economic equilibrium analysis *(vollständiges Kreislaufsystem)*. The way this works in practice is that the Economics Ministry collects survey data on detailed developments in many sectors of the economy and the public sector. A simplified graphical representation of the *Kreislaufsystem* is given in figure 3–1. The data that are collected get extended to the coming year in a process that relies heavily on intuitive assumptions about expected developments in the economy.[19]

For each category, the economic analyst tries to work out, by a process of successive approximation, a reasonable or plausible congruence between supply and demand. This procedure, in contrast to an econometric model, allows for a good deal of "ad hocery" in determining the relations among variables. The main advantage of the *Kreislaufsystem*, therefore, is its detail and flexibility to adjust to changing circumstances and accommodate political preferences. The major relations in the model are not determined by formally measured coefficients but by "finger-tip feelings." An economic forecaster explained the advantage of the *Kreislaufsystem* this way:

> When you have an econometric model (for the whole economy) you get no differences; all conflict is worked in and made consistent and logical. But it doesn't work that way in reality. We look at the partial analyses and through discussions try to resolve what the main problems are. For a decision process this approach is more useful. . . . For a prognosis, a macromodel is better; for concrete measures to be taken by the government, our models work better. . . . Our work is facilitated by not fixing the relations among the variables. The outcome depends much more on our own understanding and judgment of the situation.

The discussions in the economic-budget area take place between the Planning and Budget Divisions in the Finance Ministry and between the Planning Divisions

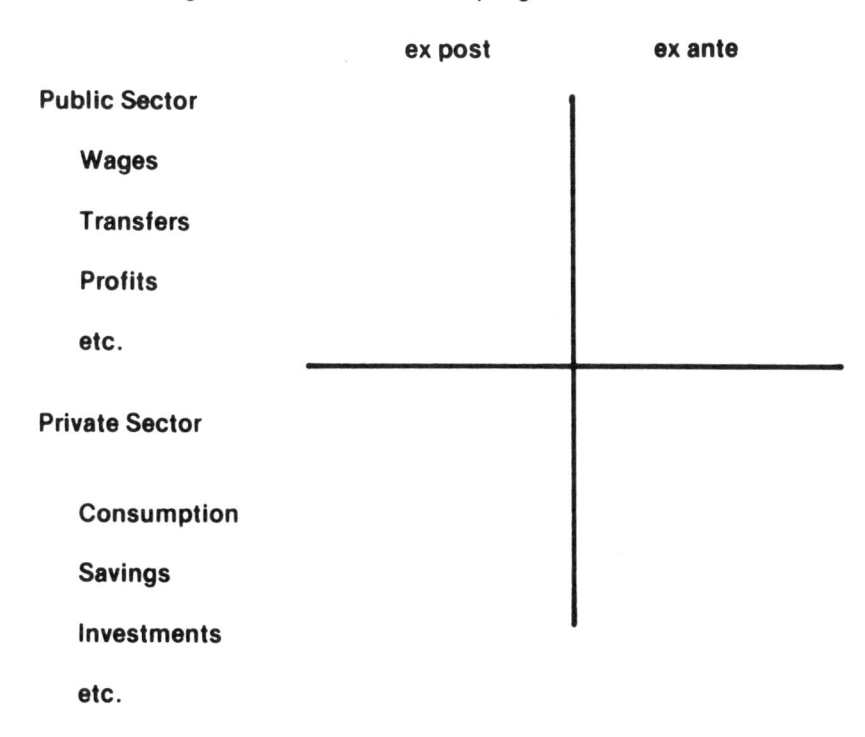

```
                        ex post           ex ante
Public Sector
    Wages
    Transfers
    Profits
    etc.
                    ─────────────────┼─────────────────
Private Sector

    Consumption
    Savings
    Investments
    etc.
```

Figure 3-1. The *Kreislauf System*

in the Economics and Finance Ministries. The Budget Division negotiates with the spending ministries in the winter over substantive budgetary issues but provides only very general financial guidelines based on the Finance Planning Division figures. At the same time, the Economics Ministry begins its work on estimating the major features of the economy for the coming year: wages, investments, the foreign sector, consumption, and so forth. Once these analyses are completed, they are sent to the Finance Ministry, where budgeters make a tax estimate based on the most recently projected figures. The estimated tax yield is then compared to the expected expenditure volume resulting from the spending ministry negotiations. These tax-adjusted expenditure estimates are subsequently sent back to the Economics Ministry, where policymakers consider whether the anticipated deficit or surplus and volume of spending fit with their expectations of the major developments in the economy.

A finance official described what happens when the two views do not fit: ". . . we talk with them about it and calculate the thing through again. It goes back and forth this way. We may begin to wonder that it still does not fit with what they consider right. In this way we gradually get closer and closer to an agreement on what are the right amounts. . . ." The outlines of the budgetary and economic figures are also sent to the respective units in the Economics and

Finance Ministries that deal with fiscal aspects of budgetary policy, business-cycle policy, and the composition of the debt and monetary policy. The amounts will be checked with the Bundesbank and the Finance and Economics Committees in the Bundestag. In June the division directors consult with the assistant secretaries and the ministers and form a final agreement, which is then sent to the cabinet in the late summer. During the back-and-forth negotiations, one main source of disagreement, as one budget official described it, was that "The Planning Division sees the budget from above to below. . . . We, on the other hand, are concerned with the building of the budget from the bottom up."

The National Accounts Model accommodates this iterative form of decision making by not specifying rigidly the interconnections among variables. If the interconnections were rigidly specified, either the recommended figures would have to be imposed on the rest of the government or they would simply be ignored. If the econometric model, in other words, were to produce nonnegotiable results, it is difficult to see why they should be accepted by other participants who do not share the same preferences. The usefulness of the National Accounts system, therefore, is precisely its susceptibility to compromise. If accommodating the top-down and bottom-up functions of the budget can be considered a worthy purpose, then the National Accounts system serves to support that goal.

The Goal Projection and Incremental Budgeting

The National Accounts Model is the foundation for the yearly *Goal Projection* that is normally presented to the Bundestag in January of each year. The *Goal Projection* is not a probability estimate of future economic and fiscal developments. Rather its purpose is to project future conditions that should occur if the government takes the necessary measures. The political questions raised by the *Goal Projection* are: Should the government take any action? And if the government does decide on some measure, what sectors will suffer and what sectors will benefit?

The development of the *Goal Projection* involves two distinct steps. The forecasters start with a predominantly technical calculation to find out how the economy will progress without any special measures taken by the government. Once these probability figures are determined, the forecaster then draws up projected goals based as much as possible on expected actual developments. At this stage, however, the projections begin to reflect the broad outlines of the government's political program that is supposed to promote the achievement of these goals. Initial assumptions and outlines are then discussed with higher, political levels in the administration, including the chancellor, the economics minister, and the finance minister.

The *Goal Projection*, therefore, is a statement by the top political leadership of what it would like to see happen with the economy and the budget. "Economists make the original calculations and proposals," stated a division director, "but these, and the assumptions that underlie them, will be tested to see if they fit with the main political goals. It is an iterative process."

The possibilities for policy manipulation are limited, however, according to an economic forecaster: "The chancellor cannot say that he wants a zero inflation rate and through some trick make that come out in the model. But he can set priority items and see how variations in the others might give the right results, even if these measures haven't been taken. In this way, political preferences are contained in the yearly projections."

The top political leadership only recently became involved in the decisions concerning the *Goal Projection*. During the 1960s the Committee of Division Directors decided the assumptions and goals without having their judgments overruled by superiors. Today, most officials see the influence of the directors committee as important but certainly not predominant. One of the reasons for the change may be the policy under the Social-Liberal coalition of replacing career bureaucrats with political appointees all the way down to the director level. A second reason may be that the macroeconomic function of the government has made the macrobudget policy more politically salient.

The most striking feature of the *Goal Projection* is moderation. A comparison of the projected yearly amounts with the actual developments reveals a cautionary pattern. The trend line, as figure 3–2 indicates, underestimates booms and recessions. The range for the projected values varies less widely than that of the actual figures. It appears that standard rules of thumb influence policy: a 1 to 2 percent real-growth rate is projected during recessions, while a 4 to 5 percent rate is set for boom periods. When actual growth falls within the 2 to 4 percent range, the projections conform to reality; when growth is either faster or slower, the discrepancies between goal and result widen.

The greater stability of projected-over actual-growth rates is due to prediction inaccuracy. The multiyear financial-planning scheme, for example, which projects a growth trend in GNP over the next five-year period, arbitrarily sets a goal of 4 percent real-growth per year. The scheme also sets the yearly growth in public expenditures as a constant or slightly rising percentage of GNP. Because GNP is projected to grow at a definite, regular rate, the growth in overall public expenditures follows a similar path. Although the shape of the business-cycle curve is more fully known for next year than it is for a five-year period, what is known about the curve is mainly the direction in which the economy is going, not the extent of the rise or the fall. Consequently, to be safe, policymakers postulate a 4 percent growth rate for the good years and a 1 to 2 percent rate for the bad years.

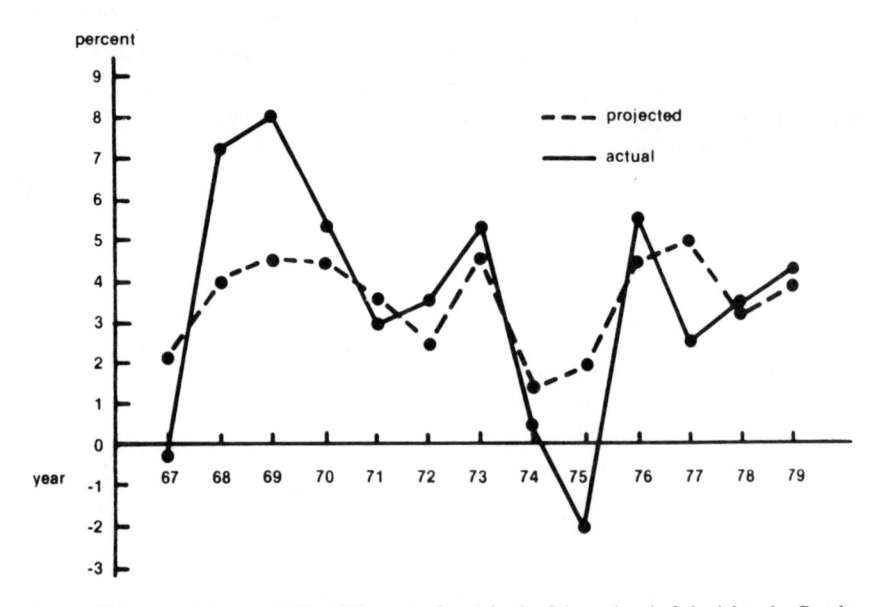

Source: Jahresprojektionen, 1967–1978, to be found in the Jahreswirtschaftsberichte der Bundesregierung, Duetscher Bundestag Verhandlungen, Anlagen und Drucksachen (Stuttgart: W. Kohlhammer Verlag).

Figure 3–2. Gross National Product, Actual and Projected (Percentage Annual Change)

The consequence of this is that the manifest function of the yearly projections is to set broad economic goals; the latent function is to accommodate economic policy to the main features of the public budget. What is known about budgets in general is what the *Goal Projection* provides in particular: namely, a fairly regular yearly percentage increase in expenditures. Eighty-five percent of the federal budget is fixed through legal and other means, and the percentage of mandatory expenditures at the state level is even higher. Most of the mandatory laws and regulations work to produce regular yearly percentage increases that are not easily changed in the short run. The calculational problems of handling billions of marks in expenditure also tend to produce yearly budgetary outcomes that reflect last year's budget plus a percentage increase.[20]

If budget plans regularly propose an 8 to 12 percent nominal growth in expenditures each year, they easily fit satisfactorily into the framework of the *Goal Projections*. "My experience has been that when it comes to the projections, the Economics Ministry is as cautious as anyone," explains an official in the Budget Division. "Agreement here has not been so difficult. There seems to be objective boundaries with these projections."

Another budget official agreed:

"Probably the greatest difference [between what the Budget Division and Planning Division considered correct] was 4 billion marks this past year (1975) in a budget of 160 billion. Earlier the differences were not this great. . . . The percentage is not normally more than 2 percent and usually less. Generally a compromise is worked out that lies somewhere in between the two proposals.

The top political leadership is unwilling to project to the public a pessimistic economic future. The failure of the *Goal Projection* to account for the minus-growth rates in 1967 and 1974 to 1975 partly reflects this caution. The top leadership, however, is also intent on keeping the coalition government together and maintaining support for the government's program. Officials responsible for choosing the initial assumptions in the *Goal Projections* realize that extreme positions do not gain acceptance by the political level in the administration: "When we make a proposal [for the *Goal Projection*] the extreme of what is possible given the economic situation is not proposed. Rather we try to propose something more in the middle which gives latitude for some variation each way during the negotiations." Under normal economic conditions it is also unlikely that the extreme positions will describe the actual developments. In fact the forecasters are only able to predict a range of growth, roughly from 2.0 to −1.0 percent for a bad year and from 4.0 to 7.0 percent for a good year. The extreme of what is possible is not chosen, however, meaning that the good year becomes 4.0 to 5.0 percent and the bad year becomes 1.0 to 2.0 percent. With these figures as guides to the budget policy, the requirement of anticyclical variation is not so great.

More accurate predictions, therefore, might introduce greater conflict into the planning stage of the budget cycle. By analogy, the climbers of the mountain may find their only comfort in not knowing how difficult the final stretch of terrain really is. The Finance Ministry, for example, would have viewed the 1974 to 1975 deficit spending with more alarm if it had known in advance that the deficit would grow to more than twice its projected size. As it turned out, the size of the deficit in 1974 to 1975 caught the policymakers pretty much by surprise, thereby presenting them with a fait accompli.[21]

Since the planning of the federal-budget policy occurs before future economic developments are fully known, an incomplete picture of developments reduces the potential conflict between the economic and other criteria for judging the budget. By agreeing not to base policy on possible extreme fluctuations in the business cycle, budgeters and fiscal policymakers more easily reach a compromise on the size of the yearly budget increase. The political uncertainty of conflicting criteria is thus subjectively resolved through the factual uncertainty of measuring future developments. Apparently uncertainties are not always additive; at times they work to subtract from each other.

A Fixation with the Nominal Growth in GNP

If policymakers in Bonn do not use formal economic criteria for drawing up the federal budget, what criteria do they use? Are economic considerations taken into account at all at this stage of the budget cycle? Most officials in both the Economics and Finance Ministries felt that during the planning phase of the budget "the political aspects are most important and the economic considerations secondary. . . . The economic effects of this process are a difficult result and not a goal." The independence of the budget process prompted one economist to exclaim: "The formulation of the budget has its own internal logic. It has to do with the minimum needs of the ministries plus percentage increases. In this way, the Budget Division is entirely separate from the Planning Division in the Finance Ministry."

A major consideration is the nominal-growth rate in gross national product. Each year the nominal growth rate in GNP is set at 8.0 to 10.0 percent. One purpose of this fixed yearly amount is to keep the public sector at a constant or slightly increasing proportion of GNP. As one official summed it up: "Everything will be hung on 8 percent. It means that we take the nominal-growth rate and approach the budget in this way."

Orienting budget growth on nominal growth in GNP does not conform to sound economics, but it does have its uses in the structured negotiations that comprise the budgetary decision process. A budget official described its usefulness:

> This fixation on the growth rate is an aid. It is something that is general and understandable. It is possible to present something in terms of the growth rate. It is also an aid to reduce inappropriate claims for funds (by the spending ministries). You get somewhere with an absolute number. You state each year a percentage. . . .

Other officials emphasized that the orientation on the growth rate is useful in negotiations with those outside the federal government: employers associations, unions, state governments, and interest groups.

For those involved in budgeting, the nominal growth in GNP represents an understandable figure—one people can relate to and use in their own calculations, even if they happen to work as budget directors in the Transportation Ministry or some other ministry. The growth rate is a specific amount that can act as a ceiling under which budgeters can run for shelter when spending demands get too stormy. During negotiations with spending ministries, labor unions, or other levels of government, the expected nominal growth in GNP is also the central figure around which discussions revolve. The figure generally represents a commonly understood amount that lawyers, bureaucrats, and economists can use and manipulate. The unions, the employers, and the states produce separate and different estimates of GNP growth.[22] The labor unions tend to project a faster rate of growth in support of their interest in continued wage and salary expansion. Since the outcomes of these negotiations in effect set a floor on what actual wage developments turn out to be, the federal government has an incentive for bargaining purposes to estimate a somewhat slower growth rate.[23]

The nominal-growth figure is also a central consideration in the distribution of the sales-tax revenue between the levels of government. If one level of government grows disproportionately fast compared with the other levels, its budget gradually gains ground as a percentage of total GNP. Under the sales-tax distribution, which is set every two years by statutory law, the faster growing level has a claim to a larger share of the tax revenue, thereby reinforcing its tendency to grow faster than the other levels. A fixation on the nominal-growth rate in GNP thus serves to protect the absolute size of each level's revenue source. Even the federal government has balked at the implications of losing tax revenue to the states because of economic management.[24]

The consequences for economic policy of a fixation on the nominal growth in GNP are not all negative. Because projections are not very sound, the Finance Ministry is not prepared to add marks to a spending ministry's budget to compensate a change in the economic indicators. Why raise expectations only to leave them unfulfilled? If developments do not work out as badly or as well as projected, it may be unrealistic to expect that the Finance Ministry could get any money back once it had been promised. Even more remote is the possibility that the Finance Ministry might try to get Bundestag approval in order to raise income-transfer benefits, thereby fighting the projected lack of consumer demand during the coming recession. Consequently the fixation on the nominal-growth rate may not harm economic management, which is concentrated in the implementation phase of the budget anyway, and may aid the budget policy by providing a commonly accepted orientation point that binds participants together.

A word must be added about the evaluation of the debt policy during the planning stage of the budget cycle. For most of the Federal Republic's history, the size of interest payments has not amounted to more than 2.0 to 3.0 percent of budget volume and, therefore, according to one debt manager, the amount "does not restrict the budget too much nor has to be carefully watched." But despite the small size of the debt, its potential impact on the private–capital market generates considerable concern and represents the central issue in deciding how large the debt may grow. The belief among officials responsible for the debt is that the German capital market is much smaller than in a country such as the United States and, therefore, a dramatic rise in public borrowing, as occurred in 1974 to 1975, can have a significant impact on interest rates and hence on the incentive to borrow in the private sector. An official in the debt division described the major task of debt policy as "inherently one of adapting debt policy to monetary policy . . . the debt has no purpose in and of itself apart from the realm of economic policy."

Two main indicators in the private economy inform the public debt policy. One indicator is the private–savings rate: when the rate is high, the rule of thumb is that the government may borrow more. The other indicator is the direction in which the interest rates are moving. If the rates are moving up, the government should follow a cautious borrowing policy. In 1974 the unusual situation arose in which, despite a high savings rate, interest rates appeared to move in the upward direction. The government correspondingly restricted borrowing and tried to avoid a full-blown deficit-spending policy. Seen in retrospect, the capacity for borrowing was much greater than perceived at the time. As interest rates began to fall, therefore, in 1975 and the recession continued to deepen, little effort was made to cover the growing deficit created by falling tax revenues and increasing stimulus costs. In 1974 the debt rose from approximately 3.0 billion to 10.0 billion marks; by the end of 1975, the debt amounted to 41.0 billion marks in a total federal budget of 160.0 billion.[25]

The degree to which the government should become active in the capital market is calculated in the *Kreislaufsystem*. A supply-demand equation is worked out for the capital market during the budget-planning stage. The decision to increase the deficit to supplement tax income depends in part on the need to consider the effects of public borrowing on the demand for credit in the market.

The consequence for the budget policy is illustrated by the dispute between the Planning and Budget Divisions in the Finance Ministry early in 1974 over whether the lower tax yield should warrant cuts in the proposed budget figures. The Planning Division opposed the cuts because of the beginning recession, while the Budget Division favored them on financial grounds. Eventually the dispute went to the cabinet where it was decided that cuts would be made as long as investments were not included. One of the economic arguments supporting the cuts was the possible adverse effects of further public borrowing on the rise in interest rates.

Loose Coupling

Budget planning involves reconciling contrary interests into a workable political program. Economic analysis that subsumes all conflict into predetermined coefficients in a formal model ignores the use of the information in a conflicting policy environment. Consequently formal measures of the appropriate size of the public budget and econometric models of the whole economy have gained little influence in the policy process in Bonn. The formal models do not allow government organizations to engage in strategies that aim at producing a politically acceptable program.

The most striking feature of the economic analyses that are actually carried out is their lack of behavioral connections between components, which are essentially comprised of a series of partial submodels that relate only loosely to each other. The partial models taken together form a whole, but changes in one do not necessarily effect changes throughout the system according to any predetermined mathematical hierarchy. Rather the interconnections among submodels form the discussion points among institutional participants in the decision process. Yet within each submodel, interconnections are specified in a mathematical way under the assumption that changes in one part of the submodel are very likely to cause predictable changes in other parts.

A system in which there exists loose interaction among components but tight interaction within components corresponds to Simon's notion of nearly decomposable systems "in which the interactions among the sub-systems are weak but not negligible."[26] One of the properties of a nearly decomposable system is the ability to construct stable subsystems relatively independently of each other, yet still bring them together into a recognizable whole at a later point in time. The advantage of the ability to construct stable subsystems is that it allows the problem solver to devote attention and effort to one area without at the same time worrying equally about all the other areas.

In the context of economic policy, the existence of stable subsystems produces a two-stage form of problem solving. During the first stage, budgeters consider in detail the composition of the budget, financial analysts treat the composition of the debt, and tax specialists work on the specifics of taxation without, at the same time, considering equally the ramifications of each change within each area on the components of all the other areas. In this first stage, therefore, the calculational and strategy requirements of the participants are greatly reduced because each problem-solving group needs to primarily consider only its own area.

In the second stage, only the aggregate of each area need concern the other areas, while the composition of each area is taken as given by those outside it. In practice, for instance, the total macrobudget must accommodate to a degree the overall economic picture, as must the aggregate size of the deficit, but the composition of each of these areas is worked out by the respective institutions responsible for debt and budget policy. Once again the calculational and strategy requirements are reduced because adjustments need to be made only among the submodels in an aggregate way.[27]

A second advantage of the ability to construct stable subsystems is their greater resistance to disruption. If a specific disturbance within any one of the subsystems produces ramifications for all or most of the other systems, the possibility for sabotaging the whole would be greater than if the disturbance were isolated within one area. If a macromodel specifies a particular size for the deficit, but the debt analysts consider the amount unrealistic given the composition of the capital market and other financial considerations, the inconsistency can bring down the entire model; whereas, with loose connections, no one component threatens the overall structure in quite the same way.

By allowing each institutional participant to concentrate on its own area, a comprehensive appraisal of all effects and relations is not required. Components of the whole can be built sequentially and semi-independently of each other without jeopardizing the subsequent need to bring them all together into a workable whole. It is not surprising, therefore, to find a degree of institutional overlap in the economic-budget area. The Finance Ministry, for instance, needs economists to develop econometric models that predict government spending and revenue based on the detailed calculations and strategies carried on between the Finance Ministry and the spending ministries. Economic analyses are not centralized in the Economics Ministry, for analyses of public spending, tax yields, and debt composition are made in the Finance Ministry. Only later, in an aggregate way, are these components adjusted to the values prescribed for the other sectors of the economy.

In addition to the loose interconnections among components, the *Goal Projection,* and in particular the projected nominal growth in GNP, serves to bring the components together by providing an overall scheme that is generally accepted and recognized by the diverse participants. Why? Because it produces stable expectations among participants in the same way that the base amounts do in the budget negotiations. The reason is that the nominal-growth referent is not to actual GNP changes but rather to predicted changes that generally hover around 8 percent yearly. Economists can accept it because the actual changes are not known in advance and a stable GNP growth represents a desirable economic goal. Budgeters can accept it because it reduces the anticyclical requirements of spending and creates the basis for regular budget growth as a percentage of GNP. If strict criteria were adhered to, contradictions between economic and financial purposes would develop in various facets of the decision process; but because the *Goal Projection* assumes a regular growth in GNP and other calculations are based on it rather than the actual growth, many of these contradictions do not arise or appear in rather diminished form.

The nominal growth rate in GNP is also used by the Finance Ministry as a strategy to maintain financial criteria as determinants of budget policy. In the first stage of negotiations between the Finance Ministry, spending ministries, and labor unions, the nominal rate serves the same purpose as the financial-planning figures—either as floors or ceilings for negotiations, depending on the expected size of the tax yield. During the second stage of negotiations between the Economics Ministry, Finance Ministry, and chancellor's office, the fixation on the nominal growth rate serves a more subtle purpose. During boom periods the growth rate is underestimated because it reduces the need to cut ministry proposals on stabilization grounds but increases the need to cut proposals on financial grounds. As is well known, to promote cuts for economic purposes is much more difficult politically than to appeal to financial stringency. During recession periods, the growth rate is overestimated because the opportunity for spending ministries to demand increases to stimulate the economy is reduced while the allowance for growth on financial grounds is increased but not beyond the anticipated figures in the financial plans. This hedge against reality, therefore, is useful for the Finance Ministry because it diminishes economic-management criteria and enhances financial determinants of the budget policy.[28]

What kind of analysis best complements an interactive decision process? The German experience with economic analysis suggests that a model that squeezes contradictory and opposed budget purposes into the economic purpose greatly oversimplifies and distorts reality. What seems to work best is a loosely coupled system that allows for sequential and semi-independent construction of submodels. The loose connections between the submodels form the bargaining points at which participants try to reconcile the diverse purposes into a workable program. During the planning phase, certain common assumptions about projected growth rates aid in preventing the bargaining positions from moving too far apart for accommodation. In this way the requirements of accommodation in a loosely coupled system are greatly reduced to just the aggregates of the subsystems, allowing participants to worry less about satisfactory criteria for making specific judgments in their own policy areas.

Notes

1. Official in the chancellor's office, in fall 1975.
2. For a discussion of the various purposes that budgets serve, see Karl-Heinrich Hansmeyer and Bert Rürup, *Staatswirtschaftliche Planungsinstrumente* (Tübingen: JCB Mohr, 1973), ch. 1; see also Aaron Wildavsky, *Budgeting: A Comparative Theory of Budgetary Processes* (Boston: Little, Brown and Co., 1975), ch. 1.
3. Allen Schick, *Budget Innovation in the States* (Washington, D.C.: The Brookings Institution, 1971), pp. 3–8; and "The Road to PPB: The Stages of Budget Reform," *Public Administration Review* 26 (December 1966):243–58.
4. See Aaron Wildavsky, *The Politics of the Budgetary Process*, 2nd ed. (Boston: Little, Brown and Company, 1974), pp. 47–55 for an analysis of this role in the U.S. House of Representatives. In most western parliamentary democracies, the guardian role is played by the Finance Ministry. For Germany, see Hans Clausen Korff, *Haushaltspolitik: Instrument öffentlicher Macht* (Stuttgart: Verlag W. Kohlhammer, 1975), pp. 13–25.
5. Korff, *Haushaltspolitik*, p. 38. See also Andrew Shonfield, *Modern Capitalism: The Changing Balance of Public and Private Power* (London: Oxford University Press, 1965), pp. 265–297, who argues that not until the sixties did macroeconomic analysis enter into the budget calculations at all. Even after the intrusion of Keynesian thinking into the Economics Ministry under Dr. Erhard, the Finance Ministry continued to adopt a cautious approach, which put heavy emphasis on good budget management—meaning frugality and accountability. It is also important to note that the 1969 Finance Reform, while abolishing the old extraordinary/ordinary budget categories, does require that borrowing not exceed expenditure for investments, thereby indicating a continuing concern for balanced budgets and "orderly housekeeping" (Shonfield's phrase, pp. 272–273).

6. Günter Schmid and Hubert Treiber, *Bürokratie und Politik* (Munich: Wilhelm Fink Verlag, 1975), pp. 122–123.

7. Ibid., p. 112.

8. Renate Mayntz and Fritz Scharpf, *Policy Making in the German Federal Bureaucracy* (New York: Elsevier, 1975).

9. See, for example, William Capron, "The Impact of Analysis on Bargaining in Government," in *The Politics of the Federal Bureaucracy,* ed. Alan Altshuler (New York: Dodd, Mead, and Co., 1975), pp. 196–211.

10. Paul Diesing, *Reason in Society: Five Types of Decisions and Their Social Conditions* (Urbana: University of Illinois, 1962), p. 203.

11. Harold Garfinkel, *Studies in Ethnomethodology* (Englewood Cliffs, New Jersey: Prentice Hall, 1967), p. 270.

12. E.S. Quade, "Systems Analysis Techniques for Public Policy Problems," in *Perspectives on Public Bureaucracy,* ed. Fred A. Kramer, 2nd ed. (Cambridge, Massachusetts: Winthrop Publishers, 1977), pp. 163–164.

13. Charles Lindblom, *Politics and Markets: The World's Political-Economic Systems* (New York: Basic Books, 1977), especially ch. 3 and 19.

14. Charles E. Lindblom and David K. Cohen, *Usable Knowledge: Social Science and Social Problem Solving* (New Haven: Yale University Press, 1979).

15. Aaron Wildavsky, *Speaking Truth to Power: The Art and Craft of Policy Analysis* (Boston: Little, Brown and Co., 1979), especially ch. 5.

16. "Etagengespräche in engem Korsett," *Suddeutsche Zeitung* (12–13 July 1975):31. "Business-cycle pessimists among the Cabinet members advocate, despite declining tax revenues, an expansive budget, especially in the programs represented by their respective ministries."

17. Dieter Biehl, Karl-Heinz Jüttemeier, and Harald Legler, "Zu den konjunkturellen Effekten der Länder-und Gemeindehaushalte in der Bundesrepublik Deutschland 1960–1974," *Die Weltwirtschaft* 2, special edition (Kiel: Institut für Weltwirtschaft, 1974), p. 30; and *Jahresgutachten der Sachverständigenrat, 1970–71* (Stuttgart: Kohlhammer Verlag, 1970), pp. 322ff.

18. Dieter Vesper, "Vergleich der Ergebnisse des Neutralhaushalts mit anderen Konzepten" (Berlin: Deutsches Institut für Wirtschaft, Winter 1975), working paper obtained directly from the institute.

19. Karl-Heinz Raabe, "Gesamtwirtschaftliche Prognosen und Projektionen als Hilfsmittel der Wirtschaftspolitik in der Bundesrepublik Deutschland," (Bonn: August 1973), obtained directly from the Economics Ministry.

20. Wildavsky, *Budgeting,* ch. 1.

21. The discrepancy between projected deficit and actual for 1975 amounted to 23.0 billion marks. This discrepancy came about partly because of the failure to predict the impact of the Tax Reform on tax revenues, but it also reflects the failure to estimate the extent of the economic downturn. See the *Jahresprojektion 1975 and 1976,* in the *Wirtschaftsberichte,* contained in *Bundestag Verhandlungen,* Anlagen und Drucksache, 7/3197 and 7/4677.

22. Michael Jungblut, "1977—Welche Karte Sticht? Selten waren die Prognosen der wirtschaftlichen Entwicklung im kommenden Jahr so widersprüchlich," *Die Zeit* (7 January 1977):7.

23. See Jack Knott, "Conflict Behavior and Accommodation: The Case of Labor Relations in Weimar and the German Federal Republic," unpublished paper.

24. See chapter 6 for an analysis of this issue.

25. *Finanzbericht* (West Germany: Bundesministerium der Finanzen, 1976): 158–164.

26. Herbert Simon, *The Sciences of the Artificial* (Cambridge, Massachusetts: The MIT Press, 1969), pp. 99–100, 86–88, 90–92, 95–97.

27. Ibid., p. 100. Simon argues that one of the characteristics of nearly decomposable systems is: "In the long run, the behavior of any one of the components depends in only an aggregate way on the behavior of the other components."

28. See Frank Levy, Arnold Meltsner, and Aaron Wildavsky, *Urban Outcomes: Schools, Streets, and Libraries* (Berkeley: University of California Press, 1974) for an analysis of attempts by city managers to hedge against uncertainty by underestimating revenue, thereby putting themselves in the more enviable position of giving out bonuses rather than taking back promises.

4 Planning and Flexibility: Sharing Uncertainty among Organizational Goals

Has the economy entered a recession?
Maybe yes.
Or maybe no.[1]

—Alfred L. Malabre

Planning is preferred so long as things turn out as expected. When projections are grossly inadequate, however, policymakers are more likely to prefer flexibility to planning. Why commit oneself to decisions that will be regretted later? This wait-and-see decision making came to dominate the budget policy after the 1973 oil-price hike. The impact was to shift the emphasis of macroeconomic policy from the medium term to the immediate. It also placed the burden of fiscal policy on the implementation phase of the budget cycle, thus concentrating policy on discretionary, short-term responses to the evolving and uncertain economic developments.

The budget plan continued to dutifully target an 8.0 percent nominal growth rate in GNP, less than 5.0 percent inflation, and under 2.0 percent unemployment; but actual economic developments came to follow a much more erratic course. The yearly *Goal Projection,* for example, foresaw a 4.0 to 5.0 percent real growth for 1974, whereas actual growth languished at 0.0 to 1.0 percent. Throughout the 1970s, moreover, real growth in GNP varied considerably. In one year, the economy grew at 8.0 to 9.0 percent real growth; in another year it actually experienced a negative growth rate of -3.0 percent. And during the most erratic period, 1974 to 1976, forecasters in the Economics and Finance Ministries complained that projections tended to be accurate for not more than four to five months.

These discrepancies between planned and actual amounts extended the uncertainties of accommodating conflicting budget criteria to the implementation of the budget policy. But unlike the budget plan, policymakers in the implementation phase cannot hedge against reality by pretending that developments will be more stable than they are. During the execution of the budget, policymakers know that the economy is in a recession and that the planned figures no longer serve as accurate guides to policy. They face strong pressures in the short run, therefore, to take discretionary measures to alter the planned amounts.

But policymakers are also cautious: though they know a recession has arrived, they do not have a full understanding of its severity or duration. Neither do they completely control the available instruments for doing something about it. If they are not careful, opposition may arise to their preferences.[2] Taking discretionary measures to fine-tune the economy throughout the budget cycle is thus not without its costs and risks as well as its benefits.

Disagreements in economic theory over discretionary measures are well documented.[3] Those economists who oppose discretionary measures propose that the government should limit its economic management to the automatic stabilizers built into the modern budget. Especially the "automatic" rise in unemployment compensation and other welfare benefits is supposed to assure a greater government budget stimulus in a recession. These theorists also argue with considerable justification that the available policy instruments—expenditures, taxation, and the debt—are so inflexible that their lagged effects exacerbate rather than diminish the severity of the business cycle. On the contrary, those who favor discretionary action maintain that doing something is better than doing nothing and that, while some measures are badly timed, most efforts have the desired effect of counteracting swings in the cycle.

The political costs and benefits of discretionary expenditure measures are debated less often. Yet efforts to fine tune the economy in later stages of the budget cycle depend heavily on the importance that is attached to the symbolic and political impacts of discretionary stabilization measures. The problem with automatic stabilizers is that they are automatic (no one takes credit for them); no special cabinet meetings take place; no intentional decision is made that gets interest group and public support. Discretionary measures, in contrast, receive widespread publicity, require an agreement process to get them passed, and make the government appear as if it is working to fight the economic difficulties. Consequently political pressures mount for decisive short-term actions, especially during election periods.

The political disadvantage of fine-tuning in the later stages of the budget cycle lies in the potential disruption of the government's spending program. Discretionary anticyclical spending disrupts expenditure policy in several ways: it reopens for negotiation just concluded allocation agreements; promotes expenditure items previously seen as unnecessary or inappropriate; widens the gap between the time required for budget planning and the shorter time referent associated with economic management; and produces lasting changes in ministry budgets that are not even considered in the decisions to stimulate the economy.[4]

The government's attempt to resolve the uncertainty between short-term discretionary economic management and longer-term expenditure policy explains the step-by-step–decision making and indecision that characterized policy between 1974 and 1976. Besides subjectively resolving uncertainty, as occurred in the planning of the budget policy, decision makers can also shift the uncertainty onto others, thereby sharing the consequences. For a time, the government felt compelled to take action to counteract the growing recession. But by 1976 the government had had enough. It decided to retreat from using the budget for economic management and turned instead to the monetary instrument. Using expenditure policy for short-term economic management, the government found out, may inadequately serve antirecession policy while jeopardizing the needs of substantive program planning.

Planning for Contingencies

The federal government originally had hoped to use expenditure policy for short-term–economic management by establishing in the budget plan a special economic-stabilization budget alongside the normal core budget.[5] When economic developments dictated an increase in public spending, under this scheme the individual ministries would then receive the additional expenditure items contained in the stabilization budget. The reverse was also supposed to happen: if the economic situation demanded expenditure restraint, the ministries would not obtain the additional funding. The purpose was to plan for contingencies. The spending ministries and the Finance Ministry would prepare in advance even the potential stabilization expenditures of each ministry. A planned discretionary budget, it was believed, would grant quicker release of funds and a more rational integration of macroeconomic spending into the ministries' normal budgets. By planning both the core and contingency budgets at the same time, policymakers hoped to partially avoid the twin problems of decision lag and expenditure disruption.

A preplanned contingency budget is supposed to work as follows: the overall budget, which is passed by the Bundestag in the fall, contains a core and contingency component, and both are approved as constituting the spending programs for the individual ministries. If the economy languishes, the total amount is allocated; if the economy grows rapidly, some items will be held back. During normal-growth periods, therefore, the main practical task of fiscal policy amounts to attempts to cut the overall combined figures. But to gain more leverage over the spending ministries during these long growth periods, the Finance Ministry has had to sell the contingency budget a little differently—as a financial control measure. "We wanted a restrictive normal budget," explained a budget official, "but to carry that out politically, we have had to say to the ministries: for economic stabilization reasons you get only a little, but when the economy goes well, you will get more. That is a political tactical aspect." In other words, the attempt was made to place the emphasis on potential future additions rather than belated actual reductions, and this reverse strategy was accomplished by preparing a restrictive normal budget during the planning stage and by promising more for the execution phases.

During strong economic expansion in 1971 and 1972, the Bonn government planned a contingency budget alongside the core budget. The contingency budget was based on certain expectations about how the economy would develop over the coming year and amounted to approximately 3.0 to 4.0 billion marks. It contained items that could be saved, stretched out, or given out more speedily depending on the circumstances. Policymakers hoped that the contingency budget would reduce conflict, avoid disruption, and provide a more flexible policy instrument for economic management.

The Finance Ministry found instead that once the overall budget included known items, efforts proved futile to cut any of them out for economic management. The planned contingency budget tended to raise expectations for the spending ministries that proved very hard to alter later if the situation did not warrant the additional expenditures. A finance official stated that, "If you change it [the contingency budget] later on, the relevant ministries will feel deceived, which brings down the carefully constructed structure of expectations. The whole thing begins to fall apart."

If a contingency budget is planned in advance, but the economy continues to do better and better, the right economic policy is not to give the ministries the extra funds. But if you do not give them the funds, stated a budget official, "you leave them standing high and dry. This is clearly not possible from a political point of view."

Contingency planning is supposed to add flexibility and adaptation to the budget policy, but the Finance Ministry has learned otherwise. Once a contingency budget is drawn up, political considerations make it very difficult to alter in any way. Consequently if the contingency budget is drawn up far in advance of the time when the money is actually spent, the only hope that its contents will suit the needs of the moment is a development in the economy that proceeds according to the original planned figures. However, if the economy does not proceed along anticipated lines, the contents of the contingency budget will soon not fit the emerging needs. The success of preplanned contingency budgets depends, therefore, on the ability to predict economic developments at least over the normal eighteen-month to two-year budget-planning–time frame. Without this ability, the Finance Ministry loses the main advantage of contingency planning—meeting unforeseen circumstances with flexible policy instrumentation—but with this ability, the underlying rationale for contingency planning no longer holds because events are already known in advance.

Predicting the Future

With few exceptions the Finance Ministry has found itself in need of contingency plans because events have not unfolded as anticipated. The 1973 to 1976 period produced one of the most unpredictable business cycles in recent German economic history. The business spurt in 1973 brought unexpectedly high tax surpluses; the 1974 recession callously persisted into 1975. Middle-level federal officials in Bonn made forecasts that proved unreliable and offered programs that were ineffectual. Scepticism developed toward efforts to make and prepare the budget policy too far in advance of its execution, and decisions once made were reexamined to accommodate newly understood developments.

Especially business-cycle analysts worried about the declining ability to forecast the future or even accurately interpret the economic significance of the present. Yet other middle-level officials frequently and voluntarily expressed concern over the failure to achieve satisfactory predictions. "The coefficients, the models, the forecasts have all miscarried," observed a finance official. "If the forecasters had been right, we would now be in the middle of a wonderful boom."

Looking at the prognoses ex post often revealed wide discrepancies between prediction and outcome. "Are the prognoses right?" asked an official in the chancellor's office. "Each time we make one it turns out worse than the one before. More are wrong than right. With stabilization policy you are always running a little behind, and never quite catch up. Each month the developments run differently than expected. It is a constant battle with the statistics."

As a rule, the prognoses were wrong. In 1974 and 1975, for example, the economy experienced a negative-growth rate of -3.0 percent, but the previous fall the government had predicted a -1.0 percent rate. "The crux of the problem," concluded a planning official, "is that estimates for the future vary quite a bit, making it hard to know if the data are reliable or not."

The inability to pinpoint the magnitude or duration of trends in the economy produced a change in the way contingency budgets are drawn up. Instead of planning them one to two years in advance during the planning stage of the regular budget cycle, the contingency budgets now are drawn up at times of need throughout the fiscal year. A budget official described the time constraint:

> Contingency budgets really only have an effect in the special antirecession programs *(Konjunkturprogramme)* that are passed in the Cabinet. Consider the time problem: a contingency budget must be drawn up now in May [1975], but this budget will only eventually take effect some time in 1976, almost a year or so away. That the economic requirements of that time will now be known is very unlikely. The contingency budget, therefore, must really be decided later. This is why more conflict is involved.

The problem with planning the contingency budget during the overall budget's planning phase is that it will become outdated before it is needed. "It might be that next year a completely different type of contingency budget is required," ran a typical comment. "A contingency budget drawn up in advance is therefore not satisfactory. It is more rational to wait until a later time and see what is actually needed in the economy."

To keep the necessary flexibility for unpredictable developments, the Finance Ministry now draws up certain contingency programs, but as one official observed, "These are only kept in the Budget Division and surely are not discussed with the ministries themselves. . . . You need an almost 90 percent assurance that these funds will be spent before they will be actually discussed with the ministries. There is a strong 'announcement effect' associated with these programs.'' This means that the contingency budgets, as now constituted, are synonomous with the special antirecession programs that are drawn up periodically throughout the year as economic need arises.[6]

Extending the Conflict

Drawing up special budgets periodically at times of perceived economic crisis does not avoid the original problem: the need for ready-made programs that do not disrupt expenditure allocation. Special budgets that arise later in the budget cycle lead to a reallocation of resources and renegotiation of agreements that were often painfully worked out during the planning phase. The burden of anticyclical policy thus extends to the later planning and execution phases of the budget cycle. Conflict arises at later stages due to the discrepancy between the initial resource-allocation agreements worked out in planning and the new macroeconomic policy opportunities for increased spending that arise later on. For this reason, the ministries fight less over the macrosize of the special antirecession programs than they do over their composition. Varying compositions affect the relative allocation of resources among the ministries' programs. "It is not primarily the macrovolume of the programs that is so difficult to decide," was the commonly expressed opinion, "but rather the bringing together of the parts."

Deciding the composition of the antirecession programs, according to a budget official, "involves additional conflict over issues that were supposed to be settled at one time. . . . To bring added conflict through a contingency budget is simply not wanted (in the cabinet). Once the decisions have been made and a consensus reached, new proposals only open the thing up again."

Altering the budget later in the year also created certain difficulties for the Finance Ministry in its relations with the spending ministries. "The spending ministry more often than not proposes items that we have just a few months before refused to approve," a budget official explained. "On the basis of program substance, we had just agreed that these measures are not worth the cost. Now we go ahead and do them. I don't see that as so sensible for the economy." Reopening just-concluded issues that probably took effort to negotiate in the first place is not a good way to conduct business. Finance Ministry officials especially worried about the maintenance of trust with the spending ministries when agreements do not bind either side for the duration of the budget period.[7]

How might the passage of antirecession programs alter the composition of the budget? One effect has already been suggested: previously denied expenditures on substantive grounds are subsequently approved for economic management. A budget official complained: "These (antirecession) investments must be ready to be given out quickly . . . therefore, you give away projects that are ready. But what about better projects that are not ready?" Of course, if everything could be done over the middle term, giving out inferior projects now and superior ones later does not jeopardize the substance of programs. But under more realistic conditions in which there is not enough to go around, spending on inferior projects under the pressure of the moment may prevent spending on superior ones in the future. More than one budget official expressed concern that they avoid following "a senseless substantive policy just because it might make stabilization policy sense."

Because the greatest part of the stabilization programs consists of investment expenditures, the fear that the pressing stabilization needs will determine the substantive policies in the long run is not unfounded. The general feeling was that "the political situation has so developed that only with investments is it possible to stimulate the economy." The almost exclusive reliance on investment spending for discretionary policy has its proponents and detractors. Those who oppose the predominant use of investments argue that this type of expenditure has the greatest long-term effects and thereby contradicts the purpose of short-term anticyclical policy. Opponents also point to the fact that during the boom years, 1970 to 1973, investment expenditures stagnated, while consumption costs increased dramatically.[8] They argue that because Germany has experienced longer periods of boom and only short interruptions of recession, the long-term effects of stabilization policy have left the investment part of the budget under-developed. Investments are cut in restrictive-policy periods and only increased during the relatively less frequent periods of expansive policy.

Those who favor the investment emphasis for discretionary policy argue that only these expenditures, which are given out anew each year, are flexible enough for short-term variation. The Finance Ministry, for example, cannot postpone paying its employees for six months, but it can postpone the construction of a new access road to a freeway. Whether rightly or wrongly, many officials also expressed the judgment that investment expenditures produce a larger multiplier effect than do consumption expenditures. For this reason, a smaller initial program is thought to have a larger eventual impact on the economy. But regardless of which side is right or wrong, the fact that investment expenditures do dominate the stabilization programs results in a mixing of the allocation, redistribution and stabilization purposes so that conflict over these issues is extended throughout the budget cycle.

At the federal level 50 percent of all investments are made in the Transportation Ministry; and if investments for military installations are excluded from the calculation, over 75 percent of the investments are in the transportation area.[9] Consequently discretionary antirecession measures that include investments are necessarily concentrated in only one or two sectors of the economy and the public budget. Discretionary policy, therefore, is not primarily an effort to increase overall demand; rather it aims to a large extent at combining allocation and distribution decisions with the need to stimulate the economy. For this reason, the composition of the antirecession programs receives as much if not more attention than the macroamounts. The decision makers do perceive that the actual developments have diverged from the goal projections, but how much of the gap to fill and with what substance is a mixture of economics and politics. Is North Rhine-Westphalia having a crucial election? Are the important Ruhr coal fields experiencing high unemployment? Is the construction industry under pressure? Can Volkswagen survive the oil crisis? A former division director stated that, "Stabilization policy is much more directed toward specific problems in the economy that are politically relevant than toward the general economic situation in the Federal Republic or in the world." The special programs will be in turn largely oriented to solve these particular problems rather than the more abstract target of aggregate demand.

Providing a Special Checking Account

In support of the need to give expenditures out quickly, the Bonn government has developed a special procedure for financing antirecession programs that does not restrict the individual ministries' normal budgets nor requires the regular, formal approval of the Bundestag.[10] The emphasis on investments determines the importance to the various ministries of the antirecession programs, which tend to be concentrated in the areas of urban infrastructure and transportation.[11] Spending ministry personnel also emphasized that the special antirecession programs are "politically advantageous for the minister," but the most important benefit tended to be financial. "In effect, the ministry's budget is unburdened by these special measures. This produces two results that are important for our budget practice. The first is that we are able to realize additional savings in the budget; and secondly, we can incorporate additional items into subsequent budgets that we wouldn't have been able to do otherwise."

Prior to September 1974, however, the special antirecession programs had not provided the ministry with these two financial benefits. Earlier programs had to be officially included in the ministry's regular budget, thereby forcing the ministry to spend the extra funds during the fiscal year or to reduce its budget by the unspent amount for the following year. As an official admitted, "This practice can become a tremendous burden and rigidity for our budget. We prefer not to do it that way." He mentioned that three years after the 1967 antirecession programs the ministry had found itself in a tight budgetary corset due to these antirecession expenditures.

The last three stabilization programs in the 1974 to 1975 period were not financed through the normal ministry budgets but rather by the setting up of a special stabilization fund in much the same way, as one official expressed it, to the setting up of "a special checking account at the bank." The ministry had to give out the contracts covered in the programs within a distinct time period, but as far as the budget account was concerned, it could pay for these expenditures over the next two years. The ministry did not bring the expenses into the formal structures of the regular budget but simply paid for them out of reserves held at the Bundesbank.

For similar reasons, the ministries preferred special antirecession-program procedures to formal supplementary budgets. Under the supplementary budget scheme, the approval of the Bundestag and Bundesrat is required, the financing goes for specific items, and the extra funds must be spent within the fiscal year or they are debited against the next year's regular budget. The new stabilization financing requires no detailed passage by the Parliament, which finds it politically difficult to oppose a program that is designed to relieve unemployment and stimulate growth. Despite the concern for unnecessary expenditure, the Finance Ministry also supported the special antirecession programs in preference to the regular supplementary budget procedure because the latter "disrupt(s) too much the decisions that have already been made."

Deciding the Macroamounts

How large should the antirecession-investment programs be? It is possible for the government to state that it wants to increase production capacity from, for example, 84 to 88 percent and reduce unemployment from 4 to 3 percent, but it is not feasible for the government to accurately measure what it needs to do in order to achieve these goals. In 1967 the Economics Ministry attempted to measure the overall multiplier effect of the discretionary expenditure programs, but the results did not clearly indicate whether the effect had been 1.2 or 2.0.[12] In addition, these measures took a great deal of time to carry out and proved less capable of accurately estimating the effects of a contractive policy. For these reasons, the Economics Ministry did not attempt to measure the multiplier effects of the special antirecession programs in 1974 and 1975.

Judgment determines the overall size of the antirecession programs, not an econometric model. A key element in making the judgment is the existence of free stabilization reserves held at the Bundesbank.[13] The federal government will attempt to match the amount of the reserves belonging to the states with its own share, thereby giving a rough estimate to the potential outline of extra macroeconomic spending. But similar to the imprecision by which the debt is economically measured, the direction of change for discretionary measures is much more important than the absolute amount. "If investment expenditures were projected to grow at 10 percent, we might propose that they grow at only 8 percent," explained an economics official. "The exact figure is not as important as that they are increased or decreased."

Another official responsible for business-cycle analysis agreed: "We can only estimate the situation and try to go in the right direction. . . . If the extremes [for an investment incentive] are 5 to 10 percent, we probably will choose 7.5 percent."

Similar to other policy areas, when scientific or technical criteria are not available for determining measurement, decision makers tend to rely on familiar rules of thumb to make calculations.[14] The following is a description, given by a budget official, of how he decided to propose one amount or another for an investment program:

> We may receive the instructions that a 10.0 billion mark impulse is needed for the economy, which is 1.0 percent of GNP. The exact multiplier is not known, but I will assume a 2 to 3 amount. We then conservatively need a program of 5.0 billion. I send memos to the ministries and get estimates of what is possible. In the end, because of this process, I may make a proposal of only 2 to 3 billion.

His proposal is not the end of the process, however, for other officials and political groups also become involved in the decision. The final figure may end up only 0.5 billion because of time problems, differences of opinion, or the need for public support. As this budget official remarked, "The resulting amount has nothing to do with economics or science. . . . The size of these programs is almost always an unsolvable problem." The first two special antirecession programs in 1974, for instance, were approximately 900 million marks each. Why? As one official explained it, "because we wanted something around 1.0 billion, and 900 million looked a little less."

The desire to have these programs appear less than 1.0 billion marks reflects the government's concern during the 1974 recession with the rising rate of inflation. When describing the 1974 period, a former division director pointed out that, "The Bonn government took measures very cautiously because it feared that the inflation would go further." Although the inflation was a modest 7.0 percent in 1974 to 1975—an amount not generally seen as very high in many countries—for the West Germans, who have a past that makes them sensitive to inflation, "anything over 5 percent is seen as dangerous and given high priority." But despite the fear that a large investment program would raise the inflation rate, the government felt that it had to do something to alleviate unemployment in certain regions and sectors.

The sectoral and regional features of unemployment in 1974 to 1975 were an indication to some policymakers that the economy faced what is termed "structural" rather than business-cycle determined slack. Because the investment programs did not get at the basic structural problems facing the economy, "the investments were not necessary nor desirable from our point of view," argued a budget official.

For many officials, especially in the Economics Ministry, "A relatively significant reservation about these [investment] programs was that we had before us a structural change in the economy which we should not hinder." To many policymakers, a large investment program in traditional policy areas might somehow prevent necessary structural adjustments in the economy that were considered essential for long-term growth.

The positions on both of these issues—structural change and inflation—tended to divide along party lines in the coalition government. The Social Democrats expressed more concern for unemployment and the business-cycle slump, while the Liberals put more emphasis on market-structural adjustments and inflation. Since the Liberal, Hans Friedrichs, headed the Economics Ministry, and the Social Democrat, Hans Apel, led the Finance Ministry in 1974 and 1975, these two ministries found themselves taking divergent positions on the size of the investment programs. The political-party division reflected the uncertainty about an adequate definition of the economic-policy problem, for the old understanding of the relation between inflation and employment no longer sufficed; and the existence of severe pockets of unemployment and slack together with an overall export surplus suggested to many policymakers that traditional stimulus measures would not work.

The timing problem also influenced the overall size of the stabilization-investment programs. Many officials believed that if the investment stimulus did not come at the turn-around point in the recession, it would do little good. According to an economics official, for instance, "The investment incentive [in December 1974 to January 1975] came at the beginning of this year, which was probably much too early. Industry had no intention of investing at that time, despite the incentive." Because the depth and duration of the recession proved very difficult to predict, a persistent uncertainty endured with respect to selecting the right moment for the stimulus. Disagreement over this aspect of the timing issue prevented whole-hearted support of any measure that was considered to take effect too early in the downswing. The last antirecession program in September 1975 was by far the largest (5.0 billion DM as compared to 1.0 billion for each of the others) despite its approval near the end of the recession; the turn-round point had finally arrived.

Decision lag exacerbated the timing problem. More than one official described why it might take six to seven months before an initial idea eventually takes effect: "If I now [in October] propose an investment incentive, it will first have to go through our ministry, then to the cabinet, then to Parliament, and will still take another few months to execute. In the end, it will not start having effect until May or June." Programs do not go into effect immediately, it takes time to draw them up, to gain support, and achieve final approval. Extra antirecession expenditures were not supposed to simply increase aggregate demand but rather were designed to supplement and complement the ongoing investment programs in the individual ministries.

A decision lag would effect the correct timing of the investment programs within the development of the business cycle. Yet there is some evidence from the 1974 to 1975 period that the requirements of the decision lag also produced smaller antirecession programs. Decision makers worked under a more severe time constraint than usual due to the unpredictability of the trend of the recession. After the passage of the first program, the government optimistically hoped that the recession would bottom out, making further measures unnecessary. But as the slump continued to worsen, policymakers realized that something more had to be done right away. This pattern of successive decisions repeated itself four times before the downturn had run its course. In each case policymakers had little more than a couple months to draw up the special programs, despite the two-year duration of the recession.

The two antirecession programs of 1967 amounted to 3 to 5 billion marks each, despite the much milder nature of that recession.[15] One policymaker estimated that to have had a comparable impact to 1967, considering inflation and the worse economic situation, the 1974 programs would have had to amount to "at least 15.0 billion marks." Why was the 1974 discretionary expenditure response so much less? In part the uncertainty over the correct policy, given the structural and inflationary tendencies, prevented agreement on one course of action. The Tax Reform, had fortuitously reduced overall tax levels, thereby making an expenditure stimulus less necessary. But in addition to these important off-setting tendencies, most officials involved in the drawing up of the antirecession programs felt that the time constraint had also prevented larger programs. One official, in reference to the 900 million spent for the first program in March 1974 concluded that, "If 5.0 billion had been required, that would have been hard to do within this time period. All we could have done, a'la Keynes, would have been to set up public-works projects that had people digging ditches."

Another official, when asked if 5.0 billion would have been a possible target for the 1974 programs, responded, "No . . . to an extent, the issue of capacity is important given the time period. We could not build that many roads."

An economics official, after mentioning that the three programs in 1974 had contained additional investments of 3.0 billion marks that were given out rapidly and successfully, added that, "But if it had been necessary to increase the investments to, say, 4 to 5 billion, that would have been much more problematical and would have taken a longer time to fulfill. In the middle-range financial plans, we look for areas of flexibility and try to work with them."[16]

If it were not considered necessary to integrate the extra investment spending into the middle-range programs of the individual ministries, larger projects might have been undertaken of the public-works type, which, from the point of view of the Finance Ministry, make little economic sense in a substantive policy framework. This is perhaps one reason why the Finance and Economics Ministries could claim an inability to devise larger programs given the time constraint, while the spending ministries consistently proposed larger spending than was eventually approved. The other factor was the difficulty of reaching agreement over the relative positions of each ministry in the overall program.

Planning and Flexibility

What has prediction uncertainty done to the process by which the budget policy is made? One problem is that a gap has emerged between the time needed to plan the budget substantively and the flexibility needed to adapt the budget to economic management. A division director described the problem as follows:

> Economic-stabilization-policy data cannot be gathered more than three to four months before the budget is decided, or they are simply wrong. In fact a shorter period would be preferable. For budget planning, on the other hand, you need a period of around ten months. In order to do this, therefore, you have to neglect the stabilization side. The projections must anticipate a twelve-month period for the budget. But that is the problem. The projections are no good after three to four months. . . . If you want to draw up a budget over the longer-term, you can't decide every three months what you are going to do.

The concern over the economic effects of the budget has reduced the time for some aspects of budget planning below the usual eighteen-month period. The budget people especially do not like the uncertainty that economic management introduced into their attempts at planning the financial and substantive components of the budget.

People involved in debt management also expressed concern over the inability to predict the capital market, as indicated by the comment that, "It is practically impossible at the beginning of the year to say this and this debt level is [economically] correct. You simply cannot predict the developments accurately enough." The uncertainty produces cautious, temporary advice that must be looked at again in a few months: "There is no decisive judgment, therefore, that comes out of the analysis. We simply say that from the present view, the credit level looks satisfactory." Would six months represent an adequate interval on which to base a judgment? The answer was: "Six months is still too long. We still would not be able to say for sure."

The miscarriage of the prognoses has meant that the tax income estimates have proven false: "The long awaited tax income has still not arrived despite the projections that it would be here already. For that reason we had to pass the supplementary budget last summer."[17]

A member of the Budget Committee in the Bundestag confirmed this sequential approach to the recession: "Income estimates may be way off, as they were this past year. This means that the government has had to go step by step through the year. X billion has to be added to the budget because the income did not suffice."

One reason for the unexpectedly low tax yield was the 1974 Tax Reform. Although the reform was not planned or even subsequently intended as an economic-management measure, it had that kind of effect at the right time. A business-cycle analyst, commenting on the reform, discounted its economic purpose: "These perceptions and decisions, however, came successively, one after the other. It was not planned in advance. . . . I want to emphasize again that the decisions [in this case, on the antirecession-investment programs] were taken successively, one at a time. We had one program, then another."

The budget cycle was effected in different ways by these considerations. The drawing up of the 1976 budget, for example, was postponed until early in the fall.[18] A main explanation for the shift was the uncertainty over the economic developments for 1976. Not until after the August Cabinet meeting did Finance Minister Apel engage in discussions with individual ministries over specific percentage increases for spending programs. The Economics Ministry decided to postpone its yearly economic goal projection for 1976 until later into the summer of 1975 (usually it is done in May or June). As a budget official explained, "The Economics Ministry feels that the business-cycle development for this year is not clear enough to make projections for the coming year as well. We therefore must wait for this projection until a later date."

As the problem of unemployment grew, so did the size of the later antirecession programs. The greater investment spending resulted in a revised procedure for drawing up the government's investment plan under the Financial Planning Scheme. An official responsible for investment planning emphasized the shortened time perspective: "We do not make such detailed plans as before nor do they include such a long planning period. The figures must be regularly revised, or they will soon be too old to be of any use." An innovation is the "Flexibility Report," which serves to indicate which investment items might be quickly brought together into a special antirecession program.

In all these ways, the prediction uncertainty of the 1974 to 1975 recession resulted in a shrinking of the time frame for budget planning. The drawing up of the budget was postponed as was the making of economic projections. The reliability of data was considered not to extend beyond three to four months. Especially budget officials expressed concern about the ten- to twelve-month period normally required for the planning of the substantive programs in the budget. If adaptation of the budget to economic developments meant jeopardizing this planning period, many of them were opposed to using the budget for economic management at all. Inability to predict or determine the future, however, reinforced a step-by-step approach to policymaking. Any other strategy would have resulted in policy built on false assumptions.

Uncertainty, Organizational Goals, and Economic Management

The inability to predict economic developments over the entire budget cycle has forced budget planners to orient the initial macrobudget on assumed, regular rates of growth in expenditures and national product. But during the later planning and implementation phases, actual developments may not conform to the earlier assumed regular growth rates. If developments turn out worse than expected, as they did in 1974 to 1975, the government will find itself, due to the *automatic*

Planning and Flexibility 75

stabilizers built into the budget, giving out more for unemployment compensation and receiving less in tax-yield revenues. Policymakers must also decide whether to engage in any discretionary action to prevent further deterioration between projections and developments. For these reasons, the uncertainty that economic management introduces into macrobudgeting is concentrated in the later planning and initial implementation phases, thereby producing an actual expenditure trend that has an anticyclical bias (see figure 4–1).

The practice of economic management in the 1970s has involved budgeters in at least two major kinds of uncertainty. The first type is based on a lack of cause-effect understanding of a general problem in society.[19] This fundamental form of uncertainty, which is here referred to as *diagnostic uncertainty*, centered in 1974 to 1975 around the controversy over the concurrent existence of unemployment and inflation, contrary to orthodox economic theory. Policymakers had to decide what (if anything) should be done; but with no known or understood trade-off between the two variables, the choice of what to do became increasingly difficult.

Although the initial policy came from a theoretical ambiguity, finding a satisfactory political solution was hindered by the bureaucratic and partisan structuring of its various dimensions.[20] The officials at the Bundesbank worried about protecting the currency; budget managers placed high priority on controlling the growing deficit; and both groups favored placing more emphasis on

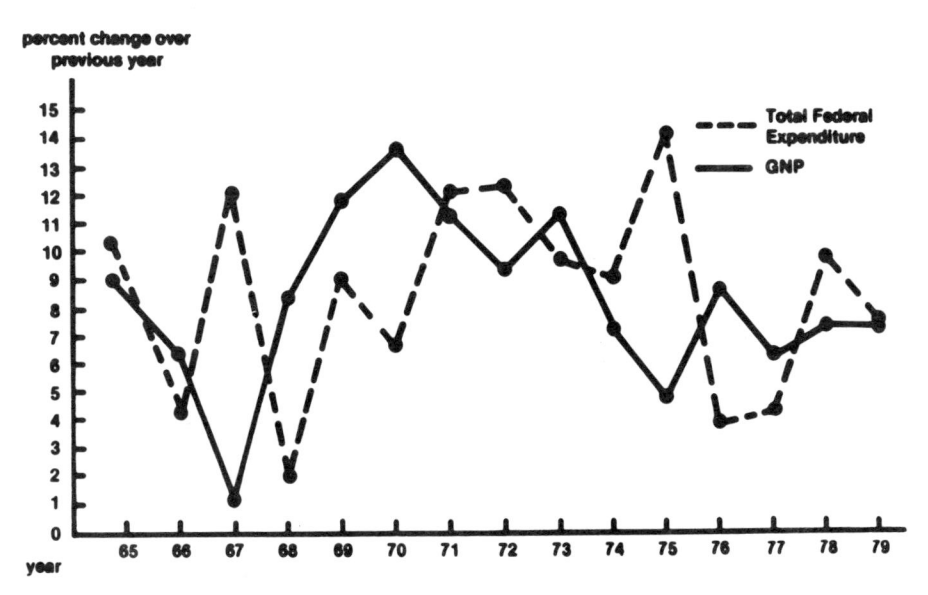

Source: *Finanzberichte*, 1968–1980 (Bonn: Bundesministerium der Finanzen).
Note: Figures for 1979 are according to budget plan and economic projection.

Figure 4–1. The Anticyclical Bias of Federal Expenditures, 1965 to 1979

curbing inflation than either the long-term growth officials concerned with structural changes or the business-cycle officials occupied with unemployment (see figure 4–2). The various dimensions of the problem also followed political-party lines due to the make up of the coalition government. The Liberals tended to accept the structural explanation and the importance of inflation, while the Social Democrats placed greater emphasis on unemployment and traditional fiscal policies.

An inability to diagnose the policy problem may hinder the formation of a consensus around a common program. Sapolsky, for example, argues that when there is not general agreement on strategic strategy, weapons projects fail to gain full deployment, development, or support, the result being that they often are funded sporadically. He presents evidence that a strategic disagreement was involved in the research program on the Fleet Ballistic Missile communications hardware, "and thus the research program languished halfway between initiation and deployment."[21] A similar lack of purpose characterized the initial antirecession programs in 1974. The size of the programs, for example, was noticeably smaller than in 1967, despite a higher rate of unemployment in the 1974 to 1975 recession. The Bundesbank, certain elements in the Economics Ministry, and the Budget Division in the Finance Ministry only reluctantly supported additional stimulus measures due to the uncommonly high rate of inflation. There was a feeling that the government needed to do something to fight the growing unemployment, yet there was also very little enthusiasm for a large stimulus package that might push up prices even further.

A second type of uncertainty present in the 1970s was the inability to accurately predict economic changes in production, employment, prices, and tax

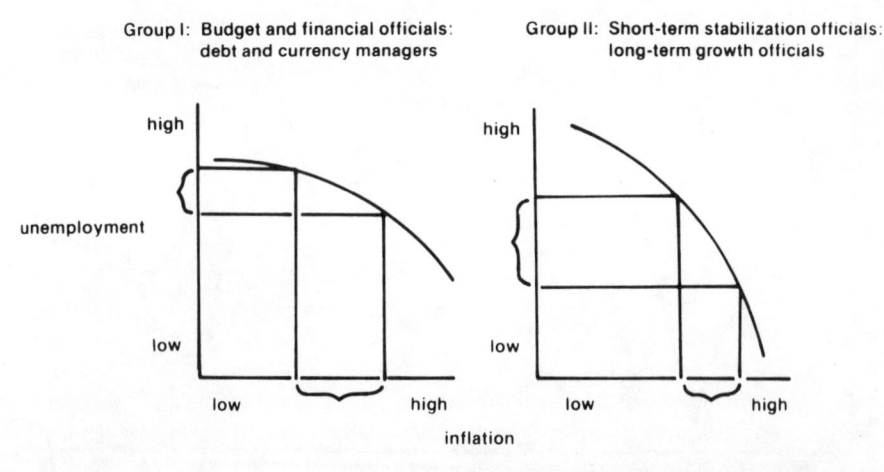

Figure 4–2. Bureaucratic Structuring of the Trade-Off between Inflation and Unemployment

yields more than a few months in advance. This *measurement uncertainty* is distinguished from diagnostic uncertainty in that it is not primarily concerned with theoretical understanding or consistency. Instead, what is at issue is the extent of the problem's presence. How big or small the problem is forms the central question, not whether the correct interconnections among the problem's dimensions are sufficiently understood.

The main effect of measurement uncertainty on economic management was to shorten the normal time frame for budget planning, thereby introducing informal changes in certain aspects of the budget throughout the fiscal year. The most notable examples of informal, recurrent changes were the special antirecession-investment programs, which did not form part of a ministry's regular budget but could be passed at any time throughout the year. The passage of the supplementary budget, although a formal addition to the regular budget, also represents an alteration in the course of the budget to accommodate changing circumstances. Finally, the debt policy changed substantially from the restrictions of a small deficit to prevent interest rates from rising to the acceptance of uncommon debt as interest rates gradually fell and the recession continued to worsen.

Caiden and Wildavsky have found that uncertainty in poor countries produces what they term "repetitive budgeting"—an informal, remaking of the budget throughout the fiscal year.[22] Formal-budget documents in poor countries are passed each year but do not correspond closely to what is actually spent. Each ministry faces unforeseen bottlenecks between supply and demand, political instability, and little redundancy to insulate it against unanticipated consequences. In the advanced, industrial country of West Germany, the environment in which the budget is made little resembles the multiple uncertainties of poor countries. Yet economic management has placed demands on the formal budget that are difficult to meet. Consequently in both instances uncertainty in the policy environment caused repetitive, informal changes in policy to take account of new developments.

Uncertainty produces repetitive budgeting in poor countries because it gives the finance ministry greater control over the dispersal of funds as the contingencies of the situation evolve. The motivation for repetitive budgeting is to hedge against uncertainty caused by bottlenecks and instability. Similarly the German Finance Ministry hedged against uncertainty by trying to control the flow of funds throughout the year. Instead of passing contingency programs far in advance of need, thereby awakening desires in the spending ministries that may have proved difficult to deal with if circumstances had not warranted the additional expenditures, the Finance Ministry worked toward a minimal base budget that could then be informally supplemented later on through the special-investment programs.

Halting short-term–budget planning also represents a case of uncertainty avoidance as described by Cyert and March, who write that organizations hedge against uncertainty by avoiding the requirement "that they correctly anticipate events in the distant future by using decision rules emphasizing short-run reaction to short-run feedback rather than anticipation of long-run events."[23] But will an organization avoid uncertainty at all costs? An organization might prefer to accept a degree of uncertainty if the goal it is pursuing is considered worth the risk. A trade-off of this sort is generally operative in capital-investment decisions. If an investor is willing to put a large sum of money into a highly risky venture, he anticipates that the success of the venture will provide him with much greater returns than he could get from less risky alternatives. Uncertainty avoidance is not an objective for its own sake but rather one of many organizational goals that must be weighed against each other.

If organizational goals are incompatible, the attempt to avoid uncertainty in the pursuance of one goal may introduce greater uncertainty in the attainment of other goals. The federal government discovered that avoiding uncertainty in the pursuit of discretionary fiscal policy collided with avoiding uncertainty in substantive budget planning. Short-term, halting action to stimulate the economy shifted uncertainty from the Macroeconomic Policy Division to the Budget Planning Division, which preferred a longer time frame for its activities. If an organization can achieve what it wants with less uncertainty, it will choose that course of action; but if the organization cannot attain a highly prized goal without introducing uncertainty into its other operations, it may still choose the uncertain course if the alternative to doing so is too disagreeable. The Bonn government delayed the drawing up of the 1976 budget and postponed the yearly *Goal Projection* until later in the spring, despite the greater uncertainty these actions caused for the expenditure function of the budget policy.

A hypothetical economic manager, therefore, may be conceived of as facing a situation in which there exists a trade-off between the uncertainties surrounding the *demand* for fiscal-policy action (prediction of the needs in the economy) and the uncertainties involved in the *supply* of fiscal-policy programs (time needed to draw up meaningful investment packages). The demand uncertainty at time T_1 is initially low because the needs in the economy are readily measurable, but as predictions are made for times T_2 and T_3, demand uncertainty rises. Eventually the uncertainty should again fall in later time periods as the types of variables that are predicted take on a less detailed and coarser orientation.[24] Supply uncertainty at time T_1, however, is initially very high because little time is available for the agreement process or the physical activity required to draw up meaningful stimulus programs. But in times T_2 and T_3, the supply uncertainty diminishes as the right programs are worked out and agreed upon. In the more distant futures, supply uncertainty may again begin to rise because of the difficulty of planning investments so far in advance of substantive needs. As figure 4–3 indicates, if the experience with investment programs in West Germany is any guide, the two demand-supply curves should converge somewhere in the T_2 time range. During 1974 and 1975, this period amounted to around four to six months.

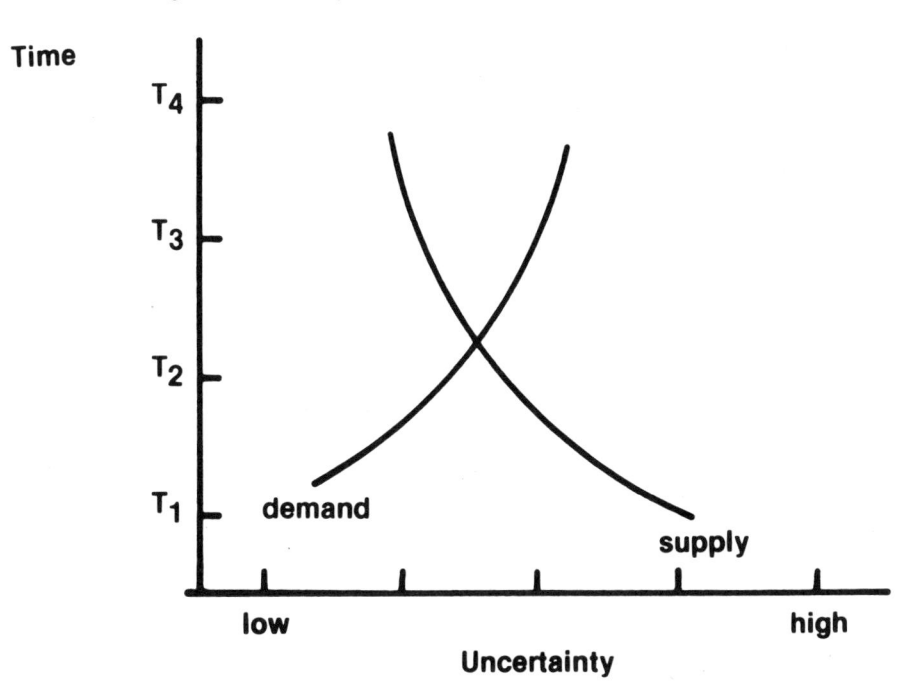

Figure 4–3. Demand and Supply of Fiscal-Policy Programs

If the economic manager takes a long time to draw up the stimulus program, he runs the risk that it will not meet the needs of the economy at that time. But if he decides to wait and see what the needs will be, he may lose the opportunity to have enough time to draw up a meaningful stimulus package. There is probably no satisfactory solution to this economic-management–budgeting-dilemma; for if the federal government wants to fine-tune the economy (and strong political pressures push in that direction), it will force the Finance Ministry into approving items that it just recently rejected on substantive grounds. Thus by the beginning of 1976 the Finance Ministry only reluctantly supported discretionary anticyclical-expenditure policy and increasingly pushed for a greater emphasis on the monetary-policy instrument. By the end of 1976, it had its way.

The federal government's fine-tuning economic management also had to contend with considerable uncertainty in its dealings with the state and local governments. Since these local administrations actually spend the anticyclical funds, their participation and support are essential for the success of economic policy. The state governments' perspective on short-term–economic management, however, differs significantly from that of the federal government. They generally are more concerned with meeting social needs than with macroeconomic policy. The inevitable federal-state conflict that resulted eventually led the

Bonn government to cut its grants in aid to the states, despite continued high unemployment.

Notes

1. Alfred L. Malabre, "Has a Slump Started?" *Wall Street Journal*, 1 November 1979, p. 1.

2. A discussion of decision lags is found in Assar Lindbeck, "Is Stabilization Policy Possible?—Time Lags and Conflict of Goals," in *Public Finance and Stabilization Policy*, ed. Warren L. Smith and John M. Culbertson (New York: American Elsevier Publishing Co., 1974), pp. 269-308.

3. For an excellent example of this debate, see Milton Friedman and Walter W. Heller, *Monetary vs. Fiscal Policy* (New York: W.W. Norton, 1969).

4. See Albrecht Zunker, *Finanzplanung und Bundeshaushalt: Zur Koordinierung und Kontrolle durch den Bundesfinanzminister* (Frankfurt am Main: Alfred Metzner Verlag, 1972), pp. 97-224 for a discussion of the timing problem involved in coordinating multiyear financial planning with yearly budgeting. Financial planning tries to extend planning horizons, whereas fiscal policy in practice works to shorten them.

5. Article 8 of the *Grundgesetz* provides for the budgetary handling of special stabilization items, including the antirecession-program spending: the regular budget (section 6002, title 97101) does not contain any figures for stabilization programs, but the government may spend funds from this title up to the amount of stabilization reserves held at the Bundesbank, or if more is needed, through borrowing—so long as the Bundesrat gives its approval.

6. For a more detailed treatment of these antirecession programs, see chapter 9, tables 9-1 and 9-2.

7. For a discussion of the importance of establishing trust in budgetary relations between the Finance Ministry and the spending ministries in Great Britain, see Hugh Heclo and Aaron Wildavsky, *The Private Government of Public Money: Community and Policy Inside British Politics* (Berkeley: University of California Press, 1974), especially pp. 15-20, 61-63, and 120-123.

8. See, for example, Institut Finanzen und Steuern, "Information über die Entwicklung der Oeffentlichen Finanzwirtschaft in der Bundesrepublik Deutschland von 1964-74" (Bonn: Institut Finanzen und Steuern, 1974). See also Dieter Vesper, "Die Personalausgaben der Gebietskörperschaften von 1961-1972," *Vierteljahresheft* 2 (West Berlin: Deutsches Institut für Wirtschaftsforschung, 1975), who writes that "Stabilization policy—in so far as expenditures are concerned—is in fact only pursued through the variation of investment expenditures" (p. 18). Vesper also states that, because of the persistently strong demand in the Federal Republic, "the government has been forced to cut investment expenditures." See Dieter Vesper, "Ein Vortrag über staatliche Wirtschafts—

und Finanzpolitik," (West Berlin: Deutsches Institut für Wirtschaftsforschung, 1974).

9. These figures were provided to me directly by the budget office in the Federal Transportation Ministry in Bonn.

10. Under the special stabilization-program scheme, the Bundestag has only thirty days in which to either approve or disapprove of the programs. But as one member of the Budget Committee complained, "We are not allowed to change the amounts, discuss adequately the total figures, or make proposals of our own." The legal basis for the stabilization programs is found in the *Grundgesetz*, article 104a, paragraph 4. See *Das neue Haushaltsrecht* (Bonn: Bundesministerium der Finanzen, 1969), p. 33.

11. The September 1974 program, for example, contained 122 million marks in investment for transportation out of a total of 250 million. If defense and internal security are added, the figure rises to 192 million. Out of the 700 million marks in this part of the program that was jointly financed by the federal government and the states, 540 million went for municipal infrastructure investments. See, "950-Mio-DM-Sonderprogramm zur regionalen und lokalen Abstützung," *Aktuelle Beiträge zur Wirtschafts- und Finanzpolitik* no. 121 (Presse- und Informationsamt der Bundesregierung, November 1974).

12. This information was obtained directly from the Economics Ministry.

13. Hans Korff, *Haushaltspolitik: Instrument öffentlicher Macht* (Stuttgart: Kohlhammer Verlag, 1975). The special stabilization reserves are created by holding a portion of tax income or credit at the Bundesbank according to articles 5 and 7 of the Stability and Growth Law (Gesetz zur Förderung der Stabilität und des Wachstums der Wirtschaft, 8 June 1967). The federal government with the approval of the Bundesrat can order that it and the states freeze up to 3 percent of last year's tax yield at the bank. The federal government with Bundesrat approval can also raise the income-tax rate up to 10 percent in case of economic excess demand and freeze these surcharges at the Bundesbank. The unfreezing of these jointly created reserves also requires the approval of the Bundesrat. Reserves created voluntarily, however, by each level of government, may be released without the approval of the other level.

14. See, for example, Morton Halperin, *Bureaucratic Politics and Foreign Policy* (Washington D.C.: The Brookings Institution, 1974), pp. 147–155.

15. See, for example, "Das Tal ist diesmal tiefer," *Die Zeit,* 15 August 1975, p. 22, and "Zweimal Rezession," *Suddeutsche Zeitung,* 30 July 1975, p. 7.

16. Hans Korff, a former budget director in Bonn, writes that "In order to prepare the expenditures [for an antirecession program], at least a period of one month is required. For larger projects, this time is far from sufficient." A bit later he explains what he considers a drawback of using mainly investment expenditures for stabilization programs: "Their disadvantage is that they require a great deal of administrative time to prepare. The difficulty of spending 1.0

billion marks in public (investments) is widely underestimated." See Korff, *Haushaltspolitik,* pp. 44–45.

17. "Der Zeitpunkt des Aufschwungs Bleibt unsicher," *Suddeutsche Zeitung,* 19 June 1975, p. 17 and "So wurde 1975 zum Jahr der Fehl-prognosen," *Welt am Sonntag,* 28 June 1975.

18. "Etagengespräche in engem Korsett, *"Suddeutsche Zeitung,* 12–13 July 1975, p. 31.

19. James Thompson, *Organizations in Action* (New York: McGraw Hill, 1967), p. 159.

20. See Charles Perrow, *Complex Organizations: A Critical Essay* (Glenview, Illinois: Scott, Foresman and Co., 1972), pp. 152–154 for a discussion of the rise in internal uncertainty due to increased subunit links to the outside environment.

21. Harvey M. Sapolsky, *The Polaris System Development: Bureaucratic and Programmatic Success in Government* (Cambridge, Massachusetts: Harvard University Press, 1972), p. 240.

22. Naomi Caiden and Aaron Wildavsky, *Planning and Budgeting in Poor Countries* (New York: John Wiley and Sons, 1974), pp. 71–78.

23. Richard Cyert and James March, *A Behavioral Theory of the Firm* (Englewood Cliffs, New Jersey: Prentice-Hall, 1963), p. 119.

24. This is the position taken by Karl-Heinz Raabe, subdivision director in the Economics Ministry for Macroeconomic Forecasts. See his, "Gesamtwitschaftliche Analysen, Prognosen, und Projektionen und Ihre Rolle in der Wirtschaftspolitik," 12 December 1974; obtained directly from the Economics Ministry in Bonn.

5 Meeting Social Needs: Economic Management and State Budgeting

In 1967 we had great hopes that through the budget and other instruments we could control the business cycle. But to brake a boom economy with public expenditure has proven to be impossible . . . the budget is a result of a drawn out political compromise and not scientific adjustment. The pressure of public opinion is very strong on the state level, and the first task is to meet the social needs.[1] —State Budget Director

The federal government's management of the economy is intimately tied to federal political relations. Economic management is concerned with the impact of total public spending on the aggregate trends in the economy. In West Germany federal-government spending accounts for only about 25 percent of this total, while the major component of the public budget is the spending of the state administrations. In the German federal system they implement and administer most federal laws, control all grants in aid to the municipalities, and take responsibility for (and in practice heavily influence) local debt policy. The state governments constitute, therefore, a major uncertainty in the task environment of federal macroeconomic officials.

The central role of the states in public spending would not be a large problem for federal officials if state budgets followed federal macroeconomic-policy guidelines. But unfortunately state budgets often run directly counter to federal actions, especially during times of economic expansion.[2] Some federal officials attribute the relatively poor macroeconomic-management record of the states to the fact that "most state budgeters are lawyers who know little and care less about macroeconomic policy." This sentiment is used to support proposals for improving macroeconomic policy by centralizing fiscal decisions in Bonn (see chapter 7).

Though it is true that the state economics ministries lack the expertise and influence of the federal Economics Ministry, the explanation for state economic management is not found in the dominance of lawyers or the lack of macroeconomic training. Much more crucial for understanding state behavior is their position in the federal organizational structure: state governments deal primarily with administration, whereas the federal government is mostly concerned with policy formulation and policy analysis. State budgeting and politics in turn reflect this policy-administration dichotomy.

As largely administrative entities, the state governments must live with the budgetary features of large-scale bureaucracies. They have a very high personnel component to their budgets, including well-organized public-employee unions. They also have numerous administrative contacts with the general public through their service activities, in addition to being the target of most lobbying efforts by private-interest groups. Not surprisingly state budget directors give foremost attention to the political allocation of spending. But as the financial managers of large bureaucracies, the budget directors must also hold down costs. They try to maintain their state's credit rating, assure adequate financing of programs, and avoid any significant long-term increases in debt.[3] Setting the state-budget policy, therefore, is largely a tug-of-war between financial control of the bureaucracy and political allocation among competing groups.

These administrative and service tasks make economic management prohibitively costly. The first problem is that employee unions and service recipients do not view kindly stabilization cuts during economic expansions, giving fiscal policy an inflationary bias.[4] Second, the recognition of the problem in the economy often lags too far behind for useful preventive action by the government. Worse still, the effort and negotiation to reach a decision adds further uncertainty.[5] Stagflation even raises doubts about the appropriate direction for expenditure change. Economic management thus requires that state governments risk cherished financial and political goals for economic purposes that are hard to achieve and not well understood—an unhappy recipe for decisive action.

Yet legal and constitutional provisions and the central place of the states in intergovernmental grants in aid do not allow their budget directors to escape economic management altogether.[6] What they can be expected to do, because of the unsuitability of their budgets for economic management, is to emphasize, even more than the federal government, accommodation strategies for reconciling conflicting budget criteria. The macroeconomic policy that such accommodations produce is not likely to be recognizable in textbook economics, but it is more likely to succeed in state politics where the foremost task is to meet programmatic needs. Is this desirable?[7] Judgment should be reserved until after we have examined the management of the economy at the state level.

Fiscal Policy and State Budgets

The states administer the laws, and the federal government makes them—an exaggerated yet valuable observation about German federalism. The German Basic Law gives the federal government responsibility for legislative, regulative, tax, and distributive policies and the state governments the tasks of administration and execution of legislation.[8] In practice the division is not nearly so neat. Laws are not always as detailed as they might be, leaving important policy decisions to those who implement them. The states also directly influence policymaking through their representatives in the Bundesrat. The 1969 Finance Reform gave clout to this arrangement, for any measure affecting the financial relation between the state and federal governments—a preponderance of the legislation—requires the Upper House's approval.[9] In addition, efforts to create a *cooperative federalism* have tended to blur a neat functional division between the two levels in the fields of education, regional planning, and agriculture.[10]

Formidable developments toward joint planning have not abolished the policy-administration distinction. Except in the fields of police protection, state roads, education up to the university level, and state and local administration, the states must share with, or defer to, the policymaking perogatives of other levels of government.[11] Most federal agencies do not have field offices but must rely on state administrations for implementation. (Important exceptions include the postal system, federal railway system, and the military.) The states are responsible for the implementation of federal and state laws and for the direct provision of services to the populace. Although the states formally have independent legislative competence, certain policy areas are reserved for the exclusive right of the federal government and certain other areas to legislative concurrence. In the latter case, the states may legislate in these policy areas only if the federal government has not already done so. In practice the federal government actively legislates in twenty-six policy fields.

The dominant emphasis on administration at the state level is reflected in the composition of state budgets. Personnel costs comprise a much larger proportion of total expenditures than at the federal level. Between 1971 and 1978, personnel costs comprised 42.5 percent of the total outlay. In constrast the proportion of the budget that has gone to personnel costs at the federal and local levels is 16.6 percent and 29.1 percent respectively. (In the United States, the percentage of total state spending that goes to wages and salaries has hovered around 18 to 19 percent between 1975 and 1979.)[12]

Over the past two decades, personnel costs have generally increased faster than other budget components. Between 1966 and 1971, a fast growth period, personnel costs grew 88.1 percent; the other components of the budget grew at only 36.4 percent. Especially personnel costs for education, research, and cultural institutions showed enormous increases, growing for this period by 132.5 percent.[13] Personnel expenditures at the state level, between 1965 and 1975 grew faster than the rest of the budget and faster than the gross national product. A similar pattern emerges for total governmental expenditure on personnel (see figure 5–1). During boom periods and recessions personnel costs have expanded faster than GNP and have showed less fluctuation than investment expenditures.[14]

The large personnel component and statutory requirements make state budgets highly inflexible instruments for fiscal policy. Figure 5–2, for example, shows the mandatory character of the 1976 budget in Baden-Württemberg. Less than 5 percent of the budget is manipulable in any way. Approximately 55 percent is tied up in either federal legislation or personnel costs. Another 30

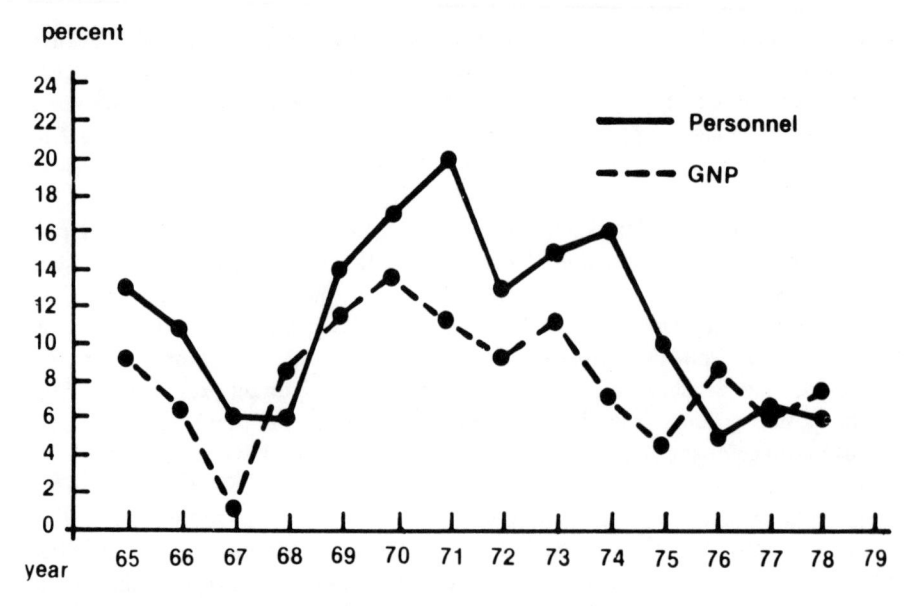

Source: *Finanzberichte, 1970–1980* (Bonn: Bundesministerium der Finanzen).
Note: Figures for 1978 for the states and municipalities are estimates.

Figure 5–1. Total Governmental Personnel Costs (Percentage Annual Change)

percent is based on legal obligations of one kind or another. None of these categories can be changed in the short run for economic management.

The second effect of the division of labor between policy and administration is that the states more than the federal government are directly responsible for delivering governmental services to the populace. In the areas of social welfare, education, police, the courts, cultural activities, and so on the states deal with people through their public employees. In addition, approximately 22 percent of state spending subsidizes municipalities. The provision of state aid to the municipalities, moreover, is not restricted to state programs but extends to many local services. The states must contend, therefore, with three large political constituencies: public-employee unions, private-interest groups, and local government officials.

Private-interest groups, like individual ministries, do not make the general welfare their main concern. To promote overall well-being for the economy is not their purpose. If criminal or terrorist activities increase, lobbyists for improved police protection are not deterred by the state of the economy. Similarly, concerned parents oppose reductions in educational services, environmentalists reject relaxing of pollution laws, and so forth. These groups want the provision of the particular service regardless of economic management.

Meeting Social Needs 87

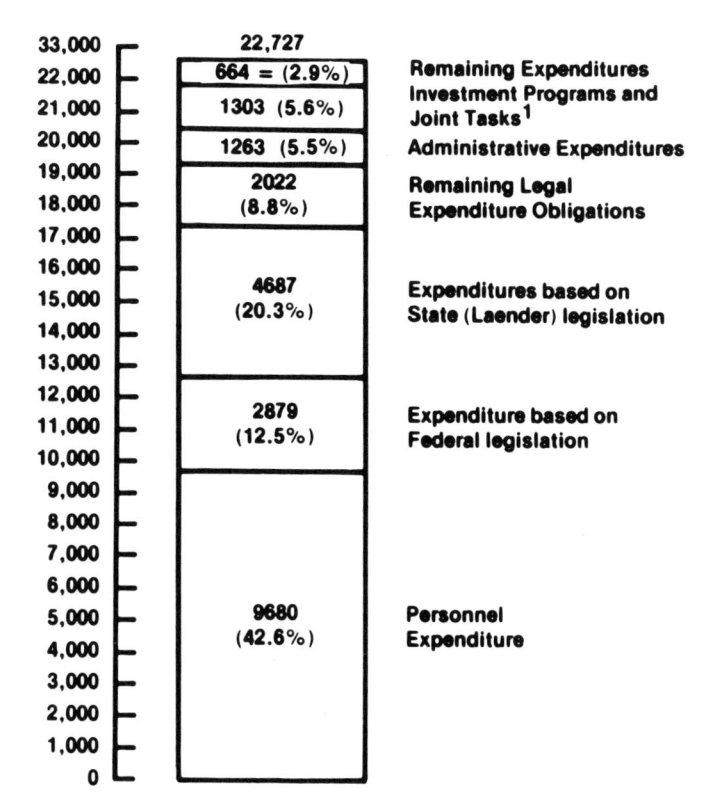

```
33,000 ─    22,727
22,000 ─   ┌──────────────┐
           │ 664 = (2.9%) │   Remaining Expenditures
21,000 ─   ├──────────────┤   Investment Programs and
           │ 1303 (5.6%)  │   Joint Tasks¹
20,000 ─   ├──────────────┤
           │ 1263 (5.5%)  │   Administrative Expenditures
19,000 ─   ├──────────────┤
           │    2022      │   Remaining Legal
18,000 ─   │   (8.8%)     │   Expenditure Obligations
17,000 ─   │              │
16,000 ─   ├──────────────┤
15,000 ─   │    4687      │   Expenditures based on
           │   (20.3%)    │   State (Laender) legislation
14,000 ─   │              │
13,000 ─   ├──────────────┤
12,000 ─   │              │
11,000 ─   │    2879      │   Expenditure based on
           │   (12.5%)    │   Federal legislation
10,000 ─   │              │
 9,000 ─   ├──────────────┤
 ...
 5,000 ─   │    9680      │   Personnel
 4,000 ─   │   (42.6%)    │   Expenditure
 ...
     0 ─   └──────────────┘
```

Source: Calculated from Robert Gleichauf, "Ein Haushalt harter Realitäten und Grossen Risiken," Speech delivered to the BW Parliament on the occasion of the submission of the Budget Proposal for 1975–1976, p. 52 in the statistical appendix.

[1] The Joint Tasks expenditures are quasi-mandatory. Once these are deducted, the nonmandatory share of the budget (including the category, "Remaining Expenditures") amounts to 829 million DM (3.6 percent). The quasi-mandatory part of the Joint Tasks amounted to 1138 million DM in 1976.

Figure 5–2. The Mandatory Character of Baden-Württemberg's Budget, 1976

Public employee wage demands in either expansionary or inflationary periods are designed to prevent real-money losses, making public-personnel costs rise at least as fast as income. During recessions, wages tend to be "sticky" in the downward direction, bringing about the expansionary effects of public-personnel costs. Altering this pattern for fiscal policy invites severe opposition from the public-employee unions, who favor deficit spending during recessions but resist stabilization cuts during booms.

The intergovernmental lobby has also become a powerful force in federal politics.[15] Municipal politicians and officials sit as members of the State Parliaments *(Lantage)* and use these bodies to lobby against using state subsidies and grants to the municipalities for stabilization policy. Like the other levels of government, they prefer to shift budgetary uncertainty onto others by demanding a steady source of income, not one which fluctuates with the economy. If the money is available, their bias is against cuts in local grant programs because programmatic needs are too great.

Each constituency accepts some cuts in funding with less severe opposition during times of recession. These periods strengthen the position of the State Finance Minister because he can simply argue that no more money is available. During the 1974 to 1975 recession, for instance, some states pushed against the legal limit for borrowing.[16] Even though the legal limit can be manipulated in practice, the occasion to have to do something about it gives the budget director a strong case against further borrowing.

The problems in the economy on the other hand become much more evident during recessions than during expansions. The political pressures to bolster employment and sagging demand grow stronger and stronger. During recessions, therefore, the budget directors must work even harder to keep down the size of the deficit, knowing that it will increase anyway as tax income falls off.

The stimulative or dampening effect of state spending depends on debt policy which lies in between the municipalities and the federal government from a fiscal policy perspective (see figure 5–3). The municipalities have followed a pronouncedly procyclical trend, having greatly increased borrowing during the boom

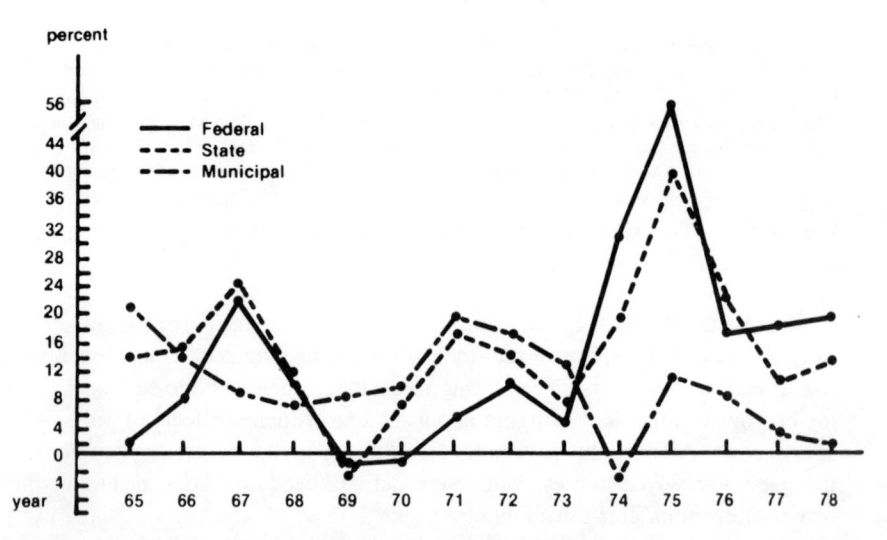

Source: *Finanzberichte, 1970–1980* (Bonn: Bundesministerium der Finanzen).
Note: The debt level is recorded for December 31 of each year.

Figure 5–3. Percentage Annual Change in Debt Assumption

periods, except for the most recent period of moderate growth. The federal government showed the greatest amount of restraint during the booms and matched the states' increased borrowing during the recession. The states did significantly increase borrowing during 1966 to 1967, a recession year, but were not able to hold down credit assumption during the subsequent long economic expansion. During the growth years, 1969 to 1973, the states' average yearly increase in borrowing amounted to 12.8 percent. Earlier, in the boom year 1965, the states had increased borrowing by 14.1 percent. In each case, the increases appear too high in light of the strong expansion in the private economy.[17]

Similar to the history of state spending in the United States, the German states have had a predominantly expansionary impact on the economy over the last fifteen years. Unlike the municipalities, the states did not show extreme caution in borrowing when funds were scarce; unlike the federal government, they did not succeed at holding back growth when funds were available. From 1964 until 1973, the longest boom period, state debt rose 165.1 percent, while the debt of the federal government rose 70.2 percent.[18] Especially during boom periods, therefore, the states failed to stabilize expenditures; they were more successful during recessions at preventing overall negative-growth rates.

Formulating the Macrobudget Figures

How did state budget directors and finance officials view the use of the budget for economic management? Some of them were opposed to varying expenditures in the short run for economic management; all of them expressed doubt about the suitability of the state budgets as instruments for anticyclical policy. The main reason given for the budget's "unsuitability" was the "composition of expenditures. . . . The states simply have other tasks [than the federal government] such as schools and police—and these are very personnel intensive areas." State officials repeatedly volunteered the view that personnel costs give the state budgets a "very compulsive character" especially during times of economic growth. Every state financial official concurred with this judgment: the budget's composition makes it an inflexible instrument for short-term stabilization policy.

The most important difficulties with stabilization policy occur during the planning stage of the budget process. At the beginning of the planning stage, budget planners make decisions about spending that will take place one to two years later. Even at the end of the planning stage, budgetary decisions affect spending one year to come. If planners are concerned about economic management, they must estimate the expected growth in GNP, price increases, capital investment, the money market, the proper size of the deficit, and the growth in expenditures.

The budget planners also need to know tax-yield estimates if they are to make reasonable judgments about providing adequate income to cover expenses.

Yet the state Finance Ministries have expressed a good deal of worry about the tax-yield estimate. Predictions that range over one to two years are not as accurate, in particular during recessions, as those that cover only a three- to six-month time period.[19]

The estimates are made by a Working Group *(Arbeitskreis Steurschätzung)* in the federal Finance Ministry,[20] which bases its calculations on the yearly federal *Goal Projection*. Unlike a probability forecast, the *Goal Projection* does not predict actual developments in the economy. Instead it postulates economic objectives and targets that are considered reasonable and achievable given the actual figures. The assumption is made that the government will take some action to bring about the desired conditions.

Although the goal projections are made in good faith and with the best techniques available, the predicted figures do not always conform to actual economic developments (see figure 3-2). If a discrepancy arises, inevitable suspicion is generated at the state level. The concern with how believable the estimates are also put emphasis on policy direction: "The absolute numbers are not accepted but rather the trend, the direction that is indicated." Most officials felt that the estimates are useful as information but were too optimistic. "Budget planning is especially difficult under these conditions," was the typical conclusion.

The problem with inaccurate predictions is the inflexibility of costs. The only way to cover an overestimated tax yield in an inflexible budget is to increase debt, making the conditions for budget planning "unpredictable and uncertain." The budget officials emphasized, therefore, that the tax-yield estimate is "the main decision criterion for the formulation of the budget." This is how it works:

> We start with the estimates of funding needs of the individual ministries. These are always too high.
>
> (How do you know that?)
>
> Well, if one ministry wants such a large increase, then we say: What if they all demanded similar increases? That would require a borrowing level at least (let us say) of five billion. And that is clearly too much. It will be simply made by a rule of thumb; there are no formulas for this.
>
> (How do you know how fast expenditures should grow?)
>
> It is a rule of thumb and nothing exact. In general, we try to orient the growth rate on the growth in GNP.

In general, three criteria are used for drawing up the macrobudget: spending needs as requested by the various ministries; the expected tax yield for the coming year; and the long-term debt policy. The spending needs are always too high, and the tax yield is the main source of income. The debt policy requires further consideration because in macroeconomic theory, the size of the deficit determines the macroimpact of the public budget on the economy.

No common debt policy is followed among the states, yet control over the size of the debt is commonly considered a major task of the Finance Ministry. Some states more than others come close to using a formula: "In the long run we use the general formula that the yearly debt assumption on average should not exceed 5 to 6 percent of current tax income. There is no scientific basis for this rule. We have simply found from experience that the amortization payments and the interest are large enough at this level that they should not be allowed to go higher." The concern over the interest payments is related to the larger fixed character of the state budgets. Since only a small portion of the budget is manipulable anyway, a significant increase in interest payments cuts further into this little amount. A budget director explained that this leads to a reduction in the "policy directed part of the budget."

Sometimes, however, the size of the deficit for a given year is simply not foreseen in advance. In 1974 one state ended up with approximately 6 billion marks in debt but had only planned to borrow 2.8 billion. As the budget official explained it: ". . . tax income fell off substantially from what was expected. We didn't anticipate this at first. The result is more or less arrived at by accident."

No one rule is appropriate for debt policy, said most budget directors, but some offered other guidelines such as "a rule which ties interest payments to not more than 10 percent of current income." Although in general, no one rule is appropriate, whenever a rule was mentioned, it emphasized keeping debt levels under control in the long run.[21]

A word should also be said about the relation of the financial plan to the drawing up of the budget. According to the Stability and Growth Law (articles 9 and 14), the federal government and the states are supposed to draw up five-year financial plans. The rolling character of these plans requires that they be revised each year to conform to current budgetary conditions. The way this law is carried out differs significantly state by state. Some states such as Baden-Württemberg or the Saarland do not publish their financial plans but use them internally in the Finance Ministry. Other states such as North Rhine-Westphalia do publish their plans largely in the format of the federal government's plan. States such as Lower Saxony or Bremen, however, draw up even more detailed and extensive plans than that at the federal level.

A tension exists between the Finance Ministry, which wants longer-term control of expenditures, and the Cabinet and Parliament, which want enough budgetary flexibility to add their own pet projects when the occasion arises. For budget directors who favored extensive use of the finance plan, it represents a "valuable tool for the Finance Ministry to keep control on expenditures. We know in advance what the expenditures should be, and that is an advantage."

The other side of the issue is that little accommodation is made for changing circumstances. One official stated that the "politicians don't like it that everything seems to be fixed by the financial plan. If an item is not in the plan for 1977, it becomes difficult to put it in. That makes for less flexibility. . . . For this reason, finance planning (in our state) is not so important." From this perspective, the main value of the plan is for internal information, and therefore, not for general publication.

The finance plan serves as a welcome instrument for placing ceilings on expenditure because cost inflation has made the estimates in the plan the strict guidelines that some Finance Ministers perceive them to be. But available evidence indicates that the plans are not well adhered to during the execution of the budget.[22] The plans have changed somewhat the yearly setting of the budget policy by orienting it on amounts contained in the plan, but the yearly rhythm of negotiations and changes does not appear to have changed much, if at all. Their main purpose is budgetary control.

In what ways, then, does economic management enter into the planning of the yearly budget? Do state budget officials employ as a decision aid the neutral budget concept or the full employment surplus budget?[23] The primary figures of interest are predictions of GNP growth and the expected tax yield. Prescribed budget figures based on formal calculations interest the state budget directors only to the extent that their own calculations differ considerably from the formal ones. One budget director summed it up: "This neutral budget concept is purely theoretical and is not used in practice." Budget officials criticized the concept because it does not define "the structure or nature of the debt" and picks a base year that "tends to project its peculiarities into the future." On a regular, yearly basis, in fact, economic management has an almost negligible impact, as typified by this observation:

> It is not possible to alter the formulation of the yearly budget plan according to stabilization policy. At this stage, stabilization policy plays hardly any role. The budget is formulated in April to May but is not passed through the Parliament until December—almost one year later. During this process stabilization policy measures do not enter because the budget is decided too far in advance . . . and other factors are more important.

The only exceptions to the insignificant role played by economic management occurred in 1967 and 1974 to 1975, the two recession periods. In both cases, the state budget officials claimed to have engaged in "deficit spending" by trying to follow the maxim that "in a recession . . . we do not want to reduce expenditures." Or a similar rule that, "we try to keep the level of investments at what they were for the previous year." For the most part, deficit spending is either unavoidable or accidental.

Rather than use any formal measure of the deficit, state budget officials apply their own version of the balanced budget concept (known in Germany as the *Saldenkonzept*). In normal years (those in which no severe recession or expansion exists) economic management plays an insignificant role. During recessions, deficit spending increases borrowing (unavoidably or accidentally) but only to the extent that it does not jeopardize the long-term debt policy. State personnel expenses and investments, for example, dipped slightly in the 1967 recession as compared to earlier rates of growth.[24] During expansions, the states strive for a balanced budget or a surplus. Furthermore, the appropriate growth rate for expenditures is oriented on the growth in GNP, especially in the negotiations with the ministries and the labor unions.

If one uses the balanced budget concept to judge state budgetary trends, a rather favorable development is recorded. In both recession years, 1966 to 1967 and 1974 to 1975, the budget showed an increase in the deficit; in the boom years, 1971 to 1973 a surplus was achieved. In contrast, when either the full employment surplus or the neutral budget measurements are used to judge the state-budget performance, the results show deflationary impulses in both recession years and an inflationary impulse in the boom years.[25] Formal measures would have required a much stronger anticyclical trend to satisfy stabilization policy. For these reasons, most state officials supported the 1975 Economy Program which proposed a drastic reduction in the size of the public debt by 1980 and a strict control over expenditure growth.[26]

The Execution Stage of the Budget Cycle

Few incentives encourage state budget directors to engage in stabilization policy, and internal financial management discourages them from doing so. The hesitancy is even greater, however, when economic forecasts cannot predict accurately six months in advance (as occurred in the most recent recession-boom cycle). The problem is the discrepancy between not knowing what to do in the formulation stage and knowing better what to do in the execution stage. The Stability and Growth Law, in response to this problem, provides for the passage of contingency budgets alongside the regular budget, as was discussed in chapter 4. These special budgets, which are financed out of reserves held at the Bundesbank or by additional debt,[27] were originally formulated at the same time as the regular budget. Since then, however, contingency budgets represent nothing more than the antirecession programs, which are drawn up at the time of need throughout the budget cycle. Yet contingency budgets do represent extra budget amounts set aside for economic management programs.

Contingency budgets on the state level, however, have both an economic-management and a financial-management purpose. Some state governments drew up contingency budgets in 1973 to 1974 during the formulation stage of the budget cycle, but these budgets were not necessarily perceived by officials in the Finance Ministry as extra amounts. "It must be planned in advance during the formulation stage or it won't work," observed one budget official. "What we say is: we are going to hold back capital spending by 10 percent, but if the economy allows, spending may increase later on in the fiscal year." But he added that the contingency budget also contains personnel expenditures and that these figures are deliberately set too low in the regular budget. By using the contingency budget, however, these figures can be adjusted upward and "in this way the contingency budget is not only used for stabilization policy." Those who spoke about contingency budgets used words such as "stoppages" and "expenditure cuts" as synonyms with it. Financial management has merged with economic management.

The closest some states have come to a contingency budget was in 1973 when the tax yield so overshot their projections that they had extra money they could not even spend. They therefore simply left it sitting at the Bundesbank. Those states that had contingency budgets, argued a budget director, did so mainly for reasons of budgetary control:

> We have the impression that the main purpose of the contingency budget is to fulfill on paper the spending wishes of the various ministries when these cannot be fulfilled in reality. I do not think that the budget has all that much to do with stabilization policy . . . this is a measure to make ministries feel that they are getting something when they actually are not.

The reason that these budget directors can blur the purpose of contingency budgets is that expenditure needs and wants have no objective ceiling or limit. Who is to say what is the correct regular amount and what constitutes an extra amount? The budget directors' bias is toward a conservative policy that allows them to control the giving out of funds throughout the fiscal year.

How is it decided how much money should go into the contingency budgets? Is the amount based on calculations of the needs of the economy? One budget official who was asked this question responded, "No, no. It only represents what the possibilities are. We couldn't have done more if we had wanted to. . . . But if the purpose had been to slow down the boom, it was far too little." How then was the figure arrived at (in this case, approximately 800 million)? He said that they looked for areas with nonessential expenditures that could be cut.

Because they were planned relatively far in advance of the actual recession that set in during 1974, the contingency budgets on the state level did not correspond to actual future needs. The contingency budgets were drawn up in 1973 and "of course no one saw how deep the recession would turn out to be." The problem became apparent in 1974 to 1975 when the federal government proposed special antirecession programs which ran into the billions of marks. The somewhat bitter feeling at the state level was that the contingency budgets did "not provide adequate available programs" and "had served little purpose" for economic management.

During economic expansions, tax income increases, making it difficult to keep a lid on the growth in costs. But the contingency budgets are passed in advance, before the ministries get actual approval to spend the funds. All the ministries really get is a promise of future funds if developments work out right. For stabilization policy, the advance passage is detrimental (Who can predict exactly where the business-cycle is headed?). But for budget control, the advance passage is beneficial (Promises are better than nothing.). The Finance Ministry can give the money out over the year without facing a fait accompli from the spending ministries, which oppose stabilization cuts in planned amounts. One state had a 10 percent stoppage of investment expenditures in 1973 and a contingency budget in 1974; but as the budget official explained, "in principle they work the same way."

To change the amounts in the budget plan according to stabilization policy is extremely difficult "especially when the changes require cuts in the budget." The problem is that the ministries know that the money is available during boom periods: "How can the Finance Ministry say to the other ministries that . . . with more than expected income we are not going to spend it, or worse still, that we are going to reduce expenditures from the expected levels? Cuts have never been instituted for this purpose during the formulation stage." Why? Because it is "not possible to know what the specific requirements of the economy will be."

Cuts or expenditure blockages have only a mixed stabilization motive. Cuts have been made because the Finance Ministry later discovered an "unexpectedly low tax yield." But this is not strictly a stabilization policy measure. During a boom the ability to spend investments in the short run may not match the funds that become available. Therefore, it often occurs that the whole amount is not spent. When this happens, the Finance Ministry usually "declare(s) that the savings are due to stabilization measures. It looks good on paper, but in reality it is a question of capacity."

Most state budget officials, who confirmed that the Finance Ministry had instituted budgetary cuts of one type or another, agreed that the cuts were distributed "proportionately as far as is possible." A budget director asked whether the practice of treating all ministries the same makes much sense for economic management. He answered his own question: "This is not a scientific or even a question of justice. It is basically a question of practical, political decision making."

The result of this procedure is that cuts are concentrated in those ministries that have the highest proportion of investments. It is perhaps this mechanism which has caused investments to decline slightly as a proportion of total expenditures, despite the proposals of the multiyear financial plans to have investments gradually obtain a larger share of the total.[28] Moreover, cutting investments means that "workers will be laid off and plans and contracts will not be met. These are heavy costs for us to bear . . . in order to pursue stabilization policy." Not every state distributed the cuts proportionately but neither did the cuts follow stabilization criteria. Internal financial or political criteria guided the cuts in every instance.

Summary and Conclusions

A budget serves many other purposes than economic management. If economic theory does not take these other concerns into account, the actual practice of stabilization policy will not conform to the theory. On the state level, the Finance Ministry is responsible for fulfilling the economic, political, and financial purposes of the budget. It is not surprising that the states pursue a budget policy that combines all three functions.

The economic purpose does not fit easily with the other two. It requires that the state adjust its expenditures according to short-term impulses emanating from the economy. Recent experience has been that it is difficult to anticipate the impulses very far in advance. If the Finance Ministry does nonetheless decide to plan ahead, it always faces the risk that its efforts will turn out to be insufficient, or even worse, inappropriate. The cost of taking the risk is high because the stabilization measures entail either further cutting already scare funds or further expanding growing programs with no clear guidelines as to any limit. These decisions touch directly on sensitive political and financial norms. Politically it is hard to act stingy when money is available or to make negotiations more difficult than they otherwise would be if no stabilization need had arisen. Financially it is hard for the Finance Ministry to accept a situation in which programs it considered unnecessary yesterday are approved today to stimulate the economy. What criterion of economy or wastefulness should apply to this inconsistent development of events?

If for these reasons the costs of risking advance stabilization planning prove to be too high, a policy of "wait and see" does not recommend itself either. Under this strategy, the Finance Ministry does not have to worry about having set out on the wrong course, thereby expending political resources it might have saved; but it does have to concern itself with disrupting negotiated settlements at a time when the political cost of doing so is greater than it might have been at an earlier stage in the budget cycle. In both cases, the Finance Ministry bears the uncertainty. For example, the state budget directors find it next to impossible to cut expenditures once they are planned and approved. But to put through cuts during the planning stage places them in the position of determining the needs of the economy one or two years hence. Since all of the directors expressed doubt about the accuracy of such calculations, few of them were willing to go ahead with stabilization plans.

The risks of these two strategies cause uncertainty. The Finance Ministries dealt with it by accommodating strict economic criteria to the political and financial purposes of the budget. The two major ways in which this has been done is through simplification of economic criteria and exploitation of ambiguous budget criteria. A layman's fiscal-policy version of the balanced-budget concept is used which greatly reduces the size of the prescribed anticyclical variations in budget policy. Exploitation of the ambiguity of budget criteria is also indicated by the dual purpose of contingency budgets which serve as stabilization funds and financial control mechanisms.

State Finance Ministries do not follow the prescribed principles of either economic or financial theory but adhere to certain informal unwritten guidelines.

1. The appropriate rate for the growth in expenditures is oriented on the expected growth rate of GNP.

2. The appropriate size of the deficit is based on the long-term-debt policy. In the short term, this translates into a strived-for policy not to cut expenditures equal to the tax-yield retrenchment during recessions; during expansions, it entails zero, or at worst, very little debt assumption.

3. The debt policy is made primarily by a comparison of the size of existing debt or of interest payments to the size of current expenditures. The size of the ratio to interest payments may vary but at most payments should not exceed 8 to 10 percent. The composition of the debt is also important, especially its long-term or short-term character.

4. The size of the contingency budget is related to debt policy and any possible extra or unexpected tax income.

5. Cuts are usually across-the-board, amount to 5 or 10 percent, and are distributed more or less proportionately, with due recognition given to the fixed or nonfixed portion of a ministry's budget. If it is not done proportionately, it is not done on economic criteria either but rather according to what the Finance Ministry considers "unnecessary" expenditure.

6. The state Finance Ministries employ a modified balanced-budget concept which considers a balanced budget to have a more or less neutral effect on the economy. *Deficit spending* entails incurring a deficit; *stabilization* means a balanced budget or a slight surplus.

7. In years in which no strong inflationary or deflationary pressures exist, economic criteria play only a minor role compared to political or financial concerns.

This mix of economic and financial-political criteria produces a result which it might be argued is preferable to a strictly traditional balanced-budget approach. The state Finance Ministries do attempt their brand of deficit spending during recessions, although one wonders if any other policy would have been feasible in the short run. During expansion, little was cut out for stabilization purposes. But enormous growth in educational facilities took place after 1969 so that any significant reductions in personnel or supplies clearly would not have met program needs.

The interviews with state budget officials also strengthen the common impression that a great deal of economic management is more symbol than substance. State governments often cannot meet investment deadlines or spend all the investment funds allotted within the prescribed time period. In a boom, the resultant surplus looks good for economic management. Contingency budgets have served as a nice sounding stabilization instrument but have been used largely for budgetary control. To many people, economic management is what the government is supposed to do. Practitioners realize that it is much more difficult than is popularly thought, and, therefore, often pretend to pursue stabilization policy while actually attending to other matters and concerns.

If it is assumed for the moment that economic theory could be advanced to the point where little room were left for simplification or ambiguity, the costs to financial-political objectives may increase conflict. Martin Landau, for example, has argued that scientific advance can generate political conflict by altering the traditional relationship between means and ends.[29] Martin Rein also makes this same point in his discussion of social science and policy.[30] Actions that were once viewed as unproblematic means to accepted ends, with further knowledge, are seen in a broader context. Conflicts are revealed that were not there before.

Budgets used to be unproblematical as means for paying for government programs. Now, however, it is better understood that budgets are a means for achieving goals for the economic system of a country. The older, more traditional ends are still there, but the phenomenon of budgeting now has more dimensions to it. But we are still learning about their relative worth and interactions.

For state governments, which have high personnel costs and other fixed expenditures, it is unrealistic, even detrimental, to require a strict anticyclical budgetary policy. As one budget director summed it up: "The pressures on expenditures on the state and municipal levels are tremendous. We are on the front line and have to deal with teachers, policemen, parents, workers, and other groups . . . (the federal government) is further removed from the public and the kinds of expectations which affect people directly."

Furthermore, the municipalities are prominently represented in the state Parliaments. As a budget director complained, "They are not about to look bad at home. They would not pass a program (for municipal subsidies) based on stabilization policy." Given these pressures and other financial factors discussed earlier, the best that is to be expected from the states under the yearly budget policy is a nonprocyclical trend. An anticyclical trend appears unworkable and detrimental to the political and financial goals of the states.

It must be added that certain instruments exist to improve the situation. One is the special antirecession programs, whereby extra or speeded-up investment spending is financed by reserves held at the Bundesbank or by subsidies from the federal treasury. The other is the mandatory stabilization reserves put aside at the Bundesbank when the tax yield is unexpectedly high. If this latter policy were to be strengthened and extended to include the municipalities, it also offers a support to states wanting to hold down expenditures.

The key to the success of these programs, however, is not the active participation of the states, although their willingness to go along is important. At the federal level of government is found the main macroeconomic institutions for making forecasts and analyses as well as for coordinating budget policy in the Federal Republic. But will the federal government willingly play the budget coordinating role?

The temptation for federal officials is to become involved in administration to make sure that their policy priorities are carried out. But greater federal involvement in administration is not likely to improve economic management. My guess is that the policy-administration conflict would merely shift to the federal level. The federal budget would become more fixed through statutory requirements, policymakers would have to deal directly with inflexible personnel costs, and interest groups would exert a greater influence on federal policy. The state administrations, for their part, blame the federal government for passing laws without adequate regard for the administrative and financial costs. They want more policy control over their own programs and less anticyclical fluctuation in their sources of income. Bonn's efforts to coordinate macroeconomic policy, therefore, expose sensitive political nerves in German federalism.

Notes

1. State Budget Director, Spring 1975.

2. For evidence of this in the United States, see Alvin H. Hanson and Harvey S. Perloff, *State and Local Finance in the National Economy* (New York: W.W. Norton and Company, 1944). Especially chapter 4 describes the fiscal perversity of state and local governments. See also, Morton S. Baratz and Helen T. Farr, "Is Municipal Finance Fiscally Perverse?" *National Tax Journal* 12 (September 1959):276-284.

3. L.L. Ecker-Racz, *The Politics and Economics of State-Local Finance* (New Jersey: Prentice-Hall, 1970), pp. 118-119. In the United States, these concerns may lead to balanced-budget guidelines in state constitutions or other traditional legal requirements for sound financing.

4. This is the point of view taken by Dr. Horst Zimmerman and Dr. Klaus-Kirk Henke, in F. Naschold, et al., "Stellungnahme zu dem Gutachten 'Untersuchung zur Mehrjährigen Finanzplanung des Bundes,'" *Projektgruppe Regierungs- und Verwaltungsreform beim Bundesminster des Innern,* p. 11. They argue that the practical experience in the Federal Republic of Germany shows that it is more difficult to reduce expenditures during a boom than to expand them during a recession. The reason given is that during a boom the participants and interest groups do not share the same preferences. Labor unions and spending ministries, for example, oppose cuts during booms, while fiscal-policy advocates support them. During recessions, however, the interests of both of these groups coincide to a large extent. Besides this, the concern for unemployment and failure is often more intense and immediate than the concern that growth is taking place too rapidly.

5. These three problems were initially analysed and discussed in the interviews with German government officials. See also Assar Lindbeck, who refers to them as the "recognition lag," the "effects lag," and the "decision lag." Especially the first and third types of lag are discussed in chapters 6 and 7. See Assar Lindbeck, "Is Stabilization Policy Possible?—Time Lags and Conflicts

of Goals," in *Public Finance and Stabilization Policy,* ed. Warren L. Smith and John M. Culbertson (New York: Elsevier Publishing Co. 1974), pp. 269–308.

6. The Stability and Growth Law *(Gesetz zur Förderung der Stabilität und des Wachstums der Wirtschaft*—StWg, article 1) requires that the states take into account macroeconomic equilibrium in their financial measures. In addition, the special-investment-antirecesstion programs usually involve all three levels of government. This practice is supported in the Basic Law *(Grundgesetz),* article 104a, paragraph 4. See also Sachverständigenrat zur Begutachtung der Gesamtwirtschaftlichen Entwicklung, "Zur konjunkturpolitischen Lage im Mai 1973," (Stuttgart: Kohlhammer Verlag, 1973), p. 165.

7. See Norman C. Thomas, "Political Science and the Study of Macroeconomic Policy Making," *Policy Studies Journal* 4, no. 1 (1975):7–15, for a general discussion of this issue.

8. Basic Law, article 30. See also Fritz Scharpf, "Alternativen des Deutschen Föderalismus: Für ein Handlungsfähiges Entwicklungs system," (West Berlin: International Institute of Management, 1974), p. 237.

9. See in this regard articles 104a, 105, and 106 of the Basic Law.

10. For a discussion of "cooperative federalism" see Helmut C.I. Liesegang and Rainer Plöger, "Schwächung der Parlamente durch der kooperativen Föderalismus?" *Die Oeffentliche Verwaltung* 7 (April 1971):228–236.

11. Nevil Johnson, *Government in the Federal Republic of Germany: The Executive at Work* (Oxford: Pergamon Press, 1973), p. 102.

12. U.S. Bureau of the Census, State Government Finances 1979, Series GF79, no. 3 (Washington, D.C.: U.S. Government Printing Office, 1980).

13. Dieter Vesper, "Die Personalausgaben der Gebietskörperschaften von 1961 bis 1972," *Vierteljahresheft* (West Berlin: Deutsches Institut für Wirtschaftsforschung, no. 2, 1975), statistical appendix and author's own calculations. For more recent years, see *Finanzbericht,* 1975 to 1980 (Bonn: Bundesministerium der Finanzen).

14. Vesper, "Die Personalausgaben der Gebietskörperschaften," pp. 3–4.

15. For an analysis of this development in the United States, see Samuel Beer, "The Adoption of General Revenue Sharing: A Case Study in Public Sector Politics," *Public Policy* 24(Spring 1976):127–196.

16. See, for example, the Budget Proposal of the Bremen Finance Ministry, submitted before the Parliament's Budget Committee on 4 June 1975, p. 7. The legal limit on borrowing is the amount of investments. However, through financial maneuvering the limit can be avoided. But it does provide the budget director with a ready-made argument against further borrowing.

17. Institut Finanzen und Steuern, "Information über die Entwicklung der Öffentlichen Finanzwirtschaft in der Bundesrepublik Deutschland von 1964 bis 1974," (Bonn: Institut Finanzen und Steuern, 1975), p. 12. Working paper obtained directly from the institute.

18. Ibid., p. 14.

19. This is based on discussions with forecasters in the federal government. See also Karl-Heinz Raabe, "Gesamtwirtschaftliche Prognosen und Projektionen als Hilfsmittel der Wirtschaftspolitik in der Bundesrepublik Deutschland," *Allgemeines Statistisches Archiv* (January 1974):1–31.

20. The members of this committee include as chairman the federal finance minister, the federal economics minister, representatives of the Federal Statistical Office, the Bundesbank, the state governments (after 1963), the leading economic-research institutes, the National Municipal Associations, and the Council of Economic Experts. See the *Finanzberichte* (Bonn: Bundesministerium der Finanzen, 1964):62; (1967):57; (1969):51; and (1970):36.

21. In practice, states have found ways to get around the legal limits on borrowing. For one thing, the law does not state whether amortization should be included in the total or not. For another, the fiscal year runs four to six weeks beyond the legal year. No policy on debt is set for this period. For a discussion of state debt policy, see Dr. Krajovski, *Schuldendiensthilfe als Finanzinstrument im Oeffentlichenhaushalt* (Meisenheim am Glan: Verlag Antonheim, 1975).

22. As far as the states are concerned, actual budgetary deviations from the finance plan 1969 to 1973 amounted to 17 percent for the current account and 27 percent for the capital account. The planned figures also changed considerably from year to year. If one compares the figures of the finance plan for 1971 to 1975 with the 1969 to 1973 planned figures, deviations often reach 30 percent for the current expenditures and as much as 70 percent for investments. See Dieter Vesper, "Die mittelfristige Finanzplanung bei Bund und Ländern," *Vierteljahresheft* (West Berlin; Deutsches Institut für Wirtschaftsforschung, January 1974):46.

23. Chapter 3 treats the difference between these budget measures and their significance for federal decision making.

24. Vesper, "Die Personalausgaben der Gebietskörperschaften," pp. 117–118, who argues that the states make the hiring of new personnel dependent on increased tax income.

25. Dieter Vesper, "Vergleich der Ergebnisse des Neutralhaushalts mit anderen Konzepten," (West Berlin: Deutsches Institut für Wirtschaftsforschung, Winter 1975). Working paper obtained directly from the institute.

26. Bundesministerium der Finanzen, "Bundesminister Apel über die Massnahmen zur Verbesserung der Haushaltsstruktur und zur Verminderung der Kreditaufnahme," (Bonn: Referat Presse– und information, 8 September 1975).

27. Article 8 provides for the budgetary handling of these items: the regular budget (section 6002, Title 97101) does not contain any figures for stabilization programs, but the government may spend funds from this title up to the amount of Stabilization Reserves at the Bundesbank, or if more is needed, through borrowing, if the Bundesrat gives its approval.

28. Vesper, "Die mittelfristige Finanzplanung bei Bund und Ländern," p. 37.

29. Martin Landau, *Political Theory and Political Science* (New York: Macmillan Co., 1972), p. 173. "But the trouble is precisely the loss of correlation between means and ends . . . whatever conflict and tension ensue, the stage has been set for the deliberate introduction of a change agent."

30. Martin Rein, *Social Science and Public Policy* (New York: Penguin Books, 1976), p. 12.

6 Federal Politics and Macroeconomic Policy Guidelines

. . . all the states are politically autonomous. You may use a macrobudget amount for economic analysis, but that does not mean that it will be implemented.[1] —Federal Economist

. . . the theorists always talk of the macrobudget as though that were some living, breathing thing. There is no consideration given to the political units that make these decisions.[2] —State Finance Official

The analysis has not yet considered intergovernmental relations. So far we have examined decision making from the perspective of each level of government separately. We have also approached decisions from inside the federal and state governments looking out; now they will be viewed as part of a larger economic and organizational setting. Considered separately, the federal government plays the key role in managing the economy, while the state and local governments pay more attention to political and allocation issues. Yet this simple distinction is not sufficient when the interaction between the levels of government is taken into account. It adds another dimension to policy decision making that alters these individual perspectives in interesting ways. We begin, therefore, with efforts to achieve joint agreement between levels of government during the planning phase of the budget cycle.

The Macrobudget as a Public Good

Federal political relations are intimately tied to economic management. This tie is due to the focus of macroeconomic analysis on the net impact of government economic activity on the gross national product. To determine this net impact, decision makers need to calculate the aggregate level of public expenditures, including all levels of government, in relation to total taxes. These aggregate amounts comprise the *macrobudget*.

The macrobudget differs significantly from ordinary budgets. The most important distinction is that macrobudgets contain figures that are summaries of taxing and spending decisions of organizational units that are largely independent of one another. Financial transactions are included from the municipalities, state governments, and the federal government. Yet no single organization, including the federal government, has primary jurisdiction over all the elements in the macrobudget. Limited jurisdictions and fragmented authority make it hard for the states and municipalities to take the macrobudget seriously. For an individual state or city to be more committed to the macrobudget than to its ordinary budget, it must accept the general welfare as more important than its own financial situation—a rare occurrence in organizational and individual behavior.

The problems of fragmented authority and limited jurisdictions are dealt with in theories of public finance by assigning differing functional tasks to each level of government. The state and local governments are supposed to concern themselves with allocation, while the federal government worries about macroeconomic policy.[3] In addition, a recommendation to separate functions by government level should apply particularly well to West Germany, which already has a form of functional division in its federal system that gives responsibility for macroeconomic policy to the central government. But before concluding that West Germany is better blessed in this respect than other systems, each component of the public-finance approach must be examined more closely.

State and Local Governments Have Little Incentive to Cooperate in Economic Management

In the theory of public finance, state and local governments will not pay the costs of economic management.[4] The argument runs: the kinds of factors that produce economic imbalances transcend a local government's jurisdiction; any measure which a local government might take, therefore, will have only a small or even a negligible effect by itself. Only if most other local governments also pursue a sound fiscal policy will the single government receive any economic benefits for its budgetary efforts. Otherwise it will bear the budgetary costs but get nothing in return. The likelihood, however, that most local governments will pursue similar policies to counteract private-demand fluctuations is very small. If most other governments pursue sound fiscal policies, any single government can receive the economic benefits without doing anything itself. Consequently each single government has a strong incentive to cheat on a cooperative solution.

The possibility that state and local governments will not cooperate in economic management is known in American economic literature as the *perversity hypothesis*. The following conditions are emphasized:[5]

1. Benefits from employment creation measures do not remain within state boundaries; debts incurred during a recession are largely paid to outsiders.
2. States and cities do not have ready access to the credit of the central bank nor can they supplement fiscal changes with monetary policy.
3. Statutory laws and constitutional provisions inhibit flexibility in state and local budgets.

Empirical evidence in support of the perversity hypothesis is not entirely conclusive. The record shows that in the upswing phase of the cycle, U.S. states and municipalities have behaved perversely; in the downswing phase, they have maintained growth rates much more successfully, therefore not reinforcing the slump in the private economy.[6] The German evidence from the sixties strongly supports the hypothesis, both in the upswing and downswing phases, although the record in the seventies is less clear.[7] Despite disagreement over the procyclical extent of state and municipal budgets, studies in both countries do reveal that neither group of local and state governments actively tries to use the budget to manage the economy. Consequently the main burden of coordinating and directing the macrobudget falls to the central level of government.

The Central Government, in Contrast to State and Local Governments, Possesses the Requisite Incentives and Capacities to Manage the Economy

The central government is not caught by the public-good problem. The country-wide policy jurisdiction of the central government should encourage it to manage the economy because doing so produces an overall greater welfare. Unlike the state governments, the central government should not have an incentive to cheat on a cooperative solution. If the federal government does not participate, it receives fewer benefits.

A central purpose of macroeconomic policy is to compensate for the overall undesirable effects of individual actions. It is precisely because economic well-being is a public good that state and local governments have incentives not to pay the costs but to "ride free." As with national defense, only the central government can be concerned with a system-wide solution.

The related literature on turbulent organizational environments reaches similar conclusions. The essence of *turbulence* is a situation in which individuals pursue policies and get reinforced in preferences that collectively produce undesirable effects in the aggregate; the way to deal with turbulence is through system-wide–joint action that mitigates the overall detrimental effects. In his discussion of turbulence, Less Metcalf, for example, writes that a macroeconomic model is valuable for analysing complex problems of coordination in a network of subsystems because it manipulates the major constraints of price levels, full employment, and balance of payments at the system level. He suggests that what is necessary as an organizational response to turbulence is "a range of 'macro-policies' with which the component organizations comply . . . adaptation requires collective action at the level of the system as a whole. Independent action may have widespread damaging effects if it triggers uncontrolled positive feedback processes, i.e., if it creates turbulence."[8]

Collective Action and Federal Competition

Is the problem of the macrobudget solved by assigning responsibility for collective action to the central government? Although macroeconomic models that employ aggregate budget figures are valuable for analyzing complex and interrelated policy problems, actually adopting macropolicies depends on the costs to the central government of achieving joint action. If the central government faces high costs because of limited capacity to influence other units, it can be expected to weigh these costs in its decision to promote collective efforts to achieve macroeconomic goals. How important these costs are, moreover, depends on how salient the collective goal is. One factor that affects salience is uncertainty. In the macroeconomic-policy area, an inability to predict and interpret economic events has had precisely this effect, thus eroding the central government's firm commitment to a single course of action. The interaction between this uncertainty and the costs of achieving joint agreement brings federal political relations into the arena of managing the economy.

The catch in the turbulence argument for macropolicies is thus found in the phrase "with which the component organizations comply . . . adaptation requires collective action at the level of the system." Collective action, or in other words cooperation among the components, is not likely to occur freely. Some components (states and cities) do not have incentives to cooperate in joint solutions. Collective action, therefore, requires some form of enticement or coercion by the central government to assure compliance. These measures may be either selective incentives, regulations, or more direct actions, but all entail certain costs. These costs will vary but will include losses of time through bargaining efforts with other units, financial losses through money enticements, political costs from opposition by states'-rights and balanced-budget advocates, and so forth. How important are these costs to the central government?

The public-finance solution to the public-good problem of macroeconomic policy assumes that governments can separate budget purposes and hence costs. The allocation purpose goes to the state governments, while the macroeconomic purpose is given to the central government. Thus the central government should not be deterred in its economic management by financial or other budget costs. But chapters 3, 4, and 5 demonstrated that the politics of budgeting work in the opposite direction. Rather than separate purposes, for political reasons budgeters are inclined to combine them in the same program. A contingency budget, for example, may also serve as a financial-control measure; an economic projection, as an aid in incremental budgeting. The other budget costs of coordinating joint–economic action, therefore, will not necessarily be ignored by the central government.

How does the German federal government fare in this respect? What capacity does it have to determine the macrobudget and what costs are involved? A further issue is: Do these costs vary under differing conditions for the federal government and the states? To begin with, the share of federal-government spending as a percentage of total public spending is only around 25 percent. If only investment expenditures are considered, the federal share falls to 16 percent.[9] The federal government is thus very dependent on the spending decisions of other levels if it hopes to influence the size and composition of the macrobudget.

The mechanisms to influence other levels' spending patterns, however, are minimal. Each level of government has independent budgetary authority. Although the state Interior Ministries have a degree of budgetary oversight over municipal debt, for most purposes the localities remain independent of higher-level intrusion into budget making. One reason is that many local officials sit in the state Parliaments and effectively prevent state decisions that excessively interfere with local autonomy. In addition, the central government has no jurisdiction over local budget-making authority and must give municipal grants in aid indirectly through the state administrations. As a consequence, if the central government intends to influence local investment decisions, for example, it can only do so through grants, but even then it must obtain the cooperation of the states.

This limited capacity imposes costs on gaining compliance for macropolicies from other levels of government. Although the federal government needs the cooperation of other levels to have an impact on the macrobudget, it also competes with them for financial resources and policy jurisdictions. Pursuing joint action for macroeconomic policy can jeopardize these other important concerns of budgeting.

A main target of budgetary competition is the mixed tax system. Yields from certain taxes are shared *(Verbundsystem)* and others are not *(Trennsystem)*.[10] The distribution of revenue from the sales tax between the states and the federal government is an especially hot political issue. The tax distribution is decided every other year through loudly debated legislation that requires the consent of the Bundesrat. Each level argues for a favorable shift in the tax's distribution when its expenditures grow faster than the other level's expenditures. The faster-growing level inevitably asserts that it deserves a larger percentage share of the total income from the sales tax due to its increasing revenue needs.

The states especially try to overestimate expenditure needs and underestimate revenue growth in order to pad their position in the bargaining with the central government over the sales-tax distribution. These budgetary strategies produce information for fiscal policy that is not entirely accurate; they also tie the overall level of growth of the macrobudget to arguments over the precise distribution of the total among levels. The reference point for bargaining is the growth rate of GNP. The Working Group for Expenditure Development of the Finance Planning Council (discussed later) has even proposed that the states' budgets should grow slightly overproportional to GNP, while the central government's budget should grow slightly less. The long-term implication of this arrangement is not missed by federal policymakers.

Joint agreement also depends on competition for jurisdiction over particular policy areas. Traditionally the states have had primary influence in the areas of education, administration, agriculture, and regional-economic development. In the late sixties, however, the states accepted federal proposals to create Joint Task *(Gemeinschaftsaufgaben)* policy areas. The states hoped that the Joint Tasks would help them get federal money for projects that overlap individual state jurisdictions (such as universities or coastal protection). But many of the states, and especially the wealthier ones, entered into joint agreements somewhat reluctantly due to the fear that they would lose their financial autonomy. The states have also resisted attempts by the central government to increase grants that go indirectly to municipalities, preferring instead to maintain their own influence over local-investment spending through state grant programs. Battles over turf thus divert the federal government's energies from macroeconomic policy.

The third issue facing the federal government is the uncertainty of economic developments and their interpretation. The 1974 to 1979 recession-boom cycle raised serious questions about the interconnections in the economy between prices and employment and the ability to predict changes in economic trends. In addition, the oil–price rise, the effects of recession in the United States, and the double-digit inflation in the European Community led many West German policymakers to conclude that world economic events were determining domestic trends and that efforts by the federal government to cope would be only partially successful.

The effect on policy of this uncertainty (as discussed in chapter 4) was a halting indecisive product. An important reason why the federal government did not pursue macro-objectives more wholeheartedly was simply that it did not know what correct policy to follow. This indecision in turn caused the state governments to lose confidence in the federal government's abilities and authority for macropolicy and even attack it for overly partisan projections and an insensitivity to state budgetary and administrative needs.

There are thus several important reasons why the federal government faces important political and budgetary costs if it seeks a collective macrobudget policy. What is left to show is whether this view of the federal government's situation is supported by the evidence. For this purpose, the next section examines the attempt in the 1970s to formulate joint economic and budgetary guidelines between the federal government, the states, and the municipalities.

An Attempt at Joint Economic and Budgetary Guidelines

The federal government has only limited options for influencing the planned-spending decisions of state and local governments. Since each level has independent budget authority, the most that the federal government can do is meet with the other levels and try to convince them of the importance of macroeconomic objectives. The most important institution set up during the 1969 Finance Reform to facilitate this type of joint consultation and planning is the Finance Planning Council *(Finanzplanungsrat)*.[11] This joint body provides evidence of the federal government's commitment to collective action to achieve macroeconomic objectives through the public budget. The investigation should also reveal the propensity of the state governments to go along with collective efforts and the kinds of concerns they have about federal-government priorities.

Membership in the Finance Planning Council consists of the finance ministers of the federal and state governments as well as representatives from the National Municipal Associations. The discussions in the middle sixties over the necessity for multiyear financial and budgetary planning provided the background for the establishment of the joint membership in the council; but an additional reason for including the states and municipalities was the concern for macroeconomic policy. And in the course of time, despite the original intention to make longer-term–budgetary planning the main item of business, short-term fiscal-policy concerns tended to dominate the sessions of the council.[12]

As originally conceived, the council had three main purposes: the creation of a unified system of financial and budgetary statistics; the drawing up of unified economic and budgetary guidelines for financial planning; and the identification of problem areas in fulfilling the macroeconomic function of the public budget. The council has successfully worked toward the achievement of the first of these purposes but neither of the last two. The economic and budgetary guidelines through 1973 contained recommendations for growth rates of investments, consumption expenditures, personnel costs, and so forth for each level of government (see table 6–1). Until 1971 the members tentatively drew up rough guidelines for year B in February of year A, reviewed them in May, and made the final decisions in October, thereby following the rhythm of the yearly budget cycle. After 1971 the membership did not even discuss the guidelines until the fall but even then failed to produce a joint document outlining the macrobudget policy.

The yearly *Financial Report* of the federal government, which contains summaries of the council sessions, tells the story. The report states for April 1971 that "no recommendations over guidelines were published (because of unforeseeable economic developments)." But in September, the council still had not reached agreement, in part because of the extended discussions over the distribution of the sales-tax revenue. Again in June 1972 the report states that no guidelines were recommended. In 1973 the basic disagreement centered around the proposed rates at which each level's fixed expenditure should grow. The federal government had rejected the investigation of the council's Working Group on Expenditure Developments, which had proposed that federal expenditures grow at a slower rate than those of the states and municipalities. The conclusion in the *Financial Report* states: "For this reason, no guidelines were agreed upon."[13]

Table 6-1
Detailed Macroeconomic and Budgetary Guidelines

	Percentage Increase 1969–1970	Average Annual Percentage Increase 1969–1973	Percentage Increase 1970–1973
GNP			
Nominal	6.0	6.0	6.0
Expenditures			
Federal	5.5	6.0	5.5
State	6.5	6.5	6.5
Local	7.0	7.0	7.0
Total	7.0	7.0	6.5
Real investment			
Federal	7.0	11.0	6.5
State	8.0	7.5	6.5
Local	8.0	8.0	8.0
Total	8.0	8.5	7.5
Personnel expenditures			
Federal	7.5	7.5	7.0
State	8.0	8.0	8.0
Local	7.0	7.0	7.0
Total	7.5	7.5	7.5
Transfers to local government			
From federal	3.5	2.5	2.0
From state	6.5	8.5	7.0
Total	6.0	8.0	6.5
Tax income			
Federal	5.9	5.9	4.4
State	9.9	8.3	7.8
Local	9.2	6.7	6.6
Total	7.6	6.8	5.8

Besides not issuing any macroeconomic and budgetary guidelines, the council also stopped talking about macroeconomic matters. Discussions of the macrobudget were postponed and restricted to the final meeting of the year in the fall just prior to the federal Cabinet's session on macroeconomic policy. In this final meeting, the federal government offers its yearly *Goal Projection* as a substitute for the original, more detailed council recommendations.

The federal government's procedure for making these goal projections, however, is clearly not intended to involve the states and municipalities. The federal Economics Ministry projects a macrobudget–growth rate for the public sector for the next year, determines from the Finance Ministry the most likely growth in Bonn's budget, and simply allots the difference to the states and cities. By designating state and local spending as the remainder, so to speak, Bonn greatly aggravated the states, leading one state budget director to declare: "The federal government really does not make recommendations any more. There are no more guidelines to speak of; the federal government has already decided before the negotiations. The three levels of government make their individual budgets separately and by themselves. The council has lost its main function."

But the biggest controversy over the way the federal government began presenting the data after 1973 centered on the failure to delineate expenditure growth according to major budget categories, including personnel, investments, and so forth (see table 6–2). State budget directors argued that they have to make choices that are more specific than the overall growth level. How much should public employees get paid? How fast will consumption expenditures grow? What will be the increase in federal grants in aid to the states? Aside from the issue of the expected tax yield, these are the questions that need answers. State officials indicated that without guidelines on salaries, for example, an overall guideline does not help much. If the salary component is out of step with the total, more than likely the total will get changed rather than the pay rates.

But the federal government did not stop there. It also greatly shortened the amount of time it allows the states and municipalities to evaluate its projected figures before a joint decision of the council is required. The federal government frequently presented the data from the *Goal Projection* to the Working Circle of the council only one week before the plenary session in the fall. In September 1975, the worst recession year, the federal government did not even provide a

Table 6–2
Economic and Budgetary Projections for the Levels of Government, 1974–1979

Expenditures and Income	Annual Percentage Change				
	1975	1976	1977	1978	1979
Expenditure					
Federal	16.5	4.1	3.0	7.0	5.4
State	10.0	5.0	5.5	6.0	6.0
Community	9.0	4.5	5.5	6.0	6.0
Total public budget	13.5	4.5	4.5	6.5	6.0
Income					
Federal	−5.8	7.1	16.9	10.9	9.8
State	0.5	7.5	11.5	10.0	10.5
Community	6.0	7.0	9.0	9.5	9.5
Total public budget	−1.0	7.5	13.5	11.0	10.0
Information Growth rate of GNP					
Nominal	4.5	9.5	10.5	9.5	9.5
Real	−3.5	5.0	5.0	5.0	5.0

Note: The projections do not include the antirecession programs.

week's opportunity for consultation and discussion of the data but rather presented them for the first time in the plenary session itself. By receiving the data so late, the state delegations have had little or no opportunity to make changes or to adequately evaluate the data's implications. A state budget director looked at the federal procedure this way:

> Look, the minister and I went to Bonn, had lunch with Apel [the then federal Finance Minister] and then went into the third session of the council for this year. There before us lay a few pages, the last page of which contained the *Goal Projection,* which you have seen. . . . It was the first time that we had seen the figures. For me, that type of meeting does not make much sense.

By waiting until September to present the data, the federal government placed itself in a strategically advantageous position to prevent any changes. Only two or three weeks later the federal Cabinet meets to hold its annual budgetary discussions, but once the Cabinet passes the contents of the goal projections, no further alterations in the data are possible. This statement by a state budget official, who is a member of the Working Circle of the council from an SPD state, is indicative of the general resentment against the lack of opportunity to change the recommendations in the goal projections:

> Were we brought into this from the start? Ha! This sheet [the *Goal Projection,* see table 6–2] was produced two weeks before the federal budget was passed. The federal government did not give opportunity for any discussion of changes whatsoever, despite the tentatively proposed tax change for 1977 and the present proposal to change the structure of expenditures. The sessions of the council last around two hours, but we got these sheets during the meeting. What does that mean for us? It means that we are going to draw up our own budget, purely on the basis of what we think is right, by our own plan. You cannot expect us to orient ourselves to data which we get in this manner.

Suspicion has developed on both sides. The states blame the federal government for not following the strict legal prescriptions contained in the Finance Reform and the Stability and Growth Law; the federal government refuses to support detailed budgetary guidelines and insists on reserving the decision on aggregate economic and budget goals to itself. The delaying action of the federal government in turn creates distrust among the state delegations, which, even if they tend to support the overall figures, reject them as official guidelines due to the way in which they are presented.

What is the explanation for the varying intransigence of each side? The answer lies in the public good character of macroeconomic policy. The states and cities cooperate in joint budget planning based on selective benefits they get for themselves; the federal government, which is primarily committed to the macroeconomic-policy goal, chooses the macrobudget instrument so long as the costs involved in obtaining joint planning do not make other more direct instruments, such as tax incentives or monetary policy, more attractice. Two factors especially influence these cost and benefit calculations. The first factor is scarcity, which affects the states and the federal government in opposite ways due to each side's different policy goals. The effects of scarcity are seen most clearly in the change from a strong economic expansion in the early seventies to the 1974 to 1975 recession. This change altered bargaining positions of the two sides but did not increase agreement.

A second factor that influenced the cost and benefit calculations of joint planning is the inaccuracy of economic projections combined with ambiguity in economic theory. This factual uncertainty on the federal level actually aided political agreement on planning the budget policy. But the states and the federal government are more distant and the relations between them are more formal and open to the public. In addition, each side bases its projections on varying policy assumptions. These factors together generate distrust between parties and governmental levels and worsen the atmosphere for agreement. Factual uncertainty thus increases the costs to the federal government of pursuing a macrobudget strategy.

From Boom to Recession

In times of need the individual state governments want help to control the budget; in times of plenty, they favor autonomy over charity.[14] Previously the state governments had rapidly growing budgets, but state revenue kept pace with expenditure increases. The states, and especially their Finance Ministries, did not want federal interference. Beginning in 1974, however, the states faced unprecedented deficits. Many of them suddenly wanted help to control spending.[15]

The federal government, primarily concerned with economic management, in good times is concerned about the inflationary impact of strong state-budget expansion and tries to dampen it; in times of recession, again concerned with economic management, the federal government subsidizes both the states, to keep their investments from falling off, and the European community, to prevent inflationary costs from overtaking revenue. But as its own budget position continued to worsen after 1974, the federal government's willingness to pursue this macropolicy through joint agreement began to wane in preference for protecting its own financial needs. Other macroeconomic instruments became more attractive.

The federal government's decision to discontinue detailed budget and economic guidelines was one approach to reducing the costs of a full commitment to joint planning of the macrobudget. It thought that this change would not matter much for macroeconomic policy because in the early seventies the states had frequently not followed the guidelines by spending more than they recommended.

But what the federal government did not realize is that the states used these guidelines not because they were concerned about macroeconomic policy but because of the selective benefits they offered or failed to offer the state administrations. Actually the states came to desire these guidelines after their financial position began to worsen. The guidelines, they thought, would strengthen the state Finance Ministries' bargaining position with the unions and the politicians. A state budget director explained that detailed budget guidelines "really strengthen the state administration vis-à-vis the Parliaments. . . . In general the states are unified in favor of these data . . . they also strengthen the position of the Finance Minister in the Cabinet. Especially in the last few years, the ministries have made higher and higher requests for funds." Another state finance official agreed that because the spending ministries increasingly want greater funding, "the data give the Finance Minister a band within which requests can move. Simply expressed, it is a help against excessive expansion."

Previously under boom conditions and fast-growing revenue, spending demands of the ministries could be more easily accommodated; but with the arrival of the recession, state deficits began to grow larger than ever before. Tax revenue did not keep pace with the growth in expenditure needs, especially in the 1974 to 1975 period in which some governments experienced an actual decline in the tax income. In addition, personnel costs, which comprise the largest single component of state budgets, have increased since 1970 in a slightly overproportional rate to the rest of the budget.[16] On this basis, the cities and states argued that their budgets should grow faster than the federal budget by 1 to 2 percent per year.[17]

If the state governments came to strongly prefer budget guidelines for their selective benefits, the federal government was moving in the opposite direction because of the costs involved. One issue of contention is the distribution of the revenue from the sales tax, which is determined every two years by statutory law according to the revenue needs of each government level. An agreement on the components of the macrobudget must also specify which level should grow faster than the others or whether all levels should grow at the same rate. On more than one occasion, the council has set investments as a high budget priority, yet these expenditures are concentrated on the state and local levels.[18] As already indicated, personnel costs also have grown slightly overproportionately to total budget needs, providing a second argument for faster growth of the lower levels. But while faster growth entails increasing tax revenues for the states and cities, it brings declining amounts for the federal government—an important cost when discussing budgetary components with other levels of government.

Besides the state governments, the federal government must deal with the national public-employee and industrial unions. The projected growth in personnel costs influences bargaining with the state employees, whereas the anticipated growth in GNP and inflation affects industrial-union contracts. Unlike labor relations in the United States, unions in federal Germany are organized largely by industrial sector rather than local plant. Wage bargaining, therefore, rather than determining costs for each manufacturer, sets minimum-wage levels for the whole industrial sector. On the plant level, labor councils have frequently succeeded in obtaining wage contracts that have exceeded the overall sectoral figures. As a consequence, projections of GNP and inflation influence minimum-wage outcomes in each sector and involve the federal government in trilateral bargaining with the unions and the employers.[19]

According to one state official, "The federal government did not want to have the detailed guidelines published. . . . A very important factor was the negotiations over wage and salary levels."

Another state official stated similar concerns: "The federal government is not prepared to do this [give out guidelines]. In the negotiations, it is the major negotiator with the unions and does not want to pull its pants down before the time is right." Especially in the 1974 to 1975 period, the government attempted to hold down wage demands due to the economic recession and inflationary pressures.[20]

Policy Preferences and Goal Projections

Besides losing budgetary ground and revenue growth to the states, the federal government also faced considerable uncertainty in projecting economic trends. The federal government makes the analyses of the economy through the goal projection, which includes data on overall budgetary growth of each level of government. But because the goal projections assume that the government will take certain policy actions, situations in which viewpoints differ give rise to attempts at alternative analyses. States such as North Rhine-Westphalia, Bavaria, and Shleswig-Holstein, for instance, have put forward proposals to have the states make their own tax estimates and goal projections. They questioned the legitimacy of applying the federal government's goal projections to their budgets.

Government officials who participate in making economic projections and forecasts, agreed that the problem of prediction has increased in the seventies as compared to the sixties.[21] One reason is that the growth potential in the economy is not what it was in the past. Overall slower growth does not hide mistaken policy choices. The officials also felt that the private living standard had reached saturation borders in many important areas, making demand shift more rapidly than previously. For this reason, they felt "these trends are not going to go away but will increase in coming years." Others emphasized the greater importance of the world economy for internal production, prices, and competition in many traditional manufacturing areas.

From the viewpoint of the state governments, the federal government refuses to publish and discuss detailed economic and budgetary guidelines because it knows they will be inaccurate. A state budget director expressed this opinion when asked why no economic guidelines have been given out since 1971: ". . . the economic development has not been projected with any certainty. The federal government is in fact the chair of the meetings [of the council] and did not want to declare that the data were unrealistic."

Another state official agreed with this assessment: "What I suspect is that at present it is very difficult to forecast future developments, and the federal government does not want its projections published."

Because the most recent projections have produced unreliable tax-yield estimates, the states have become increasingly unwilling to see them as a basis for the formation of their budgets. Of particular concern is the prediction of individual tax yields, which accrue to one level of government or another according to the mixed-revenue-sharing system. For states to know their own projected revenue, they need to have information on the anticipated yields of particular taxes that accrue to them. A state official felt that the income side is the worst problem: "How far in advance can you accurately estimate tax income? The estimates for 1976 are done with only great reservation." A budget director said that his government simply takes over the estimate of the federal government, but "in the past two years . . . the deviations from reality have been considerable and have caused us to have second thoughts."

The inability to predict tax yields in advance has made the federal government reluctant to give out these data until the most recent estimate is made, which usually comes only a few weeks before the Cabinet meeting in the fall. Waiting until just prior to the next fiscal year, however, does not give the states the option of altering or adequately discussing the projections or the assumptions on which they are based.

The inability to make accurate projections reduced the attractiveness of early agreement due to the difficulty of knowing at an early stage what conditions will prevail when the actual decision time arrives. If the tax estimate is overly optimistic, neither side wants to maintain its original position. An attempt at early cooperation prevents the other side from making the necessary adjustments later on. As a result, a time difficulty arises for joint budgetary recommendations: meaningful substantive budgetary planning takes around ten to twelve months, whereas, if accurate prediction is to guide choice, economic management must hold back decisions to just prior to the actual spending of the money.

If fiscal policy remains a high priority, keeping options open to the last minute is advantageous for the federal government when it negotiates with the states. But a side effect is to disrupt joint substantive budgetary planning. Those officials who are involved in planning hospital or university construction, for instance, do not face the same need to delay or hold out; they need and want advance information and stability in federal relations. But the officials who worry about economic developments and intend to respond to them through the public budget do face the need to keep information hidden and options open to account for changing circumstances. Agreements made early to their benefit may turn later to their detriment. Presenting evidence at the last minute prevents the states and municipalities from building a coherent coalition, but when they do, it is already too late for the decisions have been taken by the Federal Cabinet.

The federal government reacted defensively to attacks by the states and municipalities. The federal officials felt that they were blamed when the projections went wrong even though the other levels of government are responsible for many expenditure decisions. One federal official decried the failure of the states to follow budget guidelines: "What has happened to what we have put into the projections in the past? These projections are purely hypothetical amounts provided by the federal government. The deviations in practice have been enormous. The figures are so ineffective that it is questionable if they make sense any more."

Another official emphasized that if the federal government includes an investment quota of 8 percent in the projections, because the municipalities give out the most investments, the federal officials have little influence on the outcome. As he said, "When 2 percent comes out instead of 8, the projection is false. Who takes the blame? We do. They want the goodies but they want us to do the work. Certainly normative values are contained in the projections; they are goal projections after all."

If the federal government predicts a tax yield increase of X percent, but due to the recession the actual yield is much lower, the states are quick to blame the federal government. They argue that the federal government follows an overly liberal fiscal policy and does not care that their budget deficits increase unexpectedly. But because the projections reflect federal goals, the states downplay the difficulty of prediction and emphasize the unrealistic character of the objectives. And since the objectives are based on policy preferences, political-party divisions form around support or opposition to one projection or another.

The government coalition is likely to place greater emphasis on unemployment, for example, and thereby to underestimate the growth in inflation; the CDU/CSU (Christian Democratic Union), which worries more about price rises, is tempted to see in turn an unrealistically rosy employment picture. Or a state government which receives a goal projection that foresees a 5.0 percent inflation rate, a 2.0 percent growth rate in GNP, and a 6.0 percent increase in tax yields, may reinterpret the figures to 7.0 percent, -1.0 percent, and 2.0 percent respectively, on the belief that the federal government always is too optimistic because it needs to look good to the general public. In either case, the state blames the federal government for its policy assumptions rather than recognizing the very real difficulty of making accurate projections.

The worse the predictions are, the more intense the policy dispute, and the greater the attempt to find out or place blame on what went wrong. The belief of federal officials that they take the blame for wrong policy preferences when inaccurate predictions are made is indicated by the comment of a state official: "We have in this year a very uncertain economic development. The trend cannot be predicted. Should we say to the unions: no more than the price development, or what? The numbers come to us on the basis of a one-sided political decision. Each state fends for itself. We will go it alone, even if the results turn out quite differently." The figures are not seen as neutral attempts to forecast the future but as indications of policy priorities and political strategies that may not agree with the preferences and needs of other parties or levels of government.

One influence on the different viewpoints of the states and the federal government is the growing party split—the Christian Democrats (CDU/CSU) dominate state governments and have a majority in the Bundesrat, while the Social Liberal Coalition (SPD/FDP) controls the federal government with a majority in the Bundestag.

Due to the functional federal divisions that require joint planning and decision for implementation, the Bundesrat was originally intended to function as a body that represents the technical, administrative, and policy preferences and needs of state governments in the national policymaking process. But since the CDU/CSU went out of power on the federal level in 1969, it has increasingly attempted to use the Bundesrat and other bodies with state representation, including the Finance Planning Council, as political forums to influence national policy and support the party's comeback to power on the national level. When financial planning was introduced, the Grand Coalition governed Germany and the partisan use of joint-decision bodies did not arise as a real issue. Even in the Bundestag, the Grand Coalition produced a parliament-government split rather than a party split. Now the CDU/CSU has a majority in many of the states, and Helmut Kohl, the Christian Democrat candidate for the chancellorship in 1976, as well as Franz Joseph Strauss, the party's candidate in 1980, used the Bundesrat to provide Christian Democratic alternatives to coalition policies.

Conflict results from factual uncertainty in prediction and interpretation of economic events in part because of the large number of participants and the publicity generated by the plenary sessions of the Finance Council. Besides the finance ministers, numerous other advisors, aids, and government officials and politicians attend the meetings.[22] According to the Basic Law, there is supposed to be around fifteen participants, yet the actual numbers range from seventy-five to one hundred people. Each state delegation and the federal government bring along numerous advisors and other personnel. Many state officials disapproved of the large participation because of the problems inherent in parliaments. One official complained, "With so many people, the council can hardly serve as a confidential committee. People tend to shift the blame to others and make them the scapegoats, which in turn makes real work difficult. For me, it makes the work unbearable."

The participants also have little prior discussion time to evaluate and develop opinions about economic and budgetary guidelines. Despite apparent agreement in September 1975 on the need to reduce the size of the debt by 1979 and follow a very restrictive budget policy for 1976, the council made no common declarations on guidelines.

The CDU/CSU made numerous attacks on the government's policy of deficit spending, claiming that Bonn had followed irresponsible financial policies and had brought about the German recession. Budget directors in Christian Democratic states especially saw joint–economic guidelines as a means to control the demands of spending ministries and labor unions and enhance the influence of the states in deciding economic and budgetary issues. Consequently the CDU/CSU states made the failure to produce guidelines a political issue that had implications for the correct budgetary approach to the recession. The partisan split also aggravated the impasse brought about by prediction uncertainty with claims that the federal government had used the goal projection to provide statistical support for its own erroneous fiscal-policy priorities.

Public Needs and Selective Interests

The macrobudget is a useful ideal in economics but not a practical reality in politics. No decision unit concerns itself primarily with the macrobudget to the detriment of its own finances. With no enduring political constituency or policy advocates, the macrobudget exists only in theory because each decision unit makes its own choices. If the macrofigure is not broken down, the appropriate growth rate for each government remains unclear. A state government may not only decide that its finances, for whatever reason, should grow faster than the federal government's but perhaps should increase at a more rapid rate than that of some other states. The utility of a macrobudget is a little like that of program budgeting—good for everyone else. A hypothetical budget director might put it this way: "I prefer that the federal government hold down its budget growth during the long periods of boom and incur deficits in the short interludes of recession. For us, we have important services and long-term–investment expenditures that simply cannot be altered for economic management." A federal official might respond: "We're not about to subsidize state budgets in recessions and abstain from growth in booms just in order to give them a larger portion of the tax pie. The states should pay for a larger share of the stimulus packages." Magnanimity is not an organizational trait.

Uncertainty in predicting and interpreting economic events has produced greater conflict because of the formal feature of the federal system. Most state budget directors are interested in how fast the major components of the federal budget will grow and, in particular, at what rate federal-grant programs will increase. The federal government could also use similar kinds of information for planning its grant programs and making fiscal-policy recommendations. But public disclosure of actual budgetary intentions weakens bargaining positions with the unions, spending ministries, and other levels of government. Reliance on formal institutional arrangements for joint agreement thus jeopardizes more informal pathways to mutual accommodation as occurs within the federal ministries in Bonn. Making everything public invites deception. Formal attempts to draw up or recommend macrofigures inevitably embroil the participants in strategies to protect their own positions.

Not recognizing the effects of formal agreements mars the proposal of Baden-Württemberg in March 1975, which merely argues that the federal government should do what it prefers not to—the discussion and publication of detailed budgetary guidelines of the states and federation.[23] The planning would still contain a public, formal character and invoke the kinds of strategies of delay and information suppression that occurred in the 1974 to 1975 period. Although it is reasonable that a finance minister take along an advisor to the council's sessions, the proliferation of participants to almost one hundred persons can only lead to speeches that address a wider audience. More extensive informal preparation may allow for more intimate and fruitful bargaining and give-and-take meetings.

Decision premises for policy choice also do not remain constant given differing situations of resource scarcity and economic uncertainty. Depending on the position a government occupies in a federal system, its response to scarcity may vary from that of seeking outside help to control its budget to resisting mutual agreements to cut its costs. The central government, which is primarily concerned with the general economic well-being, may reject mutual efforts at joint–budget planning to reduce costs; state and local governments that depend more on outside revenue sources and policy direction, may strive for federal macroeconomic guidelines and aid for the selective benefits involved. From 1970 to 1973, during a time of strong revenue expansion, state governments in Germany ignored joint guidelines and resented federal attempts to direct macrobudget policy, but during the 1974 to 1975 recession, when many of them faced revenue shortages, they clamored for federal aid and planning to hold down expenditures. In the earlier period, the federal government sought to stabilize the economy through expenditure restraints on the macrobudget but was rebuffed by the states. During the recession, the federal government, feeling its budget squeezed between labor union, state, and European Community (EC) expenditure demands, retreated from joint budget-planning efforts to protect its own financial position.

Under improved economic conditions in the future, the spectre of central planning may again become a negative political issue for the states, thereby possibly jeopardizing the success of economic guidelines in the longer run. It is conceivable that the economic and budgetary guidelines, as originally established, may persistently run up against these two alternating bargaining positions.

A third conclusion is that prediction uncertainty may worsen the potential for joint agreement by focusing conflict on the policy assumptions built into economic–goal projections. When predictions are wrong, political opponents can claim that they are based on one-sided or biased preferences of those who make them. If more reasonable assumptions were employed, opponents might argue, the predictions would better describe future reality. The state governments, for instance, increasingly came to see the federal economic projections as containing unreliable assumptions about economic and inflationary growth. Their response was to accuse the federal government of paying more attention to short-term–fiscal policy than to important concerns of responsible financial management and longer-term development. The federal government's delaying tactics disrupted expenditure planning and shortened the time frame for macroeconomic policy, which in turn reinforced the states' belief that the federal government was trying to enforce wrong policy priorities. But the federal government saw the states' renewed interest in mutual guidelines as a ploy to gain a more favorable tax settlement in order to reduce their unprecedented deficits.

What is the explanation for the retreat of the central government from macrobudget policy through joint planning? We now know the answer. The central government found the costs in other budget and political purposes too high. It continued to pursue macroeconomic policy but with other, less demanding instruments.

Although macroeconomic analysis is useful for analyzing complex and interrelated problems, the ability or willingness of the federal government to actually pursue a particular course of action depends on its jurisdiction and relationships with other governments. Conceivably a federal polity in which macropolicy is dependent on mutual agreement among governments can experience a kind of turbulence that encompasses the federal government. Ernst Haas, for example, has argued that the member countries of the European Community, because they must deal with complex and intractable economic-policy issues that originate in world economic problems, have increasingly attempted to keep their options open rather than foreclose them by mutual community agreements. He writes:

> The actors learned to avoid choosing with finality. Their options continue to include both the regional and extra-regional forms for making collective decisions. . . . Uncertainty concerning one's options is the hallmark of turbulence. Organizational decision making under such conditions strives for adaptation to a threatening environment of intractable issues and impatient clients by keeping most options open. . . . This trend has implications beyond the question of externalization. It throws into question the *authority* of the regional institutions to cope with the issues of highly industrialized societies and it may undermine the *legitimacy* of regional policies and processes in the mind of the public. [Emphasis in original.][24]

Actually to have manipulated fiscal-policy variables at the system level would have required that the German central government have authority over budgetary and other decisions in the federal system and jurisdiction over the geographical areas within which policy problems arise. The German federal government had neither. It stood in competition with the local units for sales-tax revenues and policy jurisdiction; issues for policy choice arose in worldwide economic disequilibriums.

The 1974 to 1975 recession came about in large part because of the decreasing demand in the United States and elsewhere in the world, that dramatically reduced German export volume (although the country did maintain a surplus on the current account). Moreover, the recession and its severe effects caught most forecasters by surprise, and the government only reacted belatedly to the growing problem. In addition to prediction uncertainty, the German policymakers learned that the major interconnections between employment, price stability, growth, and balance of payments equilibrium proved to be more complex than originally thought at the time these goals were set as the cornerstones of macroeconomic policy. The central government, as a consequence, never wholeheartedly supported budgetary economic-management efforts, and especially the Liberal Party in the coalition government opposed traditional use of deficit spending in a time of stagflation.

Thus the federal government was faced with high budget and political costs plus considerable uncertainty about how to respond. Instead of supporting collective budget action, it withheld information, delayed discussion, withdrew from full participation in the council, and worked to keep its options open in negotiations with the unions and the states.[25] The federal government was not convinced that working with the states toward a joint macroeconomic policy would improve the overall economic situation. It did believe, however, that continued efforts to promote the general welfare through the macrobudget would worsen its own financial position. The safe course was to retreat to other instruments.

The method chosen by the federal government to get out of this dilemma was to turn away from fiscal policy toward an emphasis on the monetary instrument. But in the longer run this may not be an adequate solution because West Germany is quite susceptible to interest-rate induced capital flows from other countries. The problem of dependence on world economic developments, therefore, would not be any less significant.

Another way out of the dilemma would be to place greater reliance on automatic, self-regulating-policy changes that are triggered by economic indicators. A proposal to vary revenue-sharing grants anticyclically is a case in point. The proposal, however, proved to be infeasible politically. The municipalities did not mind receiving an increased share during recessions but did oppose having no say in deciding the reduced share during booms. They also opposed having some municipalities get more than the others without having any say in the degree of discrimination. Without political agreement on the rules for the self-regulating formula, no progress was made. Consequently proposals for automatic regulators will have difficulty passing.

Of even more importance might be the attempt to reduce the need for federal bargaining. Subsidies to private firms and individuals as well as other tax measures might replace joint federal-state-local grants as the main budget avenue to stimulate or dampen the economy. The difficulty with a private-incentive approach to reducing the need for government bargaining is political—the right and the center tend to support private subsidies, while the left tends to oppose them. Governments also do not always view with favor what their citizens do with "free money." Attaching strings, however, may jeopardize the economic-management purpose. As with many policy areas, therefore, deciding what to do in economic management involves recognizing the lesser of two evils as a relative good.

Notes

1. Interview with a federal economist, fall 1975.
2. Interview with a state finance official, fall 1975.
3. Stanley Engerman, "Regional Aspects of Stabilization Policy," in *Essays in Fiscal Federalism*, ed. Richard Musgrave (Washington, D.C.: The Brookings Institution, 1965). See also, Wallace E. Oates, *Fiscal Federalism* (New York: Harcourt Brace, Janovich, 1972), pp. 4–5, 32; and, Manfred Neuman, "Zu Oekonomischen Theorie des Föderalismus," *Kyklos* 24(1971):493ff.
4. For an analysis of this issue in a broader context as a theory of groups, see, Mancur Olson, *The Logic of Collective Action: Public Goods and the Theory of Groups* (Cambridge: Harvard University Press, 1965) or Thomas Schelling, "On the Ecology of Micro-Motives," *The Public Interest* 25(Fall 1971):59–98.
5. These principles are discussed in Robert W. Rafuse, Jr., "Cyclical Behavior of State-Local Finances," in *Essays in Fiscal Federalism*, ed. Richard Musgrave (Washington, D.C.: The Brookings Institution, 1965).
6. Rafuse, Jr., "Cyclical Behavior of State-Local Finances"; L.L. Ecker-Racz, *The Politics and Economics of State-Local Finance* (Engelwood Cliffs, New Jersey: Prentice Hall, 1970), pp. 119–121; and Ansel M. Sharp, "The Behavior of Selected State and Local Government Fiscal Variables during the Phases of the Cycles 1949–1961," *Proceeding of the Fifty-eighth Annual Conference on Taxation* (Harrisburg, Pennsylvania: National Tax Association, 1966), pp. 599–613. What may be happening here is that no anticyclical actions are taken at all and local governments are growing no matter what, which might also be regarded as perverse.
7. Dieter Biehl, Karl-Heinz Jüttemeier, and Harald Legler, "Zu den konjunkturellen Effekten der Länder- und Gemeinde Haushalte in der Bundesrepublik 1960–1974," *Die Weltwirtschaft* 1, (Kiel: Institut für Weltwirtschaft, Universität Kiel, 1971). See also by the same authors, "Zu den konjunkturellen Wirkungen der Haushaltspolitik in der Bundesrepublik Deutschland 1960–1970," *Die Weltwirtschaft* 2 (Kiel: Institut für Weltwirtschaft, 1971), p. 142ff.
8. J.L. Metcalfe, "Systems Models, Economic Models and the Causal Texture of Organizational Environments: An Approach to Macro-Organization Theory," *Human Relations* 27, no. 7 (June–December 1974):648.

9. Total public real investment during the period 1970 to 1978 was divided according to governmental level in the following way: the federal government invested on average 6.9 billion DM each year, the states 7.7 billion DM, and the municipalities 27.3 billion DM. This means that the federal government's percentage of the total was only 16.6 percent, the states' share was 18.5 percent, while the municipalities invested 65.6 percent of total public investments during this period. See, *Finanzberichte* (Bonn: Bundesministerium der Finanzen, 1970–1978).

10. For a good general overview of this rather complex topic, see Robert L. Rothweiler, "Revenue Sharing in the Federal Republic of Germany," *Publius* 2, no. 1 (Spring 1972):4–25.

11. The legal basis for the five-year financial plans is contained in the "Gesetz zur Förderung der Stabilität und des Wachstums der Wirtschaft," sections 9 and 14. The basis for the establishment of the Finance Planning Council *(Finanzplanungsrat)* is found in the "Gesetz über die Grundsätze des Haushaltsrechts des Bundes und der Länder" (Haushaltsgrundsätzegesetz), 19 August 1969, section 51. For an analysis of the reform see Albrecht Leicht, *Die Haushaltsreform* (Munich: Geschichte und Staat, Bd. 146a, 1970).

12. For a discussion of Financial Planning, see, K. Schmidt and E. Wille, *Die Mehrjährige Finanzplanung, Wunsch und Wirklichkeit* (Tuebingen: J.C.B. Mohr, 1970). The description contained here is based largely on Dietrich Hosse, *Aufbau and Ablauf der Kommunikation im Arbeitsbereich des Finanzplanungsrates* (Opladen: Westdeutscher Verlag, 1975), especially pp. 27–55. Quotation is from p. 30. (Hereafter cited as *Finanzplanungsrat*.)

13. The source for these quotations is the description of the sessions provided in the *Finanzberichte* (Bonn: Bundesministerium der finanzen, 1969–1971).

14. States that are wealthier are also much less willing to accept federal subsidies in exchange for federal influence. From the interviews it became clear that the stronger states, for example, put up the most opposition to the Joint Tasks *(Gemeinschaftsaufgaben)*. See, Bernd Reissert, *Die finanzielle Beteiligung des Bundes an Aufgaben der Länder und das Postulat des "Einheitlichkeit der Lebensverhältnisse im Bundesgebiet"* (53 Bonn-Bad Godesberg: Vorwärtsdruck, 1975), pp. 75–76.

15. A federal official, for instance, gave this description of the switch in orientation: "Previously the states had said: 'Yes, we have numerous expenditures but we can finance them ourselves. And you, bad Bund (federal government) want to prevent us (for stabilization policy reasons) from fulfilling these important tasks.' " But he added that in the 1974 to 1975 period the states' argument was completely different: "By God's will (say the states), we have in 1975 such a high deficit that it is much higher than we have ever had before, and we do not want that. It is too much. We must do something."

16. This is a disputed issue in which the federal government does not agree with the states that personnel expenditures on the state level have grown overproportionately. The growth rates on the state level of total and personnel expenditures from 1971 to 1973, the figures of crucial import for the 1974 to 1975 debate, are: personnel, 15.6 percent per year; current account, 14.5 percent; and total expenditures, 15.0 percent. Thus the figures do show a slightly faster growth rate for personnel but hardly anything to greatly affect state budgets. See *Finanzberichte* (Bonn: Bundesministerium der Finanzen, 1970–1975).

17. This was the resolution passed by the conference of state finance ministers, 1973. See, Hans Wertz, "Für die Bundesländer ist Ihre Finanzautonomie unantastbar," *Handelsblatt,* 20 September 1973. Moreover, the state finance ministers were reacting to an article written by the then federal Finance Minister Helmut Schmidt, who argued that the federal government needed direct influence on local budgets in order for any macroeconomic policy to be successful. See, "Helmut Schmidt—Theorie und Thesen der Finanzpolitik," *Handelsblatt,* 3 September 1973. For the municipalities point of view in this controversy, see "Kein Kontrollrecht des Bundes über die Etats der Kommunen," *Handelsblatt,* 5 October 1973.

18. Despite the exhortation of the council to emphasize public investments, these expenditures have more or less stagnated in real terms since 1972. See, for instance, Institut Finanzen und Steuern, "Information über die Entwicklung der öffentlichen Finanzwirtschaft in der Bundesrepublik Deutschland von 1964 bis 1974." Working paper, p. 7. Since 1972 the investments have increased at an average annual rate of 6.5 percent. Moreover, the share of governmental expenditures on GNP climbed from 37.3 percent in 1970 to 45.0 percent in 1975. See, *Suddeutsche Zeiting,* 23 June 1975, p. 9.

19. See Jack Knott, "Conflict Behavior and Accommodation: The Case of Labor Relations in Weimar and the German Federal Republic."

20. After the recession, however, it was reported in the newspaper that Finance Minister Apel responded more favorably to the repeated demands of the states for detailed budgetary guidelines. Apel also argued that, "the federal government and the states should work together on a new financial constitution." He felt that the purpose would be to increase the reaction speed of the various public governments to changes in the business-cycle." "Das Steurpaket kann in Kraft treten: Bayern, Niedersachsen, Saarland stimmen zu," *Frankfurter Allgemeine* (16 July 1977):1.

21. In 1975 the problem became considerably more difficult. In April, for instance, the major economic institutes in Germany still predicted a 0.0 to 1.0 percent growth rate in GNP, although in January they had predicted a 2.0 percent rate. The real-growth rate has turned out to be negative, around -2.0 to -3.0 percent. See *Suddeutsche Zeitung* (28 June 1975).

22. Hosse, *Finanzplanungsrat,* pp. 32–33.

23. For an analysis of the proposal made in the Bundesrat by Baden-Württemberg, see Dr. Otto Erich Geske, "Koordiniering der Finanzpolitiken von Bund, Ländern und Gemeinden: Möglichkeiten und Grenzen," *Wirtschaftsdienst* 7, (1975), pp. 372–373.

24. Ernst Haas, *The Obsolescence of Regional Integration Theory*, Research Series no. 25 (Berkeley: Institute of International Studies, University of California, 1975), pp. 62–63.

25. Metcalfe, "An Approach to Macro-Organization Theory," argues that turbulence produces "reliance on internally generated information and attenuation of interorganizational relations (which) reinforce one another and reduce the viability of organizations. . .," p. 654.

7 Curing Local Fiscal Pathologies through Grants in Aid

The problem that the municipalities make the most public investments, but do so procyclically, is not yet solved in our system. There are really not enough possibilities to influence them to follow stabilization policy.

In recessions, grant income and tax revenue are lower and in booms they are higher. The corresponding allowable level of (municipal) debt varies in much the same way—exactly opposite to the requirements of stabilization policy.[1]

—Federal Financial Officials

Despite the optimism that infused the Finance Reforms in the late 1960s, the levels of government have made little progress toward achieving agreement on budget policy. Even the federal government retreated from its commitment to macrobudget objectives. Uncertainty over the causes of and cures for the recession plus a deteriorating financial position caused the Bonn leadership to adopt a strategy of keeping its options open during increasingly distasteful negotiations with the states and the municipalities. The first casualty was the macrobudget plan.

Legal-constitutional provisions could not produce voluntary joint agreement. The federal-fiscal system is characterized by financial competition, organizational rivalries, independent budget authority, and contrary partisanship. But the Finance Reforms did not rely solely on voluntary cooperation as a means to improve macroeconomic policy. They also gave greater authority to the federal government to regulate public-debt policy and provide monetary incentives through intergovernmental grants in aid. The specific instruments created were the Stabilization Reserve Fund, the *Financial Aid* grants, and the debt-ceiling policy. Each was designed with the purpose of improving the federal government's ability to influence especially the income side of state and local budgets.

Regulatory policies and grants in aid have more appeal for the federal government than does joint budget planning. Both policy instruments better meet the economic uncertainties of the 1970s and the federal government's dilemma in trying to deal with them. Unlike budget planning, these types of policies can be employed throughout the budget cycle, thereby fitting nicely with the government's shortened time horizon for economic decision making. Unlike voluntary joint agreement, state and municipal governments find it more difficult to ignore regulation or monetary incentives. Not following regulatory guidelines makes them appear as "bad apples"; not accepting available grant money is unpopular with state parliaments and the public. Thus the federal government can obtain the states' cooperation through selective incentives or regulation, even if the states do not necessarily approve entirely of the macropolicy goals.

The greater coercive power of regulatory and grant policies, however, has not made them unqualified successes. The practice of varying federal grants in aid counter to the business cycle grew into a formidable political controversy during the 1974 to 1975 recession. Some groups argued that interference by the central government on a short-term, discretionary basis violates the principles of federalism. Others, more concerned about overall economic welfare, countered that procyclical local expenditure patterns do more harm than local autonomy does good. If the swings become too violent, unpredictable variations in local tax income force cutbacks in local services during recessions and unplanned, hasty spending during booms. Each side challenged the federal government to choose between a little less federal independence or a bit more national well-being.[2]

Most of the state governments came to oppose a further extension of anti-recession grants. Some of them even set about challenging the constitutionality of the way these grants have been implemented. The federal government also became disenchanted with the use of investment grants for economic management, proposing to include them in the budget cutting program for 1977.[3] Many state and federal officials argued that investment grants cannot be varied in a way that satisfies the requirements of economic management. Grants for above-surface construction, for example, which are a prominent type of federal grant, require a minimum two-year planning phase plus a two- or three-year execution phase.[4] Smaller communities that possess a limited repertoire of investment projects are especially hard pressed to alter plans in the short run. The familiar time-lag problem between approval of an investment project and its implementation also plagued the use of these grants as economic-management measures. During the 1966 to 1967 recession, despite large increases in federal construction grants, the construction industry started its recovery more than one-half year after general business activity had turned upward—not a very impressive response to federal efforts.

But even if the capacity existed to use grants for economic management, many policymakers opposed doing so. Policymakers in the Joint Task investment areas, for example, saw their job as promoting long-term growth.[5] The grant system also serves the purpose of equalizing income among regions with varying tax yields.[6] Economic-management priorities, however, often conflict with policy measures to bring the poorer regions up to the standards of service delivery for the Federal Republic as a whole.

But before analyzing in detail the impact of federal grant-in-aid policies on federal political relations (see chapters 8 and 9), we first need to answer the question: How important are investment grants and debt ceilings as economic-management instruments? Several issues need to be explored: (1) How much do grants influence state and local spending decisions? Conceivably grant policy is irrelevant for economic management because grants do not comprise a very significant part of state and local spending. (2) But supposing that grants are important to the states and localities, can economic-management measures be imposed effectively, given the independence of state and local budgets? (3) How serious is the problem these measures address? Perhaps not all states and municipalities reinforce business-cycle swings through public spending.

This last issue, the variability of fiscal perversity by state and local governments, is of special interest because of the proposals to centralize the federal system. The centralization argument rests on the assumption that larger, wealthier, and urban state units will more likely behave less fiscally perverse than their smaller, poorer, and rural counterparts. This assumption, however, does not explain fiscal perversity for the 1966 to 1972 boom-recession cycle, the period with the best data availability. Chapter 8, therefore, offers an alternative explanation based on the political costs and benefits of imposing macroeconomic criteria on traditional budget purposes. The exercise of this strategy—the political decision to impose macroeconomic goals—is explored more fully in chapter 9.

Evaluating Institutions and Policy Instruments

The federal government and the states have independent budget authority as long as the law does not prescribe otherwise. Consequently, unlike more centralized systems, the federal government cannot directly influence state or local spending decisions. Policy instruments established by the 1969 Finance Reforms, therefore, emphasize indirect federal influence on the income side of state and local public spending; but most of these instruments have not worked well, and many officials would argue that they have not worked at all.

One such instrument employed during times of economic expansion is the federal government's right to set ceilings on capital borrowing of all levels of government. The Finance Reform allows the federal government to exercise this power through legislation requiring Bundesrat approval.[7] The policy imposes ceilings on borrowing that are based on a weighted average of each government's actual credit assumption over the past three years. But because of Bundesrat approval, most policymakers believed that the restrictions did not severely hinder state capital spending, although they did presumably have a more positive impact on the capital market.[8] As expected, the restrictions also raised difficult questions about the right of self-administration for local government.[9] Another argument against them was that they cause disruption of local investment planning. A limitation imposed in the later stages of a construction project, it was argued, introduces undue strains with contractors and other clients.[10]

The capital borrowing of local governments is supervised by the state interior ministries, which emphasize responsible financial management. This approach has worked to increase the fiscally perverse behavior of local spending. Generally, the state interior ministries judge the debt capacity of a community according to its financial strength, measured primarily in terms of tax revenue. Recessions, however, reduce tax income and the community's financial strength. As this occurs, the debt authorities become less willing to approve additional debt. In response, the community cuts back on investments, thereby reinforcing the recession.[11] Consequently federal regulations only weakly offset this more pervasive influence of the state interior ministries.

A second instrument that the Finance Reforms gave to the federal government was the Stabilization Reserve Fund. Federal legislation with Bundesrat approval may require that the states and the federal government freeze certain tax income at the Bundesbank, but significantly the municipalities are not included.[12] The advantage of the reserve system is the power the federal government has over the release of the reserve funds. With Bundesrat approval, it may release the reserves to stimulate additional spending in times of recession. The municipalities also build savings according to law, but they are not used for economic management nor are they in any way controlled by the regulatory policy of the federal government. The reciprocal of this measure, that is, the obligatory running of current account deficits during a recession, is not provided for by the Basic Law.[13] Consequently the states and municipalities decrease spending during recessions and increase spending during booms to make up for these losses.

The real impact of the Reserve Fund is its use by the federal government as a selective financial incentive to entice the states to increase grants during recessions. But the problems are formidable. The Basic Law states that the federal government may not give financial aid directly to local governments.[14] Instead it may give the money only to the states, which make it part of their programs of state aid. Under normal circumstances, there is absolutely no obligation on the part of the state governments to go along with the policy intentions of the federal government. The states may spend as much as they desire in grant areas, regardless of what the federal government prefers. The federal contribution, moreover, is made only in limited spending areas and is relatively modest in comparison to the size of the states' grant programs for local-investment projects.[15]

If the federal government decides on a policy of increasing investment grants during a recession, it will propose a special antirecession program *(Konjunkturprogramm)* which contains additional investments in these areas. To induce state participation, it generally makes the additional funds provisional upon matched spending by the state and local governments. This program will be discussed next in the Finance Planning Council and worked out into an administrative agreement between the federation and the states.[16] The Bundestag then has a period of thirty days in which to reject the plan; otherwise it goes into effect.

Economic management, however, seems to work only to increase grant spending. Instances in which the federal government has attempted to reduce categorical investment grants explicitly for stabilization reasons occurred only once. In 1973 the Planning Commissions in the Joint Tasks *(Gemeinschaftsaufgaben)* spending areas agreed to a 10 percent shift in spending to the following year. The shift did not alter the regular, planned program but had more of a symbolic character.[17]

The greater importance of symbolism over substance is not atypical. Studies of the stabilization effects of investment grants have all agreed that they have followed a more or less destabilizing and hence procyclical course.[18] Federal categorical grants to the states have shown only a slightly procyclical development; state categorical grants to local governments, on the other hand, have followed a pronouncedly procyclical trend. The other major types of grants, the untied or formula grants, have also followed a procyclical tendency. From the state to the local level, untied grants developed procyclically but in a less pronounced way than the tied grants.[19] Thus whether grants are based on formulas or discretionary actions in specific funding categories, they reinforce rather than counter swings in economic activity.

The major macroeconomic-policy instruments created by the Finance Reforms—grants-in-aid, debt ceilings, and stabilization reserves—thus leave the federal government with only an indirect and marginal impact on the local-investment cycle. The state interior ministries play the key role of overseeing local debt levels but have done so in a way that encourages destabilizing behavior. The legal stipulation that the federal government give financial aid only to the states has further placed the states in a central position over the local communities. In this instance as well, the state-grant programs have supported a destabilizing behavior on the part of the local governments. Moreover, the local communities have not yet become part of the obligatory stabilization reserve system. In sum, the federal government cannot directly influence the local-spending cycle. Major instruments which are available have marginal impact, or, as in the case of credit regulations, reinforce the local procyclical pattern.

Canceling Federal Policy: 1966 to 1967

The 1967 recession and following boom period demonstrate the procyclical character of local spending and the inability of the federal government to do anything about it. The recession-boom also shows the potential that state governments have to thwart the intentions of federal policy by simply doing the opposite of what the central government is trying to achieve.

State and local public-spending patterns reinforce private swings in economic activity. For most of the last fifteen years state and local investment expenditures have gone up and down parallel to the business cycle.[20] But in the Federal Republic, 90 percent of public investment is made in the construction industry, and during the 1970s the federal government made only slightly more than 16 percent of the total. Any federal investment program designed for economic management, therefore, must include state or local investments.[21] The problem is to get the local governments to support federal initiatives.

Cyclical swings in local public expenditure, in addition to harming macroeconomic policy, cause disruptions in the provision of local services. The main theme of the budget speeches made in 1974 and 1975 before the local parliaments, for example, was the reduction of city financial capacity and service levels due to the continuing recession.[22]

The biggest impact, however, has been on local capital spending and borrowing. Local governments slowed investments during recessions and speeded them up during economic expansions. Especially during the 1966 to 1967 recession investment declined considerably (see figure 7–1); again in the boom phase, 1969 to 1972, investment surged ahead, registering growth rates over 15.0 percent per year. Since 1972 real public investment on the local level has not grown strongly, but outlays for personnel and other current account items have done better.

Municipal fiscal decisions are made in much the same way as they are in a private household.[23] With higher income, the borrowing potential of the community increases. If ninety units of funds are needed, for example, but the local

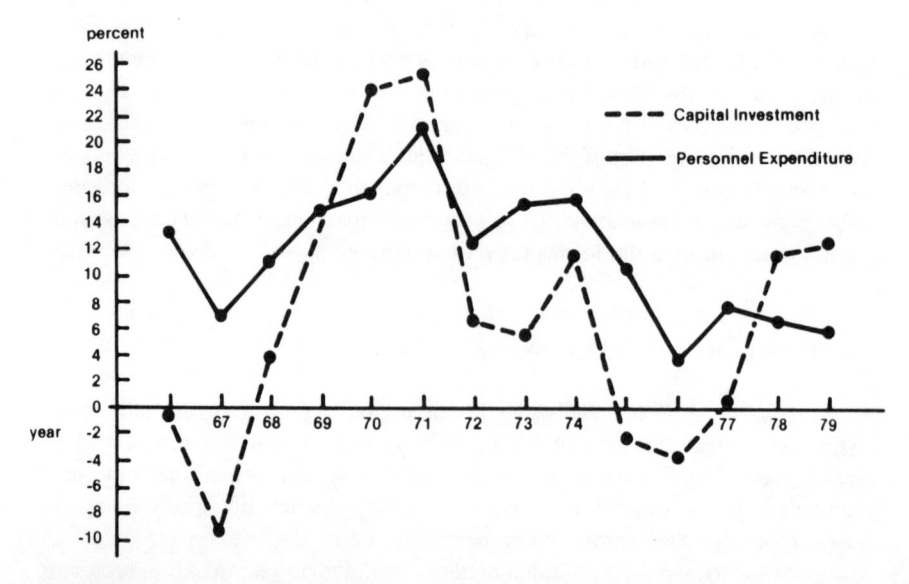

Source: *Finanzberichte, 1970–1980* (Bonn: Bundesministerium der Finanzen).
Note: The figures for 1979 are estimates.

Figure 7–1. Local Government Capital Investments and Personnel Expenditures (Percentage Annual Change)

administration takes in one hundred, it can use the extra ten units for investment, by which five to eight units meet interest payments and around two units go for amortization. But with this amount the administration can spend another ninety units for investment. In other words, the key amount is the surplus of current income that allows the community to meet its debt payments.

The 1967 recession caused a decline in current revenue which forced municipalities to cut credit by −2.3 percent. The following boom caused a growth in revenue that encouraged a renewed surge in credit, which climbed sharply at an annual average rate of 23.0 percent. Overall local government income during the recession had grown at only 3.2 percent over the previous year. The average annual–growth rate for the ten-year period 1964 to 1974 was 10.8 percent; for the boom years 1969 to 1971, it was 14.4 percent. Tax income declined more than overall income in 1966 to 1967, while revenue from grants in aid grew slightly faster than the total at 5.0 percent.

What makes grants in aid an attractive policy for countering such local fiscal pathologies is the dramatic increase in their share of total local income. At the same time, tax income as a source of local expenditure financing, and in particular investment financing, fell consistently. Taxes as a percentage of total income fell from 34.7 percent in 1961 to 29.7 percent in 1975. As a source of investment financing, the decline has been even more significant. In 1962, current income accounted for 36.7 percent of investment financing, while in 1974, the figure had fallen to 15.9 percent. Intergovernmental grants in aid have largely filled this gap, especially as a source of finance for local investments. The percentage share which tied grants comprised of local investment financing increased from 15.0 percent in 1962 to 29.2 percent in 1974.[24] For this reason grants have become a major potential source for influencing local-investment decisions.

Despite the seemingly great opportunity to alter local procyclical behavior through grants in aid, the potential to vary them anticyclically in practice is very small. Each federal state in Germany has a system of tax-equalization laws *(Finanzausgleichsgesetze)* which regulate to a large extent the untied and formula grants to the local communities. These untied grants followed a slightly procyclical trend over the last ten years and have accounted for at least 50 percent or more of total grants in aid from the states. The main reason for the procyclical growth of untied and formula grants is that they are based on tax revenue, which varies procyclically with the business cycle. Conceivably, if the states could vary the percentage share which the municipalities receive, they could mitigate the effects of the variations in tax income; but politically the states simply cannot raise the percentage in recession times and lower it in boom times in order to even out revenue flow for the communities. The municipalities view such manipulation as a violation of their constitutional right to local fiscal autonomy.

Tied grants also cannot cure local fiscal pathologies because the state governments offset federal anticyclical policy by cutting their shares in the grant programs. The federal government increased tied investment grants to the states by 23.5 percent in 1966 to 1967, a very strong economic-management action in the midst of the recession.[25] But a look at total state grants to local governments, which include these federal government monies, reveals a much less favorable outcome. State-tied grants for investment increased by an annual rate of only 1.8 percent. Although published figures are not generally available for individual programs, Thomas Hahn provides data on the percentage participation of the federal government, states, and localities in the low-cost-housing program from 1952 to 1972, which serve as an illustration of how the state governments offset federal economic-management objectives.

Federal participation in low-cost housing continued to fall in the first recession year, 1966, according to a longer-term legal provision that foresaw a declining federal share. In the following year, due to the passage of the antirecession programs, the federal share reversed course, climbing in volume by more than 500 percent. The concurrent sharp drop in the states' contribution, however, more than leveled out this anticyclical spending of the federal government. As table 7-1 shows, the states reduced spending by 1380.07 DM in 1967, slightly more than the amount by which the federal government increased spending.

In summary, it appears that grants in aid did very little to offset destabilizing local spending, thereby reinforcing the local–business cycle. Coupled with this was an even sharper decline in the revenue from taxes, causing local governments to reduce borrowing and investment. As in the analysis of economic-management instruments, the federal states occupy a key position for the success of any federal policy. Are all the states "bad apples," or do only some of them spoil the whole lot?

Individual State Differences

The aggregate of state spending has destabilized the economy. But the differences in wealth and population size raise the question whether some states might pursue a less fiscally perverse policy than others. North Rhine-Westphalia, for example, has a population of more than 16 million and produces a state-domestic product

Table 7-1
The Participation of the Federal Government, States, and Municipalities in Low-Cost Housing, 1966-1967
(in million DM and percent annual change)

	1966	1967	Annual Δ	Percent Annual Δ
Federal	246.9	1595.7	1348.8	546.3
State	3887.5	2507.5	-1380.1	-35.5
Local	222.8	205.2	-17.6	-7.7

Source: Calculated from Thomas Hahn, "Förderung des sozialen Wohnungsbaues: Dargestellt unter besonderer Berücksichtigung der Aufstellung und Durchführung der jährlichen Wohnungsbauprogramme in Baden-Württemberg," paper, October 1974.

Curing Local Fiscal Pathologies

that approaches that of many smaller foreign countries. The Saarland, on the other hand, has less than 2 million inhabitants and does not possess a large industrial infrastructure. Conceivably the wealthier and more populous states pursue a less procyclical policy than the others.

The public-finance literature argues indirectly that size is a factor that can hinder economic management. The economies of smaller governmental units, the argument runs, are too open to allow them to retain the benefits a stabilization policy might produce. The public good character of economic stabilization, as was argued in chapter 6, causes the smaller governmental units to pay the stabilization costs themselves but share the benefits with others.[26] Following this line of reasoning, the smaller federal states may not have as much incentive to take initiatives in the economic-management field as do larger states.

A similar argument led the Expert Commission for the Realignment of the Federal States *(Sachverständigenkommission zur Neugliederung des Bundesgebietes)* to propose a reduction in the number of states to five or six more or less equal units in size and tax base.[27] The commission's purpose was to create units that could sustain support for standard public services without extraordinary funding from the federal level. The commission also believed that the new states would better meet the demands of macroeconomic policy. Presumably, if the larger and wealthier states were found to be less sensitive to the business cycle in their public spending, that would support the argument for realignment along these lines.

Relative poverty is also an argument raised against pressuring states into fiscal-policy programs. The relatively less-wealthy states in West Germany have claimed that their pressing policy needs preclude an active fiscal policy.[28] Especially during periods of economic growth, fiscal-policy prescriptions to hold down expenditures may mean that poorer states have to cut back on essential public services and miss opportunities for infrastructure development. During a recession phase, these same states face severe difficulty meeting regular costs even without spending additional stabilization funds. For them, fiscal policy should be somebody else's problem because they have enough of their own.

To investigate if some states are bad apples from an economic-management perspective and some are not, we need to examine the tied-investment grants given to the local governments within the state's jurisdiction from 1962 to 1971.[29] Two time blocks are particularly important in this regard: the recession years 1966 to 1967 and the boom years 1969 to 1971. The percentage growth in gross national product for 1966 to 1967 fell to 1 percent, while from 1969 to 1971, the average growth rate was 12.2 percent. The 1967 recession was short, lasting not much more than one year. The economy began to recover again strongly in 1968 with a GNP growth rate for that year of 9.0 percent. The high point of the subsequent boom phase was reached in 1970 with a GNP growth rate of 13.3 percent.

Table 7-2 shows the percentage change in growth rates for tied-investment grants to local governments for 1966 to 1967 and the average growth-rate change for 1969 to 1971 for each of the eight regular states, excluding the city-states.[30]

Table 7-2
Federal-State Expenditure on Categorical Grants for Investment to Local Governments, 1966–1967 and 1969–1971
(average percentage annual change in extraordinary budget)

Federal State	1966–1967	1969–1971
Group 1		
North Rhine-Westphalia (NRW)	15.1	14.4
Schleswig-Holstein (SH)	15.9	9.6
Lower Saxony (LS)	16.6	7.6
Bavaria (BV)	15.4	6.4
Group 2		
Hessen (HS)	−2.9	24.8
Rhineland-Palatinate (RLP)	−6.9	18.4
Baden-Württemberg (BW)	−1.0	18.4
Saarland (SL)	−12.4	16.6

Source: Calculated from Statistisches Bundesamt, Finanzen und Steuern, Reihe 1, Haushaltswirtschaft von Bund Ländern und Gemeinden, II Jahresabschlüsse, Kommunalfinanzen und Staatsfinanzen, 1962–1971 (Stuttgart: W. Kohlhammer Verlag).

Note: 1969–1971 refers to average annual percentage change for the years 1968–1969/1969–1970/1970–1971.

For the recession period 1966 to 1967, the table shows a sharp division in grant policy between North Rhine-Westphalia (NRW), Schleswig-Holstein (SH), Lower Saxony (LS), and Bavaria (BV) as one group (group 1) and Hesse (HS), Rhineland-Palatinate (RLP), Baden-Württemberg (BW), and the Saarland (SL) as the other (group 2). The first group has a 15.8 percent average increase in grants in aid for that year, while the second group reduces their grants on average −5.8 percent. All the states in the second group fall below the midpoint and/or the average growth rate for 1966 to 1967, while all the states in the first group lie above it. The difference between the average percentage growth rate of the two groups is 21.6 percent without much variation within each group.

Dividing the states again according to growth rates above and below the mean for the boom period 1969 to 1971, the same two groups fall out. The states in the first group show an average growth rate of 9.5 percent, while the second group has an average rate of 19.6 percent. For this period the break is not so sharp nor is the variation around the mean so small. Despite this, the placement of each state in the two groupings does not change from one time period to the next, as can be seen from figure 7–2. Group 1 increased grants in the 1966 to 1967 recession and held back grant growth in the subsequent boom; group 2 did the opposite. The point of view that more financially secure and larger federal states pursue a less-procyclical–budget policy receives little support from the data on investment–grants in aid to local governments from 1962 to 1971. The less procyclical group contains such diverse states as NRW and SH. The former state is the largest and one of the most wealthy, while the latter is next to the poorest and one of the smaller states in population. In the more procyclical

Curing Local Fiscal Pathologies

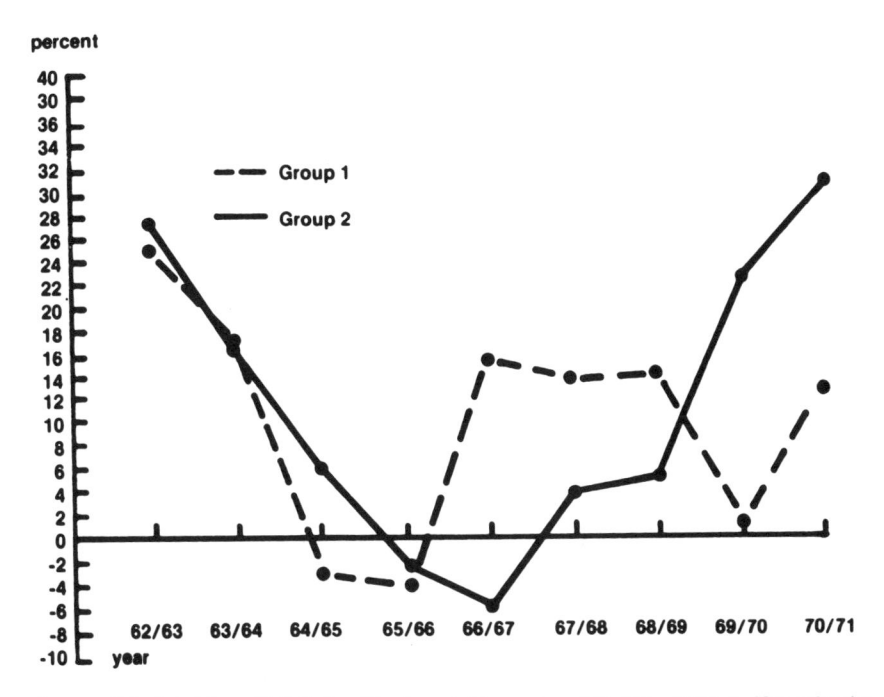

percent

Source: Calculated from Statistisches Bundesamt, Finanzen und Steuern, Reihe 1, Haushaltswirtschaft von Bund Ländern und Gemeinden, II Jahresabschlüsse, Kommunalfinanzen und Staatsfinanzen, 1962–71 (Stuttgart: W. Kohlhammer Verlag).

Figure 7–2. Categorical Investment Grants of Group 1 and Group 2 States in Extraordinary Budget, 1962–1971 (Percentage Annual Change)

group, a similar contrast in state characteristics is found. BW competes with NRW for first place in wealth and size, but the SL is West Germany's poorest and smallest regular federal state.[31]

In a similar manner, the proposal to realign the states into larger and more self-sufficient entities financially does not receive support from the data. The strongest case against realignment on the basis of stabilization policy is the differing performance of BW and NRW, two traditionally self-sufficient federal states. Both have a very similar per capita income, although the size of BW is somewhat smaller. The creation of all states comparable to BW, however, would not necessarily enhance the fiscal-policy performance of the states. A relatively poorer and smaller state, LS, for example, has the highest growth rate for 1966 to 1967 and next to the lowest rate for 1969 to 1971.

The political party of the state government also does not determine the division of the states into these two groupings. BV is governed by the Christian Social Union (CSU), NRW by the Social Democrats (SPD), and SH by the

Christian Democrats (CDU). In the second group, comparable party variations are found as well. HS has an SPD government, while BW is governed by the CDU.[32]

The federal grants taken together with the state grants do comprise a sizable proportion of total local public investment (TLPI), although the percentage shares vary from only 17.3 percent in LS to 42.9 percent in NRW for the year 1967. Presumably those states in which intergovernmental-investment grants comprise a larger percentage share of TLPI have a greater potential for influencing local governmental fiscal-policy performance. Through the use of these grants, NRW, for example, should be able to influence local governmental investment behavior more substantially than would LS.

Table 7-3 presents data that show the average percent-growth rates of investment grants and local investments for the recession years 1966 to 1967 and the boom years 1969 to 1971. The only real difference in local-investment spending between the two groups takes place in the recession phase, 1966 to 1967. The less procyclical group shows an average fall off in local-investment spending of −4.2 percent, despite a 15.8 percent average increase in state grants. The more procyclical grouping falls off even more sharply at −12.8 percent. Apparently a rather significant increase in investment grants during a recession does not deter a negative-growth rate for local-public investment. It does, however, prevent investments from falling off as far as they otherwise would have.

In the boom phase, only a very slight difference in investment-spending patterns between the two groups is found, despite the fact that grants in aid of the second grouping grow twice as fast as those of the first. During the boom, the percentage share which state investment grants represent of TLPI for the first grouping is 31.9 percent; for the second grouping the comparable figure is 33.9

Table 7-3
State Categorical Grants for Investment and Total Local Public Investment, 1966-1967 and 1969-1971

(average percent annual change in extraordinary budget)

	Grants	Investments
	1966-1967	
Group 1	15.8	−4.2
Group 2	−5.8	−12.8
	1969-1971	
Group 1	9.5	20.0
Group 2	19.6	22.7

Source: Statistisches Bundesamt, Finanzen und Steuern, Reihe 1, Haushaltswirtschaft von Bund Ländern und Gemeinden, II Jahresabschlüsse, Kommunalfinanzen und Staatsfinanzen, 1962-1971 (Stuttgart: W. Kohlhammer Verlag), plus the author's own calculations.

Note: 1969-1971 refers to average annual percent change for the years 1968-1969/1969-1970/1970-1971.

percent. Because the potential for influencing local-investment decisions of the two groups is similar, the lack of difference in local public-investment spending in the boom phase seems to fall to the dynamic of local-investment decisions.

During the 1967 recession, all four states in the first grouping increase grants in aid approximately 15 to 16 percent. The range is only from 16.6 percent for Lower Saxony to 15.1 percent for North Rhine-Westphalia. This lack of variation allows for holding economic-management constant, while at the same time varying the percent that these grants represent of TLPI.

As table 7–4 shows, the greater the percentage share of investment grants on TLPI, the less the fall off in local investment during the recession years 1966 to 1967. The two clearest cases are North Rhine-Westphalia and Lower Saxony. The latter state's investment falls off by twice the amount of the former state's investment. North Rhine-Westphalia's grants program accounts for almost half of TLPI, but it still experiences a decrease in this investment of -3.0 percent, despite the state's policy to increase investment grants by 15.1 percent. Even a fairly large grant program accounting for almost 50 percent of local investments cannot guarantee an anticyclical local-government-spending policy.

A difference in grants as a percentage share of TLPI of 25.6 percent between North Rhine-Westphalia and Lower Saxony produces only a 3.0 percentage difference in investment growth. In both cases the growth rates are negative, despite large positive increases in state grants. Nevertheless, all four investment-growth patterns for these states lie above the national average, some by more than 50 percent. If only local-public investment is considered during the recession phase, the two groupings formed by grants-in-aid patterns (see table 7–2) do not change.

In sum, the influence of intergovernmental grants on local-public investment during the 1962 to 1971 period is not considerable. During the boom period 1969 to 1971, local-public investment in the first grouping of states grows at a

Table 7–4
Categorical Investment Grants and Total Local Public Investment in Extraordinary Budget, 1966–1967

	National Average	NRW	SH	BV	LS
Percentage change in grants	7.9	15.1	15.9	15.4	16.6
Percentage change in local investments	-8.0	-3.0	-3.4	-4.5	-6.0
Grants as a percentage of local investments	33.9	42.9	35.7	31.8	17.3

Source: Statistisches Bundesamt, Finanzen und Steuern, Reihe 1, Haushaltswirtschaft von Bund Ländern und Gemeinden, II Jahresabschlüsse, Kommunalfinanzen und Staatsfinanzen, 1962–1971 (Stuttgart: W. Kohlhammer Verlag), plus the author's own calculations.

Note: North Rhine-Westphalia (NRW); Schleswig-Holstein (SH); Bavaria (BV); Lower Saxony (LS).

rate comparable to local investment in the second grouping, despite a 50 percent slower growth in grants in aid. In the recession years, local-public investment in both state groupings registers a negative growth, even though the grants in the first group increase by 15.0 percent. Apparently to counteract business-cycle swings in local-public investment requires a large grant program (up to 50 percent of local-public investment) and a consciously anticyclical policy. Even meeting these requirements, however, does not predict success during the boom phase. Very likely it will prove difficult to cut expenditures in the grant program to the extent that they can be increased in the recession. At the same time, during the boom, local governments readily utilize other sources of finance to pursue their own policy.

Avoiding Reliance on Grants in Aid

For at least two reasons the federal government needs to concern itself with local-investment decisions. If the federal government intends to pursue fiscal policy with the budget, it cannot do so alone because state and local governments make over three-fourths of all public investments, and this has been true not only for the 1966 to 1967 period but also throughout the 1970s. An analysis of the 1967 recession and subsequent boom has shown that local-investment expenditures have a destabilizing impact on private economic activity. But despite the need for central direction, the major fiscal-policy instruments available to the federal government and the states have had either a marginal positive effect or virtually no effect at all. A possible improvement might be the inclusion of the local governments in the system of obligatory stabilization reserves held at the Bundesbank. To include the local communities in the reserve system would help level out the cyclical nature of their tax revenue. Another reform might be to revise state-debt regulations so that they account for situations of economic disturbance.

Grants in aid pose a more difficult problem for economic management. Even categorical grants have varied more procyclically than revenue-sharing grants at the state level. In at least one program, low-cost housing, state action completely offset federal policy. Presumably grants that are based on formulas related to tax income—the revenue grants—should be more sensitive to the business cycle. The fact that discretionary categorical grants also behaved perversely from a macro-viewpoint suggests that the dynamics of the budget process contain elements which do not satisfy the criteria of economic management. Simply making grants unrelated to tax income, therefore, does not necessarily guarantee noncyclical trends.

The further analysis of individual state differences raised more reservations of a different kind. Despite strong increases in tied grants in 1967 in some states, local investment within these state jurisdictions still showed a negative-growth rate. Even worse, the boom phase raised doubts about the effectiveness of tied grants as a stabilization instrument altogether. Despite growth rates for tied grants, which averaged more than twice as much for one group as the other, little difference in local-investment–growth rates appeared. The rather disconcerting conclusion is: for tied grants to make a significant impact on the local-investment cycle, the states need to vary these grants in a very anticyclical manner. But if even a policy of sharp variation is to make a difference, the share which tied grants represent of total local investment also must be large.

With respect to the differences between group 1 and group 2 states, very little explanatory power is attached to the demographics of size, wealth, partisanship, and population. Rather, the explanation explored more closely in chapter 8 hinges on the political responses of the state and federal administrations to varying economic conditions. Only under rather unusual economic circumstances, it will be argued, do the finance ministries and the Cabinet make the difficult political decision to impose on other budget purposes in order to manage the economy.

Notes

1. Interviews with federal financial officials, spring 1975.

2. The form this debate took was a series of newspaper articles written by representatives of the cities, states and national government. Helmut Schmidt, "Theory und Thesen der Finanzpolitik," *Handelsblatt*, 3 September 1973; B. Weinberger, "Kein Kontrollrecht des Bundes über die Etats der Kommunen," *Handelsblatt*, 5 October 1973; and H. Wertz, L. Huber, and H. Rau, "Für die Bundesländer ist ihre Finanzautonomie unantastbar," *Handelsblatt*, 20 September 1973.

3. Hans Apel, "Massnahmen zur Verbesserung der Haushaltsstruktur und zur Verminderung der Kreditaufnahme," (Bonn: Referat Presse- und Information, Bundesministerium der Finanzen, 8 September 1975), pp. 2–8.

4. H. Schmidz, "Schuldendeckel: das falsche Instrument," *Handelsblatt*, 2 May 1972.

5. The Joint Tasks *(Gemeinschaftsaufgaben)* were established constitutionally in 1969 with the Finance Reform and represent joint-spending programs of the states and the federal government in the areas of university construction, development of agriculture, and regional economic development. Despite these late constitutional arrangements, joint spending existed in these areas since 1957, 1956, and 1951 respectively. See, Bernd Reissert, *Die finanzielle Beteiligung des Bundes an Aufgaben der Länder und das Postulat "der Einheitlichkeit der Lebensverhältnisse im Bundesgebiet"* (Bonn-Bad Godesberg: Vorwärtsdruck, 1975).

6. This is especially the case for regional economic development but is also a general goal prescribed by the Basic Law (see article 106, paragraph 3, no. 2). For an excellent analysis of this aspect of the grant system, see Reissert, *Die finanzielle Beteiligung des Bundes.*

7. The most recent legislation is "Die Verordnung über die Begrenzung der Kreditaufnahme," passed in June 1973 and referred to as the Schuldendeckelverordnung. The original amendment to the Basic Law is article 109, paragraph 4, no. 2.

8. Many of the officials interviewed who deal with this aspect of policy hold this opinion.

9. W. Büchmann, "Plannung, Kreditbeschränkung und kommunale Selbstverwaltung," *Archiv für Kommunalwissenschaften* 13, no. 2 (1974):63–77.

10. This aspect was brought out by the interviews with officials on the local level of government.

11. "Was der Bund nicht hat," *Der Spiegel,* no. 29 (1975), pp. 27–28.

12. See article 109, paragraph 4, no. 1 of the Basic Law.

13. Article 115 of the Basic Law does allow for the possibility that during a recession the federal government might assume more credit than that which covers investment expenditure. Nevertheless, the norm that credit must not exceed investments is strong and has never been exceeded on the federal level.

14. For a thorough description of these grant systems, see Robert L. Rothweiler, "Revenue Sharing in the Federal Republic of Germany," *Publius* vol. 2, no. 1 (Spring 1972):4–25 and J.S.H. Hunter, "Revenue Sharing in the Federal Republic of Germany," Research Monograph no. 2 (Canberra, Australia: Center for Research on Federal Financial Relations, The Australian National University, 1973).

15. In a specific joint program, the planning commission, administrative officials, or law may determine each partner's share. In the Joint Tasks, for example, there are fifty–fifty matching requirements. Other additional spending by the states in the general spending area, however, is not prohibited. In programs for local governments, the aggregate state share for 1971 was four times that of the federal government. Variations in state spending, therefore, can have a much greater effect. See in this regard, Heinz Kock, *Stabilitätspolitik im föderalistischen System der Bundesrepublik Deutschland* (Cologne: Bund Verlag, 1975), pp. 99–110.

16. The Finance Planning Council is described in much greater detail in chapter 6.

17. This is the opinion expressed by the interviewed officials in the Regional Development Program.

18. See, Kock, *Stabilitätspolitik* and Dieter Biehl, Karl H. Jüttemeier and Harald Legler, "Zu den konjunkturellen Effekten der Länder- und Gemeindehaushalte in der Bundesrepublik Deutschland 1960–1974," *Die Weltwirtschaft,* vol. 1 (Kiel: Institut für Weltwirtschaft, Universität Kiel, 1974), pp. 29–49.

19. Kock, *Stabilitätspolitik*.

20. H. Barbier, "Der Rahmen für ein Konjunkturprogramm ist eng," *Suddeutsche Zeitung*, 2 July 1975, p. 17.

21. "Rückläufige Finanz- und Leistungskraft: Auszüge aus städtischen Haushaltsreden 1975," *Der Städtetag* (Stuttgart: W. Kohlhammer Verlag, January 1975), pp. 16–24.

22. Biehl, "Zu den konjunkturellen Effeckten der Länder- und Gemeindehaushalte."

23. This was the most frequent explanation offered to me during the interviews with budgetary officials involved in local governmental-financial relations.

24. Richard Klein and Jörg M. Gleitze, "Gemeindefinanzbericht 1975," *Der Städtetag* (Stuttgart: W. Kohlhammer Verlag, January 1975), pp. 8–9 and 13.

25. Kock, *Stabilitätspolitik*.

26. Wallace E. Oates, *Fiscal Federalism* (New York: Harcourt, Brace and Janovich, 1972), pp. 3–64; and Manfred Neuman, "Zur Oekonomischen Theorie des Föderalismus," *Kyklos*, 24(1971):493–511.

27. Sachverständigenkommission für die Neugliederung des Bundesgebietes, "Vorschläge zur Neugliederung des Bundesgebietes gemäss art. 29 GG," (Bonn: Bundesministerium des Innern, 1973). These proposals are based on article 29 of the Basic Law which also foresees a realignment of the federal states. See also, Fritz Scharpf, "Alternativen des deutschen Föderalismus: Für ein handlungsfähiges Entwicklungssystem, *"Die Neue Gesellschaft*, 3 (Bonn-Bad Godesberg: Neue Gesellschaft, March 1974), pp. 237–244; and W. Ernst, "Wozu Neugliederung?" *Die Oeffentliche Verwaltung* (1974), pp. 12ff.

28. Kock, *Stabilitätspolitik*.

29. I am indebted to Bernd Reissert who recorded these data on yearly time-series sheets for each federal state and then kindly allowed me to use them in these analyses. The original data come from the Statistisches Bundesamt, Finanzen und Steuern, Reihe 1, Haushaltswirtschaft von Bund, Ländern und Gemeinden, II Jahresabschlüsse, Kommunalfinanzen und Staatsfinanzen, 1962–1971, (Stuttgart: W. Kohlhammer Verlag). Note especially that the state-grant figures include federal funds as well because in the published statistics the amounts are recorded together. The federal contribution does not alter the differences in state policies, however, because federal grants are given largely according to a population formula. See Reissert, *Die finanzielle Beleiligung des Bundes*.

30. The Statistisches Bundesamt, Finanzen und Steuern, does not contain these figures for the city-states.

31. The Saarland, Schleswig-Holstein, and the Rineland-Palatinate are the least wealthy and smallest in population. The most wealthy and largest states are North Rhine-Westphalia, Baden-Württemberg, and Bavaria. Lower Saxony is in the middle, and Hesse is a mixed case: small in population but near the top

in per capita income. See the, Statistisches Bundesamt, *Statistisches Jahrbuch für die Bundesrepublik Deutschland* (Stuttgart: W. Kohlhammer Verlag).

32. For an analysis of party influence on economic policy, see, Andrew Cowart, "Economic Policies of European Governments II: Fiscal Policy." *British Journal of Political Science* 8(October 1978):425–439.

8 Resisting Macroeconomic Objectives: The Regular Grant-in-Aid Programs

There is little possibility to pursue stabilization policy with grants from the federal government to the states. Practically all these expenditures are based on administrative agreements or legal contracts that cannot be altered from year to year. The only possibility is that the federal government and the states agree on the passage of special stabilization programs. . . . This appears, however, to be only realizable in rather difficult economic situations and not as a normal policy.[1]
—Federal Official

Documenting events is easier than explaining them. The patterns identified in chapter 7 by which the federal and state governments have used grants to manage the economy are especially problematic in this respect. Standard explanations are not very powerful. Business-cycle-sensitive taxes is one such standard approach that only goes part way in interpreting these patterns.[2] Untied revenue-sharing grants in West Germany, for example, are directly related to the distribution of the income tax between levels of government. Since the income tax is sensitive to the business cycle, the procyclical trend is thus predicted. The categorical grants, however, are not directly related to tax yields but depend on discretionary decisions made by the donor government. Yet federal categorical grants to the states also slightly reinforced the business cycle, and state categorical grants to the municipalities dramatically fluctuated up or down with economic activity.

The budget literature on the determinants of public expenditure, a second standard explanation, is also not entirely satisfactory. These studies either concentrate on political-party variables or on socioeconomic characteristics as the major influences on expenditure patterns.[3] But some of the states did not follow the predicted pattern in 1966 to 1967 and 1974 to 1975, nor did the federal government.

Apparently a more complicated set of forces determines categorical grants than just the business-cycle sensitivity of tax income or the size and partisanship of the government's jurisdiction. As discussed in chapter 6, joint–budget planning introduces certain costs into other budget purposes. Some of these costs are financial; others are political or programmatic costs. These same costs are involved in using intergovernmental grants for economic management. How the government perceives these costs and reacts to them is an important influence on fiscal behavior that is not covered by the standard explanations. Grants in aid played an important role in the federal government's decision to shift away from macrobudget planning to monetary and tax approaches to managing the economy.

Bureaucratic Autonomy versus Executive Leadership

Standard explanations for fiscal behavior mistakenly assume that the direction of influence over policy moves from the society to the government. But political decisions are not simply the vessels through which public demands are transferred into government supply. Godwin and Shepard argue that political leadership has its own interests and preferences that may contradict the wishes and needs of the citizenry.[4] In attending to these interests, the political leadership is not entirely passive in responding to public demand and also active in creating it. They write:

> [P]olitical decision makers might produce policies which are not desired by the citizens but are believed by the decision makers to be in the citizens' "best interests." In the second situation, the incentive structures internal to legislatures and bureaus might require that the decision makers respond to these pressures rather than to citizen preferences.

To test how leaders respond to these incentive structures, the authors suggest an analysis of *translation errors,* the difference between actual policies and the policies that citizens prefer.

Measurement of these differences in the economic-management field is a difficult task because people hold contradictory preferences. Yet there are incentive structures within the government that work to discourage the use of the budget for economic stabilization. Using matching investment grants for economic management can also entail initial and longer-term budget costs. One thinks metaphorically of the thoughtful father who agrees to pay half of the price of an old Cadillac for his son away at college. The car takes all the son's extra cash and gets only six miles per gallon in city driving; but the father refuses to subsidize the boy's living expenses. It is nice to have the car, but who is going to buy the gas? The state finance ministries often find themselves in a parallel relation to the federal government.

To explain the discretionary management of the economy requires an understanding of how and why these financial and program priorities are overruled in favor of fiscal-policy criteria. In particular, what causes the Cabinet and the Finance Minister to impose on ministry budget decisions in order to manage the economy?

The literature on decision making in foreign policy offers evidence that the willingness and ability of top policymakers to reach down into the bureaucracy in order to influence outcomes increases under crisis conditions. President Kennedy attempted to direct the specific movements of warships in the Cuban blockade, for example, even though tactical decisions of ship deployment normally reside with the commanding officer.[5] Francis Rourke argues that the influence of organizational processes over policy are highly variable. He refers to the Vietnam War in which, once public sentiment definitely turned against further involvement, the interests of the military and other agencies rapidly declined as new political directions in policy developed.[6]

The influence of bureaucratic organizations over policy apparently varies with the salience of particular policy issues to the top political leadership. Based on his experience as ambassador to India, John Galbraith describes the dominance of the Under Secretary of State over U.S. foreign relations with a small Latin American country. Despite the potentially explosive issues involved, the ambassador from the Latin country found that he could not gain the audience of the U.S. president because until the issues reached crisis proportions, they did not have enough importance to top American political leaders to merit their attention.[7] Likewise, chroniclers of the Strategic Arms Limitation Talks argue that until President Nixon and Secretary of State Kissinger began to see the political usefulness of arms agreements as antidotes to withdrawal pains from Vietnam, the individual bureaucratic organizations had determined the substance and detail of U.S. policy.[8]

Because budgeting is ordinarily the preserve of the bureaucracy, the influence of macroeconomic considerations on grant policies is also likely to be highly variable and dependent on the salience of the economic situation to top policymakers. Under severe economic conditions, the political benefits of aiding the economy are likely to outweigh the political costs of disrupting routine budgetary and financial decisions. Under more normal economic circumstances, however, the political price of budget intervention can be expected to exceed the marginal political value of tinkering with the economy. Top policymakers, therefore, probably cannot ordinarily intervene in bureaucratic decisions regarding grants in aid but only exercise their macroeconomic preferences in relatively severe, crisis situations. This is the line of argument we will now examine to explain the state differences discussed in chapter 7.

Stabilization versus Programmatic Purposes for Grants

The Finance Reform provides the first hint that macroeconomic considerations do not normally enter the bureaucratic policy deliberations regarding grants. The reform makes a distinction between types of grant programs based on their economic management or programmatic purpose. Economic-management grants, however, are decided according to special procedures that override the normal organizational routines and require the participation of the Cabinet.

The grant system in the Federal Republic developed prior to a concern for macroeconomic policy. Beginning with the first low-cost-housing law in March 1950, the German federal government increasingly became involved in granting categorical investment funds to the state governments for joint programs in specific policy areas.[9] The Finance Reform gave formal legitimacy to these grant developments. Although cofinancing schemes had existed for many years, the reform formally established the institutions of the Joint Tasks and the Financial Aid Programs. The Joint Tasks organized federal-state planning commissions to oversee university construction, regional economic development, and agricultural development; the Financial Aid Program set up low-cost-housing grants and the municipal-transportation investments. But besides creating formal planning commissions for traditional grant areas, the reform also extended federal grants into the areas of urban renewal and hospital construction.

The Joint Tasks are designed to provide long-term funding for basic structural, regional, and overall growth needs in the economy. The Financial Aid Program, in contrast, is supposed to provide a legal framework for both long-term programmatic needs in specific areas and for short-term stabilization priorities of macroeconomic policy. Statutory law defines and regulates the grants used for long-term structural and growth needs, but quicker and less formal administrative agreements determine the short-term financial aid given to the states for stabilization purposes. The short-term agreements, moreover, are not restricted to the investment areas defined by law but can extend to all other areas of state and local investment. The 1974 to 1975 antirecession programs, for example, covered not only the traditional areas of urban renewal but also many other aspects of local infrastructure. In addition, the antirecession grants give the Bundestag only thirty days to reject a proposal with no opportunity for amendments or change. The emphasis for these grants is on speed and flexibility.

Despite the intentions of the Finance Reform, the actual practice of joint decision making in the grant areas has placed important limitations on grant flexibility for macroeconomic policy. Bernd Reissert has found, for instance, a greater and greater uniformity in the distribution of granted funds among the states.[10] Prior to the reform, the federal government had not treated all the states the same and in particular had given larger subsidy quotas to the less wealthy states. But now the ability to participate fully in the programs depends more and more on the financial ability of the individual state to meet the matching requirements, which usually are around 50 percent. The states have also resisted federal intervention in particular problem areas of a grant category, thereby reducing federal influence on the details and components of grant programs. A third tendency has been for the states to resist federal interference in strictly state programs, that is, those not specifically identified by the Joint Tasks. Consequently federal government efforts to pass special grant programs buck up against these longer-term tendencies toward greater formal rigidity in federal-state financial relations.

The kinds of grants in the German federal system consist of two major types: *noncategorical* or formula grants from the federal government to the states *(Länderfinanzausgleich)* and from the states to the municipalities *(kommunaler*

Finanzausgleich); and *categorical* grants *(Zweckzuweisungen)* from the federal government to the states and from the states to the municipalities. The noncategorical grants form part of the revenue-sharing system in West Germany and are distributed as a percentage of tax revenue. The categorical grants, on the other hand, are designed for particular purposes and are decided on by individual ministries and joint–planning commissions.

Conflicting Budget Criteria Revisited

The second indication that macroeconomic considerations do not ordinarily determine grant decisions is found in the historical trends. In general, noncategorical grants have varied procyclically apparently because they are based on business-cycle-sensitive tax revenue. Of even greater interest are the categorical grants that are not usually tied to a tax (the transportation grants are an exception as they are tied to the gasoline tax), but which have varied even more procyclically than other grants.[11] The reasons seem to be twofold: (1) programmatic issues in particular policy areas conflict with the requirements of economic management, and (2) the dynamics of federal relations work against joint agreement on anticyclical-grant policy.

The central criterion for budgeting grants is the allocation of scarce resources among competitive bidders. Federal officials, for example, emphasized that the ministries and planning commissions want as much as they can get. Studies of budgeting tell us that when the money is there, ministries attempt to spend it, always want more than they can have, and do not see the requirements of the total budget.[12] Taking what you can get characterizes grants as well as other ministry spending. Because no office coordinates what the grants should be in the light of economic developments on a yearly regular basis, officials emphasized that they are not used as a regular economic-management instrument.

Second, economic management is short term in orientation, while grant spending has a longer-term perspective. Officials in the Joint Tasks grant areas expressed strong opinions against using infrastructure and regional development grants for anticyclical short-term balance.[13] Investment spending for hospitals, schools, or roads takes many years and is difficult to vary on a yearly basis. The officials argued that the purpose of economic management "is to reduce the potentially drastic swings between boom and recession." In contrast, program planning is "long-term and aimed at constant conditions for growth. It is not primarily concerned with the temporary swings up or down." Both federal and state officials supported this dichotomy and used it to argue against yearly variations in investment grants for economic management.

Recent statistical material on investment grants from the federal government support the contention that yearly variations in the size of these grants do not conform to economic management. Federal grants in the Joint Tasks areas increased in 1971 by 13.0 percent and in 1972 by 24.5 percent, two years of strong expansion in the private economy. Similarly, Financial Aid increased 18.2 percent in 1971, 123.9 percent in 1972, and 37.2 percent in 1973.[14] The strong increases occurred because of legislation passed during this period, but the advance took place during a boom in the economy. With the exception of the special antirecession programs, in the 1974 to 1975 recession phase, the strong advance slowed down considerably. These programs, however, did bring the 1974 to 1975 annual growth rates up to the previous year's level (see tables 8–1 and 8–2).

What occurred in 1975 to 1979, when the antirecession grants were disregarded, was a sharp reversal of the trend in the early 1970s: growth rates were very low or negative in many areas. The era of expansive legislative activity had worked its way out, and the initiation of the Economy Program *(Sparprogramm)* in 1976 has affected the grants directly. The central purpose of the

Table 8–1
Financial Aid of the Federal Government to the States, 1970–1975
(in million DM)

Type of Grant	1970	1971	1972	1973	1974	1975
Joint Tasks						
DM	2166.4	2448.2	3048.1	2932.5	2965.3	3085.9
Percentage Δ		13.0	24.5	−3.8	1.1	4.1
Financial Aid						
DM	1052.1	1243.2	2783.4	3819.0	3941.1	3869.4
Percentage Δ		18.2	123.9	37.2	3.2	−1.8

Source: "Massnahmen zur Verbesserung der Haushaltsstruktur," *Bulletin* (Bonn: Presse- und Informationsamt der Bundesregierung, 12 September 1975), plus the author's own calculations.

Notes: The figures given for 1975 are estimated amounts. The 1974 and 1975 figures do not contain antirecession grant amounts.

Table 8–2
Effect of Antirecession Programs on Federal Financial Aid, 1974–1975
(in million DM)

Financial Aid	1974	1975
With antirecession program		
DM	4238.4	5249.8
Annual percentage Δ	11.0	23.9
Without antirecession program		
DM	3941.1	3869.4
Annual percentage Δ	3.2	−1.8

Source: "Massnahmen zur Verbesserung der Haushaltsstruktur," *Bulletin* (Bonn: Presse- und Informationsamt der Bundesregierung, 12 September 1975), plus the author's own calculations.

Note: The figures for 1975 are estimated amounts.

Economy Program is to reduce and restructure expenditures in the coming years so that they correspond more closely to expected tax yields. The federal government, for example, projected and achieved a growth rate for the federal budget for 1976 of only 4.1 percent.[15] Included prominently in these growth-rate reductions were the grants in aid to the states, with the important exception of the antirecession program passed in August 1975 (see table 8–3).

The growth of these grants is being curtailed for many reasons, not any of which has very much to do with economic management in the sense of compensatory finance. The federal government became frustrated with the numerous conflicts involved in working with the states on these programs. Central to these controversies is the distribution issue. Bonn feels that it has helped balance state budgets through these grants but gets rewarded by losing ground in the distribution of the sales-tax revenue. One reason is that these matching grants have been a motor for growth in state budgets of approximately 20 to 25 percent yearly to around 21 billion DM in 1974.[16] These large increases gave the states a claim (at least in argument) for a greater share of the tax revenue.

A main thrust of this argument is the supposed greater increase in personnel costs on the state level, fueled in part by Financial Aid grants. From 1963 to 1974, the number of federal employees grew 21.6 percent, state employees by 44.0 percent, and municipal employees by 32.3 percent.[17] Most of the increases on the state and local levels occurred in the areas of education, health, sport, and recreation. This suggests that the future costs of investment grants lead to greater expanded current budgets. Thus investment grants, even for economic management, cause conflict over the distribution of revenue from the sales tax.

Bonn felt itself squeezed from two sides: the European Community budget has continued to grow at a faster pace than the German federal budget, and state and local budgets have also expanded faster than the Bonn budget. Many officials and politicians argued for cuts in these grants on this basis. The then Finance Minister Hans Apel bluntly made the connection between grants and federal

Table 8–3
Federal Financial Aid to the States, 1974–1979
(in million DM)

Type of Grant	1974	1975	1976	1977	1978	1979
Joint Tasks						
DM	2965.3	3085.9	2789.0	2514.1	2464.6	2464.6
Annual percentage Δ	1.1	4.1	−9.6	−9.9	−2.0	0.0
Financial Aid						
DM	3941.1	3869.4	4051.5	3690.6	3648.7	3520.4
Annual percentage Δ	3.2	−1.8	4.7	−8.9	−1.1	−3.5

Source: "Massnahmen zur Verbesserung der Haushaltsstruktur," *Bulletin* (Bonn: Presse- und Informationsamt der Bundesregierung, 12 September 1975), plus the author's own calculations.
Notes: The figures for 1975 are estimated amounts. The figures for 1976 are proposed amounts. The figures for 1977, 1978, and 1979 are planned amounts.

finances: "In order to make it clear to the federal states that we are no longer willing to put up with a further erosion of federal finances, we are going to cut the Joint Tasks in fiscal year 1977 by 10 percent. These programs have a total volume greater than 7 billion marks."[18]

A second reason for the cutback is that the great expansion in health care and education that took place in the late sixties and early seventies no longer requires enormous yearly increases.[19] Some voices were raised against the special antirecession program in September 1975 on the grounds that huge new investments in infrastructure make no sense from a substantive-policy point of view, even if they may be somewhat desirable in terms of economic management.

The importance of the dispute over tax sharing is placed in better perspective when it is realized that between 1966 and 1968, joint taxes accounted for around 50 percent of total state revenue. By 1972 the share of joint taxes had risen to 57 percent. Strong state budgetary expansion during these years was given a needed boost from shared taxes, especially after the revised tax-sharing law of 1969 to 1970.

Organizational Strategies and Interests

The arguments for and against grants in aid made by Finance Minister Apel and others may puzzle someone concerned with a rational division of labor between the levels of government. Should not joint or separate spending arrangements between governments depend on the nature of policy problems, such as spillover effects across jurisdictions, and the financial resources available at each level to pay for them? To test this proposition, Fritz Scharpf and colleagues explore the possibility that the solutions to certain problems require action by only one level of government, whereas other policies rationally necessitate mutual cooperation.[21] They reason that a policy such as environmental protection of the sea coasts cannot easily be handled by one state government acting independently because the effects of pollution are not confined within territorial boundaries of any one state. Consequently one should expect to find joint efforts in the environmental policy field. Similar arguments can be made for macroeconomic policy, energy policy, and so forth, based on a normative theory of functional adaptation.

The authors discovered that the rational necessity for collective action does not explain the patterns of successful or unsuccessful joint grants in aid efforts. They found instead that cofinancing exists in the areas of local street construction, hospital financing, and low-cost housing—all areas, which they argue, could reasonably be financed by the municipalities themselves. What is the explanation for this "irrational" behavior?

The alternative approach that they finally take is an organizational explanation. The organizational interests of the individual actors vary, they argue, depending on the advantages or disadvantages each might receive from joint efforts. On the one hand, there are the bureaucratic and political *promoters:* organizations and individuals in particular policy areas. On the other hand, one finds federal, state, and local *generalists:* finance ministers and heads of government. Transportation officials, for example, want to improve and expand the highway system but are much less concerned about policies in other areas. But minister presidents, because they tend to be held responsible for the whole government program, have a greater interest in balancing the budget, looking good to the public, and devising overall government policies. In other words, the protection or promotion of interests based on organizational roles determines the opposition to or support for joint financing efforts.

Managing the economy with grants in aid is equally dependent on these crosscutting interests that are tied to organizational roles. Individual spending ministries prefer joint, federal-state planning commissions to make policy because they remove those organizations from effective budgetary or fiscal-policy interference by the state finance ministries. To counteract this growing independence of joint commissions, the finance ministries in turn develop an interest in joint budgetary guidelines with other levels of government in order to give their positions more weight in bargaining with the spending ministries. But do not be mislead. The finance ministries' interests lie in obtaining budgetary control over expensive programs, not in promoting macroeconomic policy. Although economic management requires joint efforts, the organizational motives for engaging in mutual cooperation are not centered on the "rational necessity" of pursuing macrobudget policy through grants (see chapter 6).

The Joint Tasks spending areas are an illustration of the influence of organizational interests and strategies on economic management. The federal and state governments have set up joint planning commissions in each Joint Task policy area. Their purpose is to formulate framework plans that integrate with multiyear financial planning. Joint Tasks grants also have specific matching requirements for each policy area. University construction and regional-economic development each receive federal matching grants of 50 percent, while agricultural development receives a 60 percent matching subsidy from the federal government, and coastal protection gets a 70 percent subsidy.[22] Furthermore, the responsible federal minister in each policy area becomes the chairman of each commission. The members consist of the corresponding state ministers and normally also the federal finance minister. The commissions may only decide with a majority of three-fourths, with each state having one vote. The total vote of the federal government is equal to that of the combined state vote. This procedure means that a decision can be taken only with the support of the federal government and a majority of the states. In addition, no decision can be taken against the preferences of the federal finance minister. Nevertheless, the capacity for actual decision is real in contrast to the Finance Planning Council, which is primarily an advisory body.

The formation of joint commissions and framework plans in specific policy areas has given the individual state spending ministries a degree of independence from the finance ministries and a ready source of extra funds from the federal treasury. Consequently the spending ministries tend to support the joint commissions in order to promote and defend their own activities, while the state finance ministries have remained less enthusiastic because of the loss of financial control. In the area of university construction, for instance, the states never muster perfect unanimity in order to block proposals of the federal government. Usually some states will not go along, which allows the federal government to have its way.[23] A state budget director complained that in the joint-spending programs "only the states altogether can decide on a general policy. It does not uphold the right of the individual state for its own matters. The federal government sits over this general decision. . . ."

The state finance ministries thus feel that they have lost a measure of budgetary control over their own budgets. It is true that both the state parliament and Cabinets must finally approve the framework plans; but because joint–planning commissions decided them, they are difficult to reject. "We have practically no influence anymore," lamented a state budget director. "These planning commissions are staffed largely by the representatives of the interests involved, and they solicit parliamentary support. We in the Finance Ministry do not see only these areas, but other important expenditures as well."

A colleague in another state finance ministry concurred: "The amounts spent under the Joint Tasks are fixed to a considerable extent outside the negotiations with the spending ministries. Framework plans will be drawn up about which it is difficult for the financial administration to say anything."

Another financial worry with respect to grants is that the initial investments lead to future costs in state budgets that are not determined by the states themselves. The federal subsidy usually does not provide any funds for the maintenance and operation of the building or installation once it has been constructed. As one official explained it: "The danger in all this is that we undertake more than what we should as seen from our own budget. When the original investment is completed, it still costs us a lot of money. We estimate that in the first year the costs amount to 20.0 percent of the original investment. In five years, you see, we have paid the whole amount over again. This increasingly burdens our budget." The worry about future operation and maintenance costs has prompted one state, Rhineland-Palatinate, to publish a little booklet entitled "Future Costs," which found a receptive audience among the other state finance ministries.[24] The booklet reports that schools, kindergartens, and hospitals have the highest future costs (29.3 percent average), while traffic installations, sport arenas, and sport fields have the lowest (13.2 percent average).

A second worry is the lure of extra money. There is a certain dynamic to matching funds that leads to the implementation of projects simply because the money is available. All the state finance ministries were concerned about the prospect of spending just for the sake of spending, as revealed by this comment: "In the Joint Tasks, the matching division is set around fifty-fifty. You can imagine that the state politicians, when they think of a situation in which the federal government will pay one-half, are strongly tempted to go ahead. If you want something that costs 10 DM, and someone offers to pay 5, naturally you are much more inclined to buy it." The situation is one in which supply drives demand, which is not exactly the same as when supply determines allocation of resources among sectors.[25] In this case, supply promotes additional expenditure in many areas, some of which are considered frivolous.

Because the distribution of federal grants is moving toward a population formula, the less wealthy states need to pay as much per capita as the wealthy ones. The consequent inability to meet matching payments often leads to further debt and further restriction in the discretionary part of the budget. A state official explained that the investment grants were a partial cause of the difference in debt levels among the states: "You have to understand that the state is forced to participate. If the state does not take the amount offered, the federal government takes it back. The question to answer is whether the state is capable of the cofinancing, which has been responsible in part for the differences in debt levels among the states." Some of the wealthier states were more worried about losing budgetary control over a significant part of state-investment policy; some of the poorer states expressed concern that they could not meet all of the matching requirements. All the state finance ministries felt disquieted about simply spending because the money was available.

The growth in state budgets caused by federal grants also served as a basis for the federal government's decision to cut these grants in the Economy Program. The initial incentive for the federal government to participate in the Joint Tasks was the prospect of more policy influence in areas normally reserved for the states.[26] But an unanticipated result has been a continual growth in state budgets due to the operational and maintenance costs following the original investment. As a consequence, the federal government loses a claim on revenue from the sales tax, which is based on the expenditure needs of each level of government.

Financial Uncertainty and State-Local Grants

Recessions cause uncertainty for the finance ministry because they reduce tax income usually without diminishing costs. Especially on the state and local levels, where expenditures depend on adequate current revenue, increased deficits bring efforts to cut expenditures. Revenue sharing and grants in aid, however, give the finance ministry the option of shifting the uncertainty from itself to another government level. If a state government, for example, increases its local grants during a recession, it makes municipal revenue more steady and certain; but by increasing its grants in the recession, the state government incurs greater uncertainty for its own budget. Consequently the state finance ministry is inclined to cut local grants in order to reduce its own deficit, thereby increasing uncertainty for municipal budgets.

To change tax-sharing formulas during a recession is also exceedingly difficult. An increase in the percentage share for one level produces a decrease in revenue for the other level. The unhappy conclusion is that any one level of government can only have certainty at the expense of other levels of government. Only if the fiscal-policy goal outweighs the financial uncertainty costs, therefore, will the state or federal government pursue anticyclical policy. But because traditional financial concerns remain very important to state and local governments, a sharp rise in the deficit will probably encourage efforts to reduce financial uncertainty and abandon fiscal-policy goals.

State categorical investment grants to the municipalities do not vary yearly on stabilization criteria. In times of economic recession some states have passed their own special stimulus packages which have included local grants, but on a regular basis, traditional finance ministry–spending ministry negotiations determine the yearly variations. Some state budget directors emphasized that categorical grants have nothing to do with stabilization policy. After a long pause and a big sigh, a state budget director confided: "These grants depend on the financial ability of the state to pay, not on stabilization policy. They are not oriented to stabilization problems. The expenditure need is so high—higher than what can be met—that there is little room for stabilization policy." But not all states concurred that categorical grants never are varied for stabilization reasons. In 1973 some states postponed certain investment expenditures, including grants to the municipalities, and some states attempted to avoid cutting investment grants in the 1974 to 1975 period. But with the exception of the special stimulus packages, categorical grants have not followed stabilization-policy criteria.

Most of the noncategorical and formula grants are regulated by the Revenue Equalization Laws *(Finanzausgleichsgesetze)* and form part of the tax-sharing system in Germany. Each state has its own law but, with the exception of Bavaria, the states grant the municipalities approximately 20 to 25 percent of the yield of certain taxes. (Bavaria gives only 11 percent in this manner).[27] If this proportion is allowed to remain unchanged year after year, the transfers to the municipalities will vary procyclically. Slightly raising the proportion in recession years and lowering it in boom years would serve to even out the procyclical trend of the transfers and provide the municipalities with a less business-cycle-sensitive form of tax income. A change in the distribution formulas would also aid those municipalities most severely hit by the recession.[28]

Anticyclical variation of revenue-sharing formulas makes good sense economically, but in practice the states have not opted to do it. A budget director reacted to the proposal in this way:

> That is a nice idea, but something that would be very hard to put into practice. It is a political matter. When the state has a decent income, then it gives to the

cities generously. When the income is less, it gives out less. It is that simple. It works at the federal level in exactly the same way. When the tax yield is low, the states also get less. That is a political fact of life.

Another official raised the following question: "Everyone says that the communities should have business-cycle-insensitive tax income. That is fine and good, but we want to have the same. We have 40 percent of our budget tied to personnel expenditures. These do not go up and down with the economy but constantly grow in volume. The question is: Why should the cities get this money?"

Varying revenue-sharing formulas to compensate for imbalances of supply and demand in the private economy only works if one level of government has a surplus and the other a deficit. The other possibility is for the federal government to build up a larger debt without making efforts to reduce it. But the first of these options has never happened, and the second, beyond a certain point, is difficult to achieve.[29] Since over half of all tax income is shared by the federal government and the states, a fall off in tax yield due to a recession tends to effect both levels; but neither are the municipalities immune because about two-thirds of their revenue comes directly from taxes or indirectly from revenue sharing. In boom periods as well, all levels tend to share in the prosperity. In 1973, for example, all the levels of government had surpluses, except for the federal level, which had a rather small deficit of just over 3 billion DM.[30]

When all three levels have deficits during a recession, prospects appear slight for a resettlement of tax-sharing laws on economic-management criteria. In 1974 the National Municipal Association demanded that the localities receive 15 percent rather than 14 percent of the revenue from the income tax, but the Federal Finance Minister rejected the proposal, arguing that it would hurt the federal budget too much in a recession year.[31] Especially the prospect of the states giving the municipalities less during times of boom does not appeal to local officials, many of whom sit in the state parliaments. An alteration in standard tax-equalization laws to treat more favorably those regions hit hardest by the recession also is opposed by the other more well-off municipalities. Further, alteration of revenue-sharing formulas does not guarantee that the recipients will spend the money wisely from the point of view of the donor. Attempts by the federal government to interfere in the details of grants, for example, encountered the resistance of the states.

Why should the cities get the money? That is the big question asked at the state level. State officials know that a stable income for the cities means an uncertain income for them. But the municipalities do not like economic management either. They reject fiscal policy in favor of more money in recessions and no cutbacks in booms. The states, quite reasonably, feel that this gives them the worst of both worlds: no recuperation of funds in booms and no relief from stimulus spending in recessions. They refuse to bear the whole weight of uncertainty while the cities bear none.

Organizational Processes and State Differences

Changing the procyclical pattern of government spending requires that the Cabinet, and especially the finance minister, agree on special antirecession or stabilization programs independently of normal grant decision. But to intervene in normal spending patterns entails a political cost. Intervention disrupts or even reverses program and financial relations between the Finance Ministry and the spending ministries. Hence these usual incentive structures within government militate against short-term economic management.

But under what conditions do the political costs become bearable? The bureaucratic politics literature says that the problem must be severe enough to become salient to the top political leadership. Perhaps relatively severe economic conditions among important political constituencies is the catalyst that alters the political calculus enough for leaders to endure the cost of budget intervention.

A highly salient political issue in managing the economy during a recession is the increase in unemployment. Even more crucial may be the incidence of unemployment among politically and economically important groups, such as large construction unions or key industries that play a major role in the economy of the region or country. Although under normal conditions internal government incentives work against special subsidies, the importance to the top political leadership of responding to suffering in its major constituencies may induce intervention in regular organizational decisions. Still, the finance minister and chancellor will probably not want to respond in every case or have the ability to do so for, as Kennedy discovered, even in crisis situations the responsible organizations continue to assert their own preferences and interests.

The record reveals several instances in which public authorities took measures to help specific groups. In 1974 to 1975 the government gave a special subsidy to the Volkswagon plant in Wolfsburg because of the dislocations it had suffered as a result of the oil crisis and the decline in exports of its older model cars. In 1966 to 1967 West Germany experienced a classical, internally generated slump in demand, a lagging production, and increased unemployment. But certain regions of the country had higher unemployment rates than did others. Unemployment hit the coal fields in North Rhine-Westphalia and the Saarland especially hard; the border areas with East Germany, which are less successful economically than the rest of the country, also suffered. Both antirecession programs passed by the Cabinet in 1967 designated the coal fields and the border areas as targets for special aid.

Conceivably those states that increased grants in 1967 had experienced worse conditions. The crisis in the coal fields or the depressed areas in the border regions may have encouraged their top leaders to reject financial pressures to cut grants in order to respond to economic demands of particular groups to increase them.

Unfortunately it is not practical to look at unemployment rates according to the geographical policy regions. There is a less than perfect overlap between Labor Office districts and regions designated for economic policy. Nevertheless, a look at unemployment rates for the states as a whole (a very rough measure) again produces the two groups identified in chapter 7. Table 8–4 shows that with the notable exception of the Saarland,[32] listing the states according to unemployment rates sets the states of group 1 (NRW, LS, SH, BV), which increased grants to stimulate the economy, slightly above the other states. Further evidence that the states of group 1 experienced higher unemployment rates than group 2 is given by the weighting of the distribution shares for the second stabilization program near the end of 1967. With the exception of the Saarland, the four states of group 1 received additional population weighting in the share distribution of the stabilization grants. In group 2 especially Baden-Württemberg's share is reduced from the strict population criterion. Although the greater volume of federal grants going to the states of group 1 probably generated a good deal of publicity and some additional incentive not to cut state grants the main explanation for state differences is the state-level political response to higher unemployment in group 1 states.

This does not mean that the states of group 2 did not feel any of the effects of the recession. On the contrary, when compared to past growth rates in GNP,

Table 8–4
Unemployment Rates and Antirecession Programs, Distribution Shares, by State, 1967

	Unemployment Rate	Stabilization Program, September 1967	
		Population Share in Percent	Weighted Population Share in Percent
Group 1			
Lower Saxony	2.2	11.7	13.2
Bavaria	2.1	17.1	17.2
Schleswig-Holstein	2.1	4.2	5.7
North Rhine-Westphalia	2.0	28.1	28.2
Group 2			
Saarland	3.0	1.9	2.6
Rhineland-Palatinate	1.9	6.0	5.5
Hessen	1.4	8.8	8.2
Baden-Württemberg	.6	14.3	10.7

Source: Figures for the unemployment rate are taken from Herbert Kridde and Hans-Uwe Bach, "Beiträge zur Arbeitsmarkt- und Berufsforschung," *Arbeitsmarktstatistische Zahlen im Zeitreihen Form: Jahreszahlen für Bundesländer und Landesarbeitsamtbezirke* (Bonn: Institut für Arbeitsmarkt- und Berufsforschung der Bundesanstalt für Arbeit, no. 3.2, 1967). The figures for the antirecession program are taken from "Abschlussbericht über das erste Konjunkturprogramm und das Zweite Programm für besondere konjunktur- und struktur- politische Massnahmen, 1967–68," Part B, "Das Zweite Programm," (Bonn: Deutscher Bundestag, 5. Wahlperiode, Drucksache V/3630, 9 December 1968).
Note: The population share in column four is weighted doubly for depressed areas.

the German economy came to an abrupt halt in 1966 to 1967. Tax revenue fell off for all the states, causing a certain amount of mild panic in the finance ministries. "We never had such a tax fall off before," explained a Budget Director from a group 2 state. "The government got scared and cut expenditures in response . . . much of it in investments. . . . Politically it was very hard to avoid." The group 2 states were not immune to the recession, and some of them responded in the classical procyclical way.

A further puzzle remains: the differences in fiscal-policy performance of the states during the 1966 to 1967 recession persisted into the 1969 to 1971 boom period. The states of group 2 increased investment grants during the boom by twice the rate of the group 1 states, thereby again following a procyclical policy. The four states of group 1 expanded investment grants steadily during 1966 to 1968 in the midst of the recession, while group 2 states had very slow and even negative-growth rates for grants starting already in 1964 to 1965. By 1969 the group 2 states may have built up a backlog of projects that provided the tinder for the strong flare up in spending in 1969 to 1971, right in the middle of the economic boom. The strong increases in tax revenue and federal subsidies at this time also provided them with the opportunity to greatly increase spending. The group 1 states, in contrast, had less need for further rapid expansion in 1969 to 1971 because they had had steady growth over the past four years. Conceivably, substantive policy criteria decided the 1969 to 1971 pattern, not stabilization criteria, although the outcome did have the correct stabilization-policy effect. In other words, the later state differences in grant policy may have resulted from fiscal-policy decisions made (or not made) during the 1966 to 1967 period.

Is the political process a mere vessel that translates demands in the society and economy into policy outputs of the government? An explanation of policy outputs that relies only on demand ignores the importance of the incentive structures within government itself to supply the desired products. But complete reliance on supply also fails to take account of the broadly political aspects of policy. One reason for the persistent vacillation between supply and demand explanations is that the measurement of either supply or demand is not very precise, thereby preventing a clear evaluation of the relation between the two. People in society often hold vague and contradictory preferences that result in confusing demands on the political system. People who are concerned about police protection also suffer from inflation. They demand increased government spending to make society safe but want decreased spending to keep the economy well-off. Within the government itself similar trade-offs arise between providing better transportation, health or safety and meeting the economic demands of unemployment or price inflation.

An attempt to make supply equal demand on one dimension of policy may produce even greater discrepancies on other dimensions. A more useful approach may be to analyse the various factors that produce certain supply and demand curves for a particular policy area. The two curves may not intersect or they may cross over at a point that is unsatisfactory to those people interested in one particular policy area. But whether or not the intersection is satisfactory in a larger context depends on the impact of changing the curves on other priorities and preferences of not only other groups inside and outside government but also on those people concerned about the policy area under consideration.

In a democracy, the government faces conflicting and contradictory policy pressures; thus the demand-supply intersection for any one policy will probably not entirely satisfy that one group of people. But hopefully the compromises that are worked out make the supply of public goods more acceptable to other groups affected by the policy.

Notes

1. From an interview with a federal official, spring 1975.

2. The main types of grants referred to are those given under article 91a Basic Law *(Gemeinschaftsaufgaben:* University Construction, Regional Economic Structure, and Improvement of Agricultural Structure and Coastal Protection) and article 104, paragraph 4, Basic Law *(Finanzhilfen:* Low-Cost Housing, Urban Renewal, Municipal Transportation, Hospital Construction, and Student Housing Construction). The former block of grants is given to the states under the Joint Tasks arrangement; the second block is also given for the purpose of supporting local municipal infrastructure investment and construction. A third block of grants to be considered is that which the states themselves give to the municipalities.

3. See, for example, Richard E. Dawson and James A. Robinson, "Inter-Party Competition, Economic Variables and Welfare Policies in the American States," *The Journal of Politics* 25(1963):265–289; Ira Sharkansky and Richard I. Hofferbert, "Dimensions of State Politics, Economics and Public Policy," *The American Political Science Review* 63*(September 1969):867–879;* Thomas R. Dye, *Politics, Economics, and the Public: Policy Outcomes in the States* (Chicago: Rand McNally, 1966); and Robert C. Fried, "Party and Policy in West German Cities," *The American Political Science Review* 70(March 1976):11–24.

4. R. Kenneth Godwin and W. Bruce Shepard, "Political Processes and Public Expenditures: A Re-examination Based on Theories of Representative Government," *The American Political Science Review* 70(December 1976): 1131.

5. Graham T. Allison, *Essence of Decision: Explaining the Cuban Missile Crisis* (Boston: Little, Brown and Co., 1971), especially ch. 4, pp. 117ff.

6. Francis Rourke, *Bureaucracy and Foreign Policy* (Baltimore: Johns Hopkins University Press, 1972), p. 16.

7. John Kenneth Galbraith, *The Triumph: A Novel of Modern Diplomacy* (Boston: Houghton-Mifflin Press, 1968).

8. John Newhouse, *Cold Dawn: The Story of SALT* (New York: Holt, Rhinehart and Winston, 1973).

9. This description is based on Bernd Reissert, "Politikverflechtung als Hindernis der staatlichen Aufgabenerfüllung," *Wirtschaftsdienst* 8(1976):413–415.

10. Bernd Reissert, *Die finanzielle Beteiligung des Bundes an Aufgaben der Länder und das Postulat der "Einheitlichkeit der Lebensverhältnisse im Bundesgebiet"* (53 Bonn-Bad Godesberg: Vorwärts-Druck, 1975), passim.

11. See Heinz Koch, *Stabilitätspolitik im föderalistischen System der Bundesrepublik Deutschland* (Cologne: Bund Verlag, 1975), pp. 101–111. The federal noncategorical grants to the states are not considered in detail because they have not amounted to a very large volume, but they also have varied procyclically over the past ten years.

12. See for example, John C. Campbell, *The Japanese Budgetary Process* (Berkeley: University of California Press, 1975); and Hugh Heclo and Aaron Wildavsky, *The Private Government of Public Money: Community and Policy Inside British Politics* (Berkeley: University of California Press, 1974).

13. Zentrale Datenstelle der Landesfinanzminister, "Finanzhilfen des Bundes an die Länder 1970–75," (21 August 1975), pp. 2 and 3 of appendix.

14. ———, "Mittelfristige Entwicklung der Finanzhilfen des Bundes an die Länder 1974–79," (4 November 1975), p. 4 of the appendix.

15. *Finanzbericht* (Bonn: Bundesministerium der Finanzen, 1976), p. 71.

16. This figure includes all of the federal aid given to the states under articles 91a, 91b, 104a, paragraphs 3 and 4 of the Basic Law. See, Zentrale Datenstelle der Landesfinanzminister, "Finanzhilfen des Bundes an die Länder 1970–75."

17. "Zum Stand der Finanzplanungen in den Ländern," *Finanznachrichten* (Bonn: Bundesministerium der Finanzen, Presse- und Informationsamt, 9 January 1976).

18. "Bundesfinanzminister Apel über die Massnahmen zur Verbesserung der Haushaltsstruktur und zur Verminderung der Kreditaufnahme," *Documentation* (Bonn: Bundesministerium der Finanzen, Presse- und Informationsamt, 8 September 1975).

19. *Suddeutsche Zeitung,* 10 July 1975; *Welt am Sonntag,* 6 July 1975, p. 2. See also, Zentrale Datenstelle der Landesfinanzminister, "Mittelfristige Entwicklung."

20. J.S. Hunter, "Revenue Sharing in the Federal Republic of Germany," Research Monograph no. 2 (Canberra: The Australian National University, The Center for Research on Federal Financial Relations, 1973), p. 48. It is also important to add that the CDU/CSU state governments, until just recently have blocked any attempt to raise the overall sales tax. See, "Nackter Mann," *der*

Spiegel, no. 44, 1976, pp. 27-28 and "Das Steuerpaket kann in Kraft Treten: Bayern, Niedersachsen, Saarland stimmen zu," *Frankfurter Allgemeine,* 16 July 1977, p. 1.

21. Fritz W. Scharpf, Bernd Reissert, and Fritz Schnabel, *Politikverflechtung: Theorie und Empirie des kooperativen Föderalismus in der Bundesrepublik* (Kronberg/Ts: Scriptor Verlag, 1976), pp. 236ff.

22. See paragraph 10 of the *Gesetz über die Gemeinschaftsaufgaben* and *Verbesserung der Agrarstruktur und des Küstenschutzes.*

23. Nina Gruenberg, "Stoltenbergs Macht—Die neuen Kompetenzen des Bundesforschungsministers, *Die Zeit,* 15. no. 33 (1969):p. 11.

24. *Folgekosten Oeffentlicher Investitionen* (Rhineland-Palatinate: Ministerium der Finanzen, 1975).

25. Scharpf, *Politikverflechtung,* pp. 232-233. For an examination of supply promoting additional expenditures, see also, Naomi Caiden and Aaron Wildavsky, *Planning and Budgeting in Poor Countries* (New York: John Wiley and Sons, 1974).

26. Aaron Wildavsky argues that the policy authority will try to avoid a strategy that increases the size of the administration, for that drains away their own authority. They will prefer an incomes strategy, for example, in the area of welfare payments. See Aaron Wildavsky, "The Self-Evaluating Organization," *Public Administration Review* 32(September/October 1972):509-520.

27. Statistisches Bundesamt, "Allgemeine Finanzzuweisungen und Umlagen der Gemeinden," *Finanzen und Steuern,* Fachserie L, Reihe 1, Haushaltswirtschaft von Bund, Ländern, und Gemeinden, 4, Finanzausgleich (Stuttgart: W. Kohlhammer Verlag, 1973), pp. 4-13.

28. Congressional Budget Office, U.S. Congress, *Temporary Measures to Stimulate Employment: An Evaluation of Some Alternatives* (Washington D.C.: U.S. Government Printing Office, 2 September 1975) contains some proposals along these lines.

29. Ibid., p. 96. The negotiations over changing the distribution of the sales tax in the Federal Republic were not based primarily on economic-management considerations. The Tax Reform was not intended as an economic-management measure either. It just happened to come at a favorable time for the private economy. The main issues had to do with the Child Support Program, increases in NATO spending, and increases in the costs of the European Community. See, "Bund verlangt noch grösseren Teil von der Umsatzsteuer," *Kölnische Rundschau,* 26 April 1975; and "Finanzierungslücke wird Grösser," *Suddeutsche Zeitung,* 4 July 1975, p. 8.

30. *Finanzbericht* (Bonn: Bundesministerium der Finanzen, 1976), p. 152.

31. "Gemeinden in der Krise," *Suddeutsche Zeitung,* 25 August 1974, p. 4; "Apel erteilt Gemeinden eine Absage," *Suddeutsche Zeitung,* 26 August 1974, p. 2; and Städtetag schlägt wegen Finanznot Alarm," *Suddeutsche Zeitung,* 23 August 1974, p. 1.

32. The misplacement of the Saarland is difficult to explain given the data available. It has been suggested that the unemployment in the coal fields there did not cause as great a political turmoil as in North Rhine-Westphalia. This point was emphasized to me in one of the interviews on the federal level.

9 Imposing Macroeconomic Objectives: The Antirecession Grant-in-Aid Programs

The theoreticians and the professors always demand coordinated financial planning. But how is that to be done? If we grant money to the state governments, we naturally want to know what happens to it. But that seems to be unacceptable to those who receive it.[1] —Federal Financial Official

Grants in aid are not the workhorses of macroeconomic policy. Because grants touch sensitive political nerve endings, are regulated by semiindependent commissions, based on legal formulas, and geared toward long-term growth, they are poor instruments for economic management. Thus they do not carry the routine burden of adapting public budgets to economic needs. Their role is primarily to serve the programmatic goals of the spending ministries.

Under harsh enough economic conditions, however, procedures can be set in motion to cut through the normal routines and inflexibilities of grant–decision making. Both in 1966 to 1967 and 1974 to 1975, special antirecession–grant programs were passed to counteract downturns in the business-cycle. These special programs are important objects of study because they represent clear and concrete instances of discretionary economic management with the budget. We will examine closely, therefore, what these programs consisted of, whether they met the requirements of stabilization policy, what the motivations were for passing them, and how they were decided.

These special programs opened a floodgate of controversy between the federal government and the states, forcing the federal government to shift away from using budget policy for economic management. By examining the components of this controversy, we hope to gain a better understanding of discretionary budget policy and possibly also help avoid a comparable outcome in the future.

Two Tenets of Public Finance

Theories of public finance share two tenets about the relation of economic management and budgeting in a federal-political system. As normative tenets, government policymakers are urged to follow them when using the budget to manage the economy. Yet the tenets rest on assumptions that, in the West German setting at least, raise doubts about how applicable they are to actual budgetary decisions.

The first tenet is that the three functions of economic policy—allocation, distribution, and stabilization—are capable of being portioned out among the various levels of government. The federal government should take responsibility for stabilization and distribution policies, says Wallace Oates, while the local governments have greater competence in allocation policy.[2]

The second tenet is that each government is capable of making a distinction between the three functions for choice of policy instruments. Richard Musgrave, for example, states that the government may vary expenditures on goods and services countercyclically only "to the extent that the Allocation Branch finds itself confronted with such fluctuations in the demand for satisfaction of social wants." If these conditions are not met, the Stabilization Branch "will not raise the level of public expenditures on goods and services because this would interfere with the satisfaction of public wants as planned by the Allocation Branch."[3] In other words, policymakers must make a trade-off between stabilization and allocation policy objectives of each expenditure program.

To reduce expenditures to fight inflation raises the question whether the expenditures are desirable on their own merits. If they are deemed desirable, the problem becomes one of choosing between fighting inflation and supporting a worthwhile expenditure program. In similar fashion, to raise expenditures to fight a recession suggests that the government is paying for programs that do not justify the expense based on their own merits.[4] These budget purposes, therefore, must be kept separate, and the trade-offs made explicit.

The first tenet raises the problem of separating tiers of government into budget purposes when actual policy decisions are taken jointly by the three levels of government. Scharpf and colleagues maintain that for the German case the most useful way to analyze budget decisions is not in terms of three, separate tiers of government. Instead, they emphasize the probability of achieving joint agreement, given different types of problems and policy responses. They identify four different types of problem structures that require separate types of policy responses by the central government.[5] Business-cycle fluctuation is considered a *level problem* that requires either increases or decreases in aggregate public expenditure. The purpose of the policy is to influence the overall level of demand, not to deal with particular economic problems in specific regions, sectors, or program areas. Consequently the best policy is one that does not overly discriminate among recipients but tries to maintain a broad eligibility.

The correct problem-structures approach to a business downturn, for example, would be an across-the-board 7 percent investment subsidy to private businesses. The wrong way to deal with a level problem of this type would be to also specify certain investment areas, geographical regions, or other more detailed criteria of eligibility. Scharpf et al. argue, therefore, that if investment-stimulus grants to cities have many eligibility requirements not enough projects will become available to meet the economic needs or the cities will take a long time to implement them.[6]

The second tenet raises the question whether for actual choice of policy instrument the government can meaningfully determine the trade-off between allocation and stabilization goals. In West Germany, programs for stimulating demand in the economy overlap with efforts to deal with regional or sectoral economic problems. The German government passed the first of the joint-antirecession-investment programs in 1967. Two years later, the Finance Reform made these programs part of the Basic Law, according to article 104a, paragraph 4: "The federal government may provide the state with financial aid for significant state and municipal investments. The purposes of the aid are to guard against a disturbance of macroeconomic equilibrium, to even out unequal capabilities in the federal territories, and to promote economic growth." Federal law with the concurrence of the Bundesrat determines the types of investments to be covered by this provision. The grants are known as Financial Aid *(Finanzhilfen)* and include investments for low-cost housing, urban renewal, municipal transportation, and hospital construction.[7] Although the joint-investment-antirecession packages fall under this provision and contained investments in these policy areas, they also allow investments in a broader range of activities from swimming pools to sewage-treatment plants.

Budgetary Control and Fiscal Federalism

Scharpf's analysis accounts for state and local behavior but does not adequately explain the willingness of the federal Finance Ministry to adopt one policy type or another in response to a given problem structure. The investment-antirecession programs require the Finance Ministry to grant funds to the state governments. Although from Scharpf's perspective the correct policy would be an open-ended, general purpose grant, the federal Finance Ministry really has no incentive to pursue this course because it provides no method for determining how the money is spent by the states. The federal spending ministries also have their own policy priorities to promote through these programs and thus oppose general purpose grants as well.

The beginning of wisdom about policy implementation is that "the conditions in which administrators are expected to implement policy compel them to join in the policymaking process."[8] When the federal government grants money, the states are not likely to passively fulfill federal objectives with it.[9] David Porter concludes in his study of resource mobilization that ". . . a formal subordination to higher levels of government does not preclude vigorous efforts at the lower levels to shape programs, to perpetuate ongoing but related activities, or to modify the officially defined objectives of the aid."[10] To prevent changes in federal priorities, the German federal government would need to become more involved in the detailed selection of projects and implementation of programs.[11]

Antirecession programs are likely to get caught in this contest for budgetary and policy control. The states can be expected to have an interest in getting untied funds for disposal as they choose; the federal donor, in contrast, probably hesitates to give funds that allow the recipients to decide how they are spent. The federal government is more likely to prefer a specific catalogue of items that allows it to monitor how the money is used.[12]

In the United States, the authors of an antirecession–grant proposal for local governments argue that the aid should be "given quickly and with a minimum of extraneous conditions and requirements." They explain that the more restrictions that are attached to federal grants, the greater will be the delay in implementation at the state and local levels. But they admit that in practice "most grant programs have been bound by restrictions imposed to insure that the funds were spent in accordance with federal intentions." They express little optimism, therefore, that the antirecession grants in the future will avoid fears that the lower levels of government will waste the money.[13]

The budgetary contention between the federal government and the states in West Germany should drive their attention away from economic management and toward distribution and program issues. The conflict over the varying expenditure priorities between the states and Bonn and the distribution of funds among the states is thus likely to carry over into the antirecession–grant programs.[14]

Stabilization and Allocation Objectives

How close do the antirecession-investment programs come to the ideal of aggregate demand management? Do they maintain the separation of budget purposes preferred by public finance? Do they meet Scharpf's policy requirements for a level-type problem structure?

Public investments—the mainstay of the antirecession programs—account for only 6 percent of total federal expenditure and no more than 8 to 10 percent of state expenditure. The bulk of investments are concentrated at the municipal level, composing over 35 percent of local municipal expenditure.[15] The municipalities make investments in local public buildings, roads, subways, hospitals, schools, swimming pools, sports fields, and so forth, all of which benefits mostly the construction industry.[16]

But the antirecession programs have not even covered all areas of public investment. Most programs centered on local infrastructure and road construction, thus joining highly salient structural and regional goals of the federal government with economic management. A listing of the titles of the six antirecession programs indicates their multipurpose character (see table 9–1). The

Table 9-1
Chronological List of Antirecession Programs

Title	Date	Amount
The First Investment Program of the Federation	14 April 1967	2.5 billion
The Second Program of the Federal Government for Particular Business-Cycle and Structural Measures	August 1967	5.3 billion
Special Program for Regional and Sectoral Support for Employment	6 February 1974	900 million
Special Program for Regional and Local Support for Employment	25 September 1974	950 million
Program for the Advancement of Employment and Growth with Stability	12 December 1974	
Program of the Federal Government for the Strengthening of Construction and Other Investments	27 August 1975	5.7 billion

[a] No determinate amount. Program was comprised of a percentage investment subsidy to private industry.

programs have sectoral, structural, and growth policies built into them as well as economic stabilization.

The main emphasis of the 1974 to 1975 antirecession programs was on regional economic problems and municipal infrastructure. Table 9-2 indicates the share that infrastructure comprised of three of the four programs during this period. Looking at individual programs shows that in September 1975, for example, municipal investments centered on slum clearance, housing renovation, sewage-treatment plants, old peoples' homes, local government buildings, parking garages, and so forth.[17] All three programs state clearly that the main weight of each falls to the municipal program.[18]

The municipal emphasis means that the sectoral aspect of policy was built into each program. Consider the September 1975 program for above-surface

Table 9-2
Share of the Antirecession Programs Going to Municipal Infrastructure
(in million DM)

Antirecession Program	Municipal Infrastructure	Total Program
February 1974	600	900
September 1974	700	950
September 1975	3,150	5,250[a]

[a] The 1974 programs contain federal and state government grants; the 1975 program lists funds only from the federal government.

construction. A state official concurred with the view that this program was not aimed at aggregate demand: "The last [antirecession] program was designed especially to help the construction industry. It was not intended to help the whole economy get going again. This program was an attempt to prevent unemployment in the construction industry from falling even further. It was a sector oriented program." The September 1974 program discriminated in favor of structurally weak regions. The December 1974 program also provided a 7½-percent subsidy for private investment under a time limit of six months and added over 100 million DM to the Joint Tasks "Regional Economic Development Program" to create jobs in Wolfsburg following heavy lay-offs by the Volkswagon plant located there.[19]

German antirecession programs were not pure stabilization measures but quite definitely have contained other objectives. In addition, because the state governments do not have the same allocation priorities as the federal government, stimulus programs that reflect federal priorities do not conform to state preferences—the level that should dominate allocation according to public finance.[20] But for reasons of financial and policy control, Bonn has rejected an across-the-board subsidy.

Who Decides the Programs?

The antirecession programs constituted administrative agreements between the states and the federal government. Formally they were discussed in the Finance Planning Council and the Business Cycle Council. The Bundestag also had a period of thirty days in which to approve or disapprove. The programs often contained two sections, one section of which was financed exclusively by the federal government and was generally the smaller of the two. The other section was jointly financed by Bonn, the states, and the municipalities and was done somewhat differently for each program. In general the states and the federal government paid an equal share, while the municipalities covered a much smaller proportion of the costs. The September 1975 program, for example, used the percentage breakdown 40-40-20 for the federal government, the states and the municipalities respectively.[21]

Do the percentage breakdowns in cost reflect the decision-making influence of each level of government? For the states to decide the overall size of the programs, they would have to agree among themselves. Instead Bonn decides these programs "completely by itself," one official stated quite strongly. "The federal government makes the decisions alone. Completely." In response to a question whether the Finance Planning Council participates in these decisions, he added: "For a single state it is very difficult to judge what an overall right amount should be. There is a natural leadership role for the federal government."

Imposing Macroeconomic Objectives 171

The guide-post for the overall size of the antirecession programs has been the volume of stabilization reserves *(Konjunkturausgleichsrücklagen)* held by the Bundesbank. The stabilization reserves amounted to 3.9 billion DM in 1974, most of which had been built up during the boom years 1969 and 1970. The major share, 2.9 billion DM, consisted of obligatory reserves that may only be released by a joint decision of the Bundesrat and the federal government.[22]

Bonn's decision to orient the size of the antirecession programs on the volume of stabilization reserves contained two elements. The releasing mechanism works in a way that prevents the states from getting the money unless Bonn gives its approval. "The main incentive to participate in these programs is the anticyclical reserves sitting at the Bundesbank," one state official complained. Federal officials agreed with the importance of the reserves. One comment was: "The most important factor is not the grants but the reserves. The federal government can unfreeze this money, and that is what is used for these additional investments during a time of budget stringency."

A second incentive for the state to participate was the fear of looking bad politically if the grant offers are not accepted. When asked if his government could have turned down the programs if it had wanted, another official replied: "Impossible. Under these conditions the government and parliament would never allow a situation in which we did not accept money offered to us." Even the CDU-governed states felt pressured to participate:

> Politically, you cannot say, "No, we will not participate." [Why not?] Well, for example, if you are a CDU-governed state, the SPD on the federal level can immediately take the minister president to task and declare that he is not prepared to take measures to improve the economy. You can see how bad that would look. You can wrangle about distribution and size and what not, but you cannot turn the programs down.

The statements clearly reflect the Finance Ministry's perspective and not that of the spending ministry, which welcomed the opportunity for extra spending.

The federal government also determined the overall content of the programs and decided the general-expenditure areas such as housing, above-surface construction, or regional unemployment. State officials emphasized that the federal government "sets the criteria for the programs." But often state officials complained that "the prescriptions are too strict. They [the federal officials] gave us a complete catalogue list of measures." In addition, the federal government set conditions for submitting proposals that aimed at the timing factor in stabilization policy. The September 1974 program, for example, prescribed that the selected measures must show a sparing energy use, concentrate on small and middle-level firms, and have future costs that do not run beyond the end of 1975.[23] Needless to say, not all these criteria were met in every case.

The federal government's determination of the size of the programs was sharply contested by the states but clearly demonstrates the public good character of economic stabilization. As Scharpf argues, only selective incentives work to gain support for a level problem. The stabilization reserves enticed many reluctant state Finance Ministries to participate, as did the threat of looking bad politically, even if they opposed the macrobudget objectives.

The content of the programs is more problematic. Allocation decisions cannot be avoided despite the stabilization purpose of the grants. Oates argues that the lower levels of government have the greatest competence for allocation decisions.[24] To the extent that content decisions involve regional or sectoral emphases, the distribution of funds among the states also becomes an issue of dispute.

The Distribution of Antirecession Funds

The state governments have opposed any attempt by Bonn to employ special distribution formulas for antirecession grants. The usual grant-in-aid formulas, however, have increasingly followed a proportional criterion based on population.[25] But the antirecession programs in 1974 and 1975 deviated sharply from the proportional scheme. These programs especially aimed at regional and structural problems in poorer areas. Table 9-3 shows the population figures and the federal-funding share that accrued to each state. Baden-Württemberg received less money than the population share, as did Hamburg, Berlin, and Bavaria.

Table 9-3
Federal Share of the September 1974 and 1975 Antirecession Programs Going to Each State
(percentage down)

Federal State	Population Share, 1974	Federal Program Share 1974	Federal Program Share 1975	Unemployment Rate, 1974	Program Share Per Worker, 1
Schleswig-Holstein	4.2	13.0	6.6	3.5	87.6
Hamburg	2.8	0.3	2.3	1.6	2.8
Lower Saxony	11.7	16.5[a]	13.8	2.9[a]	35.4[a]
Bremen	1.2		1.2		
North Rhine-Westphalia	27.8	27.2	24.5	2.9	26.0
Hesse	9.0	10.6	8.7	2.4	30.3
Rhineland-Palatinate	5.9	9.5	6.2	3.0	45.6
Baden-Württemberg	14.9	2.0	12.4	1.5	3.3
Bavaria	17.5	15.4	18.3	2.3	23.6
Saarland	1.8	5.2	2.3	4.0	85.7
Berlin	3.3	.3	3.6	1.7	2.3

Source: For the September 1975 program, see "Programm der Bundesregierung zur Stärkung von Bau anderen Investitionen," *Bulletin* no. 106 (Bonn: Presse- und Informationsamt der Bundesregierung, 2 Septen 1975), pp. 1037–1043; for the (1974), program, the source is, "Zur rechten Zeit am rechten Ort: 1.000.000. Mark Sonderprogramm der Bundesregierung hilft regional und sektoral," *Sozialdemokratmagazin* (Noven 1974), p. 15; for the population share, see Statistisches Bundesamt, *Statistisches Jahrbuch der Bundesrepu* (Stuttgart: W. Kohlhammer Verlag, 1975), p. 34 plus the author's own calculations.

[a] This is a combined amount for Lower Saxony and Bremen together.

The differences are quite pronounced based on DM per salaried or wage earner. But this criterion also produced a dangerous political result: the two large Christian Democratic states conspicuously received less than the population criterion would grant. The reason was that the program stipulated that regions should receive special help that have an above-average unemployment rate and a below-average construction employment. Hans Filbinger, the minister president of Baden-Württemberg, protested the distribution of money. His government even proposed an alternative formula: the rate of growth in unemployment over the most recent time period.

The Bavarian finance minister, Alfons Goppel, and the economics minister, Anton Jaumann also strongly protested against the proposed antirecession program which they felt discriminated against Bavaria.[26] Jaumann added that Bonn had attached such a series of stipulations that "the funds flowed predominantly to the developed and economically strong regions, such as the Ruhr Valley"— a SPD-dominated area.

Hans Filbinger proposed that the federal government and the states draw up a General Agreement to regulate the antirecession-program funds warning that if Bonn did not pay greater attention to the rights of the states, it would encounter the "determined resistance" of Baden-Württemberg. In particular, Filbinger complained that the federal government had not allowed enough time in the Finance Planning Council to deal with stabilization measures. He accused the federal government of coming to the council with a fully worked out proposal for the distribution of funds.[27]

Federal officials also emphasized the importance of the distribution issue. "The overall size of the program is not so disputable as how it will be distributed among the states," one official stated. Table 9-3 indicates that the September 1975 program deviated much less from the proportional, population shares. Many of the states expressed greater satisfaction with this arrangement, and no states raised objections to the distribution formulas. The program itself contained different distribution schemes for each subpart, but of the four subprograms two of them followed the regular grants distribution formulas. The other two were 50 to 60 percent allotted according to a strict population formula.[28]

The first aspect to the distribution conflict is the relative share each state gets of the federal antirecession money; the other aspect is the state's own income. The problem is that the source of financing for the state share is the stability reserves held by the Bundesbank. The states accumulate these reserves by contributing up to 3 percent of their tax receipts, but the rate and absolute amount is determined by the federal government with the agreement of the Bundesrat.[29] The result is that some states have a much larger accumulation of reserves than some other states.

The main source of financing for the antirecession programs, therefore, was unequally distributed among the states. In fact the poorer states tended to fare the worst, while the wealthier states accumulated much more. Three of the wealthiest states succeeded at financing the 1974 and 1975 programs entirely from the reserves held at the Bundesbank. Two of the less wealthy states, the

Saarland and Schleswig-Holstein, needed to finance a large part of each program through credit.

Table 9-4 indicates the amount of reserves held by each state before and after the September 1974 antirecession program. The three least wealthy states, the Saarland, Lower Saxony and Schleswig-Holstein, consumed the largest amounts of reserves for that particular program. Two of them. Schleswig-Holstein and the Saarland, started out with the smallest base amounts.[30] The state share for the September 1975 program amounted to 89.4 million, 186.4 million, and 31.7 million DM respectively for Schleswig-Holstein, Lower Saxony, and the Saarland. This meant that Schleswig-Holstein, for example, had to find 71.2 million DM from some other source to pay for it.

Officials from these states explained that without exception the difference is made up through credit and agreed that the stabilization-reserve system provides an unequal distribution of funds to the states. This extra spending and forced borrowing had an impact on some state budgets. "In order to include the antirecession program," a finance official confided, "we had to alter the whole budget plan. This meant that other areas had to be cut to make room for the added expenditure and debt." The cuts occurred in current expenditures such as telephone units, travel time, janitorial services, and even technical-literature purchases for the schools, and many other items. In appraisal, he felt that the antirecession programs and their effects "do not always make sense."

The states, angry about these budget pressures, claimed that the matching requirements violate their budgetary autonomy as stated in article 109 of the

Table 9-4
The Anticyclical Reserves of the States, August 1975
(in million DM)

Federal State	Total Yield	Amount Given for September 1974 Antirecession Program	Column 1 Minus Column 2
Schleswig-Holstein	40.2	22.0	18.2
Lower Saxony	162.2	28.0	134.2
North Rhine-Westphalia	316.6	4.7	311.9
Hesse	95.2	—	95.2
Rhineland-Palatinate	54.9	9.6	45.3
Baden-Württemberg	319.7	—	319.7
Bavaria	225.9	5.7[a]	220.2
Saarland	27.1	16.1	11.0
Hamburg	103.7	—	103.7
Bremen	34.5	—	34.5
Berlin	56.5	—	56.5
Total	1,436.5	86.0	1,350.5
Federal government	2,500.0	—	2,500.0

Note: The amount given by decree of the federal government 13 November 1974.
[a]At time of printing, Bavaria had not yet claimed its share.

Basic Law. But the federal Finance Ministry completely rejected the illegality of matching requirements and stated instead that it had no intention of funding measures in which the states themselves did not have a financial stake.[31] Although the federal government favored the standard formulas for financing the programs (40-40-20 for the federal government, states, and municipalities respectively), the states did not comply with the federal-matching requirements but in fact gave an average of 60 percent subsidy to the municipalities (the state share was 20 percent). As a result, "a large number of municipalities were not in the position to come up with their own share of the financing for the antirecession programs," according to a member of the National Municipal Association.[32]

Allocation among Expenditure Areas

A major conflict between the federal government and the states has been the control over the selection of individual projects funded by the Financial Aid grants. The states initiated a suit against the federal government, claiming that federal determination of individual project selection violates constitutional law. On 4 March 1975, the Federal Constitutional Court ruled that the federal government may not use Financial Aid grants to influence the decisional and organizational freedom of the states.[33]

The "General Agreement on the Approval of Financial Aid of the Federal Government covered by article 104a, paragraph 4 of the Basic Law" was adopted by the Conference of State Finance Ministers in the latter part of 1974. The purpose of the proposal seems to have been to legally bind the federal government from influencing the selection of single projects. Article 3 of the General Agreement, for instance, proposes that the states have the right to select single projects and approve the granting of funds to the municipalities.

The federal Finance Ministry's lengthy comment on the "General Agreement" admits that article 3 "concerns itself with the essential point of dispute between the federal government and the states." Bonn argued for a joint decision right to choose those individual projects that best fulfill the goals of Financial Aid. The Finance Ministry believed that it had the legal right to overstep the regular boundaries of budgetary authority for the purposes of economic management.[34] But the Finance Ministry's argument also centered on budget control: "It is unreasonable financially to expect of the federal government that it turn over federal money to the states according to vague criteria, and then only a year later, as it states in article 4, paragraph 2 of the proposed agreement, to simply be informed of the money's use."[35]

The federal Finance Ministry wants to know how these funds are actually spent. "On the community level it is not clear that the funds are ever spent," observed a federal official. "They constantly save this money. If you normally get a 50-percent subsidy for a theater and now suddenly you get 80 percent, you pocket the difference and build the theater which you would have built in any case." Bonn feels that the states also "finance their budgets with these funds. . . . The states hardly deviate from what they would have spent anyway."

Some city officials supported this point of view as indicated by this city treasurer's comment:

> My impression is that the state only grants funds that they would have anyway. . . . The states try to stick to regular budget channels and more or less call these subsidies antirecession grants. [What do you mean by that?] I mean that the states have not done anything extra. We get the promise of funds and start the plans going. But by the end of the year the difference is not very noticeable.

Stabilization policy is concerned with the timing of expenditures. If a city pushes forward some projects that it had scheduled to take up later that is satisfactory for economic management. But the practice aggravated officials in the federal Finance Ministry. Without control over single-project selection, the states can simply shift items forward that they were going to carry out anyway and thereby take financial pressure off other budget areas. In the summer of 1975 the states proposed not to use the 40-40-20 formula, arguing instead in favor of the regular state subsidy of 50 percent (a 25-25-50 formula).

The federal government also tried to select individual projects on economic-management grounds. Bonn favored measures that did not have long-range costs, could be spent quickly, and have a potentially higher multiplier effect. But selecting those items when resources are scarce changes allocation priorities. The government, for example, may spend less on school construction (a long-term expensive project) and more on road repair (a shorter and cheaper project). Many of the state and municipal officials expressed the opinion that these criteria open the possibility for less than rational investment planning.

One official complained about the definition of investments as primarily buildings, roads, and other installations. In the case of a school, this means that the "teachers are consumption goods, while the building is an investment. . . . The future costs are then unwanted because they appear as consumption expenditures." He added that "if I need a school or hospital, and don't need a road, it doesn't make much sense to build a highway because the future costs are low. These decisions must be made in light of total policy needs."

When asked if the antirecession investments have been as useful as the regular investment program, another city official said that "suddenly under this program we look for projects that are not anticipated according to our plan but that get us the money and can be started right away." He was then asked for an example, and he cited the construction of two new sewage-treatment units even though, "We now have a fully functioning system which cleans the water to 98 percent, which is a very acceptable degree." He listed three other comparable instances.

The federal government may grant Financial Aid not only for stabilization but also for structural and growth problems. A city official explained the effect of this multipurpose character of Financial Aid on the antirecession programs: "The federal government has policy jurisdiction in the areas of regional and sectoral economic development and environmental protection. It sponsors these measures and puts them into the antirecession programs. If a community wants to go its own way, it gets no money."

Most of the states also drew up their own antirecession program in 1975. A state budget director explained that his administration had to significantly change what it wanted to do:

> I can give you our program. We wanted to invest 20 million in low-cost housing. The federal program does not contain that category. We wanted to invest in police protection measures—around 12 million. Again we couldn't do it. Road construction, agricultural support, and old and handicapped peoples' homes are other areas where we couldn't do what we wanted. We also wanted 75 million for state investments.

Both the Social Democratic and Christian Democratic governed states had similar examples to relate. If the federal government simply promotes investments in its regular grant channels, it changes some of the states' allocation priorities. In some cases the changes have definitely been minor; in others, more thorough revisions took place. All the state finance officials believed, however, that the antirecession programs have supported either unnecessary or undesirable public investments.

Uncertainty and Federal Relations

For economic management, open-ended general-purpose grants are preferable to fixed amount, carefully monitored grants in specific policy areas. The United States Congressional Report on revenue sharing concludes that "it seems clear that the more restrictions are attached to federal aid to state and local government, the more delays there will be in spending the money."[36] The German federal government, however, rejected open-ended all-purpose grants for the antirecession programs.

A possible explanation is that the fluctuations in social wants increasingly followed the business cycle. Scharpf argues, for example, that the 1974 to 1975 recession had regional and sectoral elements due to the impact of world economic developments. On the other hand, the 1967 recession was internally generated, yet the antirecession programs at that time also contained regional distribution formulas and select project areas. The most striking feature of the two groups of programs is their similarity: they all support investment in local infrastructure and road construction and promote regional and sectoral policy goals.

An alternative explanation is simply that the Finance Ministry was not interested in giving away money over which it had no say in how it was to be spent. Federal officials suspected that the lower units of government used the antirecession money to balance their budgets and to spend in policy areas not preferred by federal ministries. Because the federal government stands in competition with the states over sources of tax revenue, federal officials did not want to fight with one hand to get more revenue and give with the other through the antirecession grants. If money was to be given away, they tried to determine what happened to it.

Instead of separating allocation and stabilization objectives, the federal government joined them together. In many of the antirecession programs Bonn had definite policy preferences that differed from state and local priorities. Employment policy, urban transportation, low-cost housing, hospital construction, and so on are the preserves of the federal government. As money became available for economic stimulus, therefore, the federal Finance Ministry decided to spend it on programs that the federal government preferred.

But this form of intervention into state and local priorities creates fervent opposition. City officials did not like restrictions on grants and repeatedly proposed open-ended, all-purpose grants as an alternative. The state governments, however, opposed this solution because they wanted to restrict the antirecession grants to the regular, limited grant areas and the usual distribution formulas. But Bonn rejected this approach because it feared a loss of financial control over programs.

If open-ended all-purpose grants are chosen, the federal government suffers budgetary uncertainty because it has no control over the total amount spent or what it is spent on—whether it would be 1 or 1½ billion marks. For the recipients, open-ended grants are welcomed because they allow the cities to choose their own projects and contracts and reduce the paperwork and administrative monitoring. If the federal government chooses fixed-amount grants in specific areas, however, the recipients' budgetary uncertainty increases as outside priorities and expenditure-level decisions are imposed on their intentions and plans. But this is exactly what the federal government chose to do, that is, to shift budget uncertainty caused by open-ended antirecession grants onto the state governments by opting for fixed grants in specific areas. The resultant controversy increased political and institutional tensions to the point where the federal government was forced to reduce granted funds.

A more judicious federal policy would be to share the uncertainty of open-ended or fixed-amount grants with the state governments. The best example of a mixed strategy of this type is the September 1975 antirecession program which allowed the central government to choose the broad categories but the state governments to specify the projects. It is not the ideal solution for either level, but one that both can accept because it shares the uncertainty between recipient and donor.

Similarly, a possible resolution to the distribution problem is to force the states to decide between greater autonomy or larger subsidies. The wealthy states particularly resented federal intrusion into state policy, whereas the poorer states more willingly accepted such arrangements to get the additional funds. With respect to the antirecession grants, perhaps the wealthier state might accept a smaller percentage subsidy that has fewer restrictions, while the poorer states might agree to a larger subsidy on the condition that Bonn has more to say about how it is used. This mixed solution would allow the federal government to have a greater budget control over the larger subsidies and also to aid those states that need the money the most.

But even general purpose grants do not entirely separate stabilization and allocation budget purposes. A city might not consider building a centrally located underground–parking garage, for example, because of the small need and high cost. But if more money becomes available, the low-priority parking garage could become more attractive as a way to bring in more federal money. Consequently, no grant strategy leaves allocation priorities completely untouched.[37]

The federal government faces a further dilemma. It must decide the long- or short-term character of antirecession funds. If it chooses short-term measures, the kinds of projects selected will be those with low maintenance and operating costs and quick implementation. But these projects shift funds away from longer-term investment programs that may have greater programmatic value for the states.[38] In this instance as well, therefore, the federal system complicates the trade-off between allocation and stabilization purposes by giving different perspectives to each level of government.

Finally, the antirecession programs demonstrate the functional interdependence of the West German federal system. The states cannot manage the economy because they do not have the required national orientation; the central government cannot carry out economic management because it does not possess the administration. To the extent that federal-economic management has infringed on the policy priorities of the states, they have used the administration of the programs to thwart federal intentions. The federal policymakers have responded by intervening in the detailed selection of projects and implementation of programs. The clash that ensued turned the federal government away from budget policy and toward monetary policy.

The U.S. government was unhappy with the shift in policy focus because it had wanted a greater German economic stimulus. The Bonn leadership is less disappointed because inflation levels have lowered and budget restraint was the politically right course to follow. But as the economy enters the 1980s, the government may be having second thoughts. Part of the strict monetary policy has been the decision to defend the value of the mark. This action has raised German export prices and reduced demand. The Federal Republic is now paying for its antiinflation monetary policy with another slowdown similar to that of 1974 and 1975. But no one ever said that monetary restraint is all there is to economic management or that it does not entail certain costs of its own.

Notes

1. From an interview with a federal financial official, fall 1975.
2. Wallace Oates, *Fiscal Federalism* (New York: Harcourt, Brace, and Janovich, 1972), pp. 3–64.
3. Richard Musgrave, *A Theory of Public Finance* (New York: McGraw Hill, 1959), p. 25.
4. Earl Rolph and George Break, *Public Finance* (New York: Ronald Press 1961), p. 515.
5. Fritz W. Scharpf, Bernd Reissert, and Fritz Schnabel, *Politikverflechtung: Theorie und Empirie des kooperativen Föderalismus in der Bundesrepublik* (Kronberg/Ts.: Scriptor Verlag, 1976), pp. 13–29. They center their analysis on decentralized investment decisions in a federal system. Level problems arise due to positive or negative externalities Either bilateral bargaining does not suffice or common pool problems arise. The central authority needs to either increase or decrease expenditures to compensate for the decentral outcome. Distribution problems arise whenever "geographical, sectoral, personal or temporal incidence of decentral activities is of concern to the inclusive decision-making unit." Finally, interaction problems arise due to "complex patterns of interdependence." Urban agglomerations, for example, emerge from the interaction of housing patterns, transportation systems, locational decisions of industry, and so forth.
6. Ibid.
7. The titles that cover the yearly grants in these expenditure areas are Wohnungsbauförderung, Städtebauförderung, Gemeindeverkehrsfinanzierung, Krankenhausfinanzierung, and Studentenwohnraumförderung. For a good commentary on this article of the Basic Law, see T. Maunz, G. Duerig, and R. Herzog, *Grundgesetz Kommentar* (Munich: C.H. Beck'sche Verlag, 1973).
8. Charles Lindblom, *The Policy-Making Process,* 2nd ed. (Englewood Cliffs, New Jersey: Prentice-Hall, 1980), p. 68.
9. This perspective on the activism of local units receiving grants is excellently analyzed by David O. Porter with David Warner and Teddie Porter, *The Politics of Budgeting Federal Aid: Resource Mobilization by Local School Districts* (Beverly Hills: Sage Publications, 1973), passim.
10. Ibid., p. 9.
11. The fear that the U.S. federal government cannot control federal antirecession grants is also contained in Congressional Budget Office, U.S. Con-

gress, *Temporary Measures to Stimulate Employment: An Evaluation of Some Alternatives* (Washington D.C.: U.S. Government Printing Office, 2 September, 1975), p. 45.

12. See chapter 4 for an extended analysis of the antirecession programs' effect on decision making in the federal government.

13. U.S. Congress, *Temporary Measures*, p. 46.

14. Scharpf, *Politikverflechtung*, specifically mentions this fact. The reason: the increasingly pronounced regional and sectoral effects of recessions.

15. Dieter Vesper, "Vortrag über Stabilitätspolitik," Working Paper (West Berlin: Deutsches Institut für Wirtschaftsforschung, 1974), p. 11.

16. Ibid., pp. 11–12. In 1973 public investments in the construction industry amounted to 35 billion out of a total public investment of 40 billion DM. Scepticism was also expressed in 1974 and 1975 that a program oriented on the construction industry could in any way off set the huge losses in export volume. See, for example, "Konjunkturprogramm in Vorbereitung," *Suddeutsche Zeitung*, 4 June, 1975, p. 1.

17. "Programm der Bundesregierung zur Stärkung von Bau und anderen Investitionen," (Bonn: Presse- und Informationsamt der Bundesregierung, 2 September, 1975), pp. 1037–1043. Hereafter cited as "Bauprogramm der Bundesregierung."

18. "Aktuelle Beiträge zur Wirtschafts- und Finanzpolitik," no. 121 (Bonn: Presse- und Informationsamt der Bundesregierung, 27 November, 1974). See also "Zur rechten Zeit am rechten Ort: 1.000.000.000 Mark Sonderprogramm der Bundesregierung hilft regional und sektoral," *Sozialdemokratmagazin* (November 1974):15. Finally see, "Bericht über die konjunktur- und Sonderprogramme 1974–75," (Bonn: Deutscher Bundestag, Bundestags-Drucksache, 7/4677).

19. "Bonn verstärkt regionale Förderung," *Suddeutsche Zeitung*, 24 April, 1975, p. 1.

20. Heinz Koch, *Stabilitätspolitik im föderalistischen System der Bundesrepublik Deutschland* (Cologne: Bund Verlag, 1975), pp. 56–95.

21. Deutscher Bundestag, 7. Wahlperiode, Bundestags-Drucksache 7/4013, 9 September, 1975.

22. See article 7 of the Stability and Growth Law in, for example, *Das Neue Haushaltsrecht* (Bonn: Bundesministerium der Finanzen, 1969), p. 126. For an explanation of how these reserves work, see Maunz, *Grundgesetz Kommentar*. See also Hans Clausen Korff, *Haushaltspolitik: Instrument Oeffentlicher Macht* (Stuttgart: W. Kohlhammer Verlag, 1975), pp. 47–48; and "Konjunkturrücklage finanziert Regionalprogramm," *Suddeutsche Zeitung*, 10 November, 1974.

23. "Aktuelle Beiträge," pp. 2–4.

24. Oates, *Fiscal Federalism*, p. 8.

25. Bernd Reissert, *Die finanzielle Beteiligung des Bundes an Aufgaben der Länder und das Postulat der "Einheitlichkeit der Lebensverhältnisse im Bundesgebiet,"* (Bonn-Bad Godesberg: Vorwärtsdruck, 1975), passim.

26. Martin Rehm, "CSU: Bonn hält Bayern kurz," *Suddeutsche Zeitung* 20 December, 1974.

27. "Filbinger pocht auf Rechte der Länder," *Suddeutsche Zeitung,* 21 November, 1974.

28. "Bauprogramm der Bundesregierung," pp. 1037–1043.

29. See Stability and Growth Law, article 15, paragraph 2. It is also possible to pass a tax surcharge up to 10 percent, the receipts from which are to be frozen at the Bundesbank. This is discussed in articles 26 and 27.

30. The amount for Bremen is smaller than for these three regular states, but the population of Bremen is also considerably smaller (approximately 582,300 population in 1973). See, Statistisches Bundesamt, *Jahrbuch der Bundesrepublik Deutschland* (Stuttgart: W. Kohlhammer Verlag, 1973).

31. "Stellungnahme zum Entwurf einer Grundvereinbarung nach Artikel 104a4 GG," January 1975, which was obtained from the Bundesfinanzministerium, pp. 9–10. Hereafter cited as "Stellungnahme der Bundesregierung."

32. Richard Klein, "Konjunkturbelebung und städtische Leistungskraft im Widerstreit," *Der Städtetag,* no. 10 (October 1975):536.

33. Bundesverfassungsgericht, *Entscheidungen,* 39, pp. 96 and following.

34. "Zu Punkt 5 der Tagesordnung der finanzminister Konferenz am 3. Oktober 1974," Bundesrat, Bonn, 2 October, 1974, which was obtained from the Bundesfinanzministerium. See also "Stellungnahme der Bundesregierung," p. 5. Note that the General Agreement is intended to cover not only economic stabilization but also the yearly grants for growth and structural purposes. The agreement does not cover only the antirecession programs. Another article dealing with this issue is "Goppel rechnet mit zähen Verhandlungen," *Suddeutsche Zeitung,* 1 November, 1976, p. 1.

35. "Stellungnahme der Bundesregierung," pp. 4–5.

36. U.S. Congress, *Temporary Measures,* p. 45.

37. This is referred to as the *incomes effect*. With more money people simply change their allocation preferences. For a discussion of this issue in the context of budget reform, see Thomas H. Hammond and Jack H. Knott, *A Zero-Based Look at Zero-Base Budgeting* (New Brunswick: Transaction Books, 1980), pp. 50–51.

38. Karl-Heinrich Hansmeyer at the University of Cologne also has reached a similar conclusion that many of the antirecession investments were useless from a programmatic viewpoint. See, "Gemeinden sehen ihre Rechte schwinden," *Suddeutsche Zeitung,* 17 March, 1976, p. 17.

10 Bureaucratic Politics and Macroeconomic Policy

Justice, I think, is the tolerable accommodation of the conflicting interests of society, and I don't believe there is any royal road to attain such accommodations concretely.[1]   —Learned Hand

For the macroeconomist, economic prosperity is the goal by which to judge government policies. The macroeconomist views government as a sector of the economy that has a special role through its taxing and spending powers: to guarantee economic prosperity by being a counterweight to the other sectors.

But other important government goals are subsumed under the economic goal. Even decision processes are evaluated primarily on whether they meet economic goals in a timely fashion. Thus, many macroeconomists see the parliamentary decision process as too cumbersome, and the tedious Finance Ministry negotiations with the spending ministries as hindrances to sound management of the economy. Government should get on with the job and not let politics get in the way is the motto that captures this conception of government as an economic tool.

Public finance has a somewhat more inclusive view of government. It recognizes the important allocation and redistribution purposes of public budgeting as well as that of economic stabilization and tries to relate the various purposes to each other. Managing the economy confronts the decision maker from this perspective with a trade-off not only between inflation and unemployment but also between stabilization, equity, and efficiency.

Public finance, however, falls short of a political analysis of the impact of fiscal policy on other government purposes. Its weakness is that it has little to say about such important values as due process, trust in negotiations, political control, and conflict resolution. By not considering the political costs and benefits of separating purposes, public finance turns its attention solely to the correct mixture of policy products. Stabilization preferences should not alter allocation or distribution priorities, for example, for that elevates stabilization policy above the other two. It is also why public finance criticizes macroeconomics for its disregard of the relation between budget purposes. Yet compartmentalization of purposes, though quite correct from an economic viewpoint, is unrealistic politically.

There are two reasons why a more political understanding of how the government operates is important for macroeconomic policy. The first is that actual policies reflect more interests than just economic equilibrium and thus often do not conform to economic theory. An understanding of why fiscal policies look the way they do, therefore, requires the inclusion of political variables. A better understanding of government practice also should lead to more realistic policy prescriptions. Knowing what political costs are and where the benefits lie points to appropriate strategies for more successful policies.

Second, taking account of a broader range of interests changes the way policies are evaluated and instruments are chosen. If economic equilibrium alone is considered, fiscal policy's effects on financial integrity, federal-political relations, or resource distribution make little difference for policymakers. Yet each of these interests has an institutional and political advocate in government and society. Even if one does not value federalism or financial solvency, ignoring these interests or relegating them to mere obstacles to rational policy is likely to jeopardize worthy economic-management efforts. Bonn was forced to abandon a stimulative budget policy partly because of a coalition of opposing interests. This is the practical aspect of accommodating purposes.

But more important, a political analysis of economic management has little basis for fixing economic equilibrium as the government's sole purpose. Even public finance recognizes equity and efficiency as additional important values. Harvey Sapolski writes with respect to the presence of conflicting interests that the analyst should:

> . . . recognize that government programs invariably affect the interests of several partisan groups, each of which promotes a different set of goals. He must also recognize that governmental organizations are required to serve not only the goals of the programs within their jurisdictions, but also the contextual goals of government, the goals of equity, due process, fiscal integrity, and the like which are procedural norms of the society and which have their own partisans.[2]

If economic management lowers trust in budget negotiations, leads to a disregard of financial integrity, or violates local budget autonomy, these values should not be considered as unintended consequences but as part of the impact of economic management on the government and the society.

Throughout the preceding chapters, several ways in which macroeconomic policy conflicts with other important political goals were discussed. It is now time to summarize these sources of conflict and examine the various strategies that policymakers employ to accommodate these diverse purposes. But despite the many avenues that exist for accommodation, not all conflict can be avoided. Therefore, following is an assessment of the inevitable uncertainty that conflicting criteria cause and the role of political analysis in the study of public policy.

Sources of Incompatibility

Economic management creates uncertainty for expenditure policy because it introduces conflicting criteria for judging and planning budget amounts. *Ex-*

penditure policy in a federal-political system is mostly concerned with particulars not with aggregates, while *economic management* is concerned with the aggregate level of expenditure in the macrobudget. Expenditure policy thus examines the program worth of specific funding, but economic management ignores programs in favor of totals: the size of the debt, the macrobudget, borrowing, and capital spending.[3] The problem is that some measures that benefit the macrobudget do harm to the program budget.

On the economic-management side, deciding whether to increase or decrease expenditures depends on changes in the private economy not necessarily related (and often unrelated) to government programs. On the expenditure-policy side, the decision on what to spend is determined by programmatic needs in particular policy areas that may not (and usually do not) fluctuate with the business cycle. If the government is to pursue fiscal policy it must decide to what extent it is willing to sacrifice program-policy goals in particular budget areas for overall, aggregate economic objectives.

Spending additional funds that have little program worth in order to counteract slack demand in the economy also contradicts traditional norms of responsible financial management. During a recession period, receipts from tax income diminish, putting pressure on financial managers to contain the level of spending. But the economic-management response is to increase spending, thereby also enlarging the size of the deficit beyond what it would have been due to the decline in tax income. But salaries, social costs, and numerous other governmental expenditures are "sticky" in the downward direction in the same way that prices are always rising in the private economy. Consequently deficits incurred during recessions are not usually depleted during booms, except through increased receipts. Without sustained economic growth, traditional financial management no longer can be sustained as a political value because the gap between expenditures and receipts continues to widen as an intended feature of government policy.

A third conflict is between short- and long-term planning horizons. Economic management has a temporary, short-term orientation, whereas budgeting has a middle-term, more permanent purpose. Economic-management actions occur at any time during the approximately eighteen-month to two-year budget cycle. At times, expenditures that were planned during the formulation stage are altered later in the execution phase. But investments take two to three years to plan in advance, and alteration in the middle of this period disrupts prearranged credit and construction contracts and the provision of services. Yet investments are precisely the types of expenditures that have enough relative flexibility for managing the economy. If booms outlast recessions, therefore, short-term fiscal policy threatens long-term investment in growth. During the long boom from 1969 to 1973, for instance, public investments virtually stagnated, but other expenditures increased dramatically.

The short-term orientation of economic management also introduces a bias into allocation decisions. Old established programs have greater immunity to fiscal-policy cuts, while new and sometimes innovative and controversial programs serve as prime candidates for removal.[4] Fiscal-policy requirements, likewise, favor expenditures that can be given out quickly in preference to those that take longer but have higher program merit. Further, economic management tends to produce a bias in favor of investment in things over investment in people. Building roads, bridges, offices, and apartments is considered in Federal Germany to have higher multiplier effects than investments in better training for teachers, more and improved textbooks, health techniques, and personnel. These latter are routinely categorized as *consumption expenditures;* that is, expenses that do not produce growth but raise costs.

Economic management also attempts to make economic developments more regular and stable through anticyclical variations in government spending. The planning disruptions and prediction uncertainties that the private economy used to bear are now supposed to be born by the public budget. Expenditure policy, however, has the opposite purpose: to make relations among participants in government more regular and stable through shared expectations about future resource allocations. Budgeting accomplishes this by building on past agreements not by reacting to current developments, as in economic management. This is the important political function of the incremental and regular flavor of the budgetary process.

Changing expenditures in the later stages of the budget process to manage the economy endangers trustful relations between the Finance Ministry budget analysts and the spending ministry budget directors. Trust depends on common expectations that what is agreed upon will remain binding throughout the budget cycle.[5] Without common expectations, both sides have incentives to present deceptions early on in order to better get their way later in the process, thereby extending conflict over budget negotiations throughout the budget cycle. The Finance Ministry has found that setting up stabilization funds during the formulation stage only aggravates negotiations and creates distrust later on when economic developments do not warrant their release. Moreover, the less trustful the relations among participants, the less willing they are to settle disputes lower down in the administrative hierarchy. Decisions to have special antirecession-investment programs increased conflict at the Cabinet level, and disputes over whether to follow financial, program, or economic criteria for the budget frequently rose to the top political leadership.

By introducing greater fluctuation into spending patterns, economic management threatens the incremental character of budgeting. By introducing instability into the government's budget program, economic management lengthens the decision time necessary for reaching agreements. Budget officials complained that agreements concluded with the spending ministries only three months ago must now be overturned to manage the economy. Extending the decision time in turn caused a greater decision lag in deciding fiscal-policy programs, thereby making even their goals more difficult to achieve.

Economic management, finally, threatens the stability of the policy-administration dichotomy. As a level program, fiscal policy logically requires open-ended, general-purpose subsidies that interfere minimally with local allocation decisions. But the policymakers in Bonn were unwilling to grant money with no strings attached. But by attaching strings, the administrators in the states resented federal intrusion into their budget policies. And because they did not totally agree with the policy goals in the first place, the administrators' response was to try to take over policy themselves. Frustrations on both sides led to a retreat from macrobudget objectives.

Accommodating Purposes

The political process is characterized by interactive decision making. Groups that are concerned about government programs fight for their preferences; because not enough resources exist to satisfy everyone, not all needs can receive full compensation. Unless one group dictates for all the others, most groups will have to compete to gain partial support for their own preferences. Although the distribution of political power affects the outcomes of this competition, presumably in democratic systems no one group determines policy.

The danger, of course, is stalemate. How can a policy be decided on when none of the participants agree, are not willing to give up anything, nor have the power to coerce others? Critics have raised this very issue in their attacks on the Federal Republic's decentralized and fragmented public sector. Even the Americans, they argue, have a large presidential executive office that coordinates activities among the departments. The urge is to make the German public sector more closely reflect the private sector.

But there are other roads that lead to accommodation. Although the government is fragmented by independent ministries and semiautonomous state and local administrations, the central government is relatively small in size. Stability and familiarity characterize the relations of bureaus with each other. Coordination, therefore, derives not so much from formal hierarchies and central rules but from informal norms and back-and-forth discussions. There are three strategies pursued consciously or unconsciously that fit this pattern: (1) the restriction of the conflict between stabilization and budgetary criteria to relatively rare crisis situations; (2) the exploitation of cognitive uncertainty to combine budget purposes; and (3) the use of accepted norms, such as the nominal growth in GNP, to orient discussions and bargaining. Each of these strategies is considered here.

1. On a regular, yearly basis microbudgetary outcomes in the various parts of the bureaucracy predominate over macroeconomic objectives. Only under relatively severe and unexpected conditions do anticyclical fiscal-policy concerns dominate budgeting. The reason is that budgeting is concerned with programmatic and financial issues in particular policy areas; alterations in these patterns require outside imposition on the regular Finance Ministry–spending ministry relations. But since interference by top political executives changes normal agreements in the bureaucracy, it also entails a political cost that is unacceptable except under relatively severe economic conditions. Under more normal economic circumstances, the political price that must be paid to alter budgetary

outcomes to fit economic needs is too high in comparison to the marginal benefits for the economy. It is also unclear whether economic measures of the public budget are capable of indicating appropriate responses that fine-tune the economy with such precision.[6]

With worsening economic developments, however, the needs of the economy begin to outweigh the program orientation of budgetary outcomes and the political costs of imposing on them.[7] But simply because an objective becomes increasingly desirable in the aggregate does not indicate that individual organizations with particular concerns pursue policies that secure it. Each individual organization has its own incentives for participation. The Transportation Ministry is not concerned with business inventories but with providing and maintaining public modes of transport and travel. It will resist efforts to cut road-repair funds as part of a program to stabilize the economy.

Macropolicy thus requires that the Cabinet take action. The antirecession programs, for example, were passed by the Cabinet as special budgets alongside the ministries' regular budgets. In 1974 and 1975 the federal ministries decreased grants in aid to other levels on financial grounds, but the passage of the antirecession budgets brought the growth rates back to what they had been in previous years. Without special intervention by the Cabinet, therefore, the grants would have followed traditional growth trends based on available resources and substantive policy concerns.

The issue is one of bureaucratic autonomy versus executive leadership. But how does one evaluate this pattern of policymaking? Galbraith and others imply that bureaucratic autonomy is generally harmful to policy. Problems build up and then appear to explode on the leadership as crises. But not unlike castor oil, bureaucratic autonomy also has a useful purpose (though many children may scoff at the idea).

Harvey Sapolsky describes how the navy's Special Projects Office received high praise for its speed and efficiency in developing the Polaris missile system. But as Sapolsky argues, the secret of success had much to do with the ability of the office to promote the Polaris's cause and protect it from outside interference:

> If, however, the Polaris experience has any lesson it is that programs cannot be distinguished on the basis of their need to be involved politically in order to gain support and independence. . . . Competitors had to be eliminated; reviewing agencies had to be outmaneuvered; congressmen, admirals, newspapermen, and academicians had to be coopted. Politics is a systemic requirement.[8]

In this instance, bureaucratic autonomy was applauded because the Polaris proved to be a farsighted and effective addition to the nation's defense. The political skills of the Polaris leaders, therefore, served an important policy purpose.

Spending ministries, similarly, play the role of advocates for programmatic expenditures. Bureaucratic autonomy serves to protect these political values. By making it difficult to impose economic-management priorities, the German pattern of policymaking accommodated other interests. Perhaps this is a worthwhile political trade-off for a polity that values financial integrity and programmatic growth as well as economic stabilization.

2. The second strategy for accommodating purposes is the exploitation of the imprecision of both economic and budgetary criteria. In most instances trying to measure the trade-off between allocation and fiscal-policy goals has little meaning. On the budgetary side, no sensible production functions, to use the economists' term, exist for health, education, soil conservation, or most other policy areas. Comparisons across divisions and ministries is a task of considerable difficulty and oftentimes of questionable usefulness.

On the economic side, it is not possible to say that an X percent unemployment rate requires a Y amount of additional public expenditure. As a consequence, instead of separating stabilization and allocation priorities as the public-finance theorists would prefer, economic-management goals are combined with program and financial objectives. Policymakers in this way exploit the ambiguous and imprecise budgetary and economic criteria for the purposes of accommodation.

Combining budget purposes means that in practice economic management is more selective than in theory. Whereas in theory the aggregate values require aggregate responses, in practice political leaders tend to respond to the economic needs of select groups. "Fiscal policy is much more directed toward specific problems in the economy that are politically relevant," stated a former budget director, "and does not have anything to do with the general world economic situation or even the situation in the Federal Republic." The government is concerned about the lagging construction industry, the high unemployment in the Ruhr coal fields, the housing market, the Volkswagon plant's overcapacity, or any number of other specific concerns that it feels it should do something about.

If the federal Finance Ministry gives antirecession funds to the state administrations, it wants to know what policy areas the money supports and if federal policy priorities have been met.[9] Additional funds provoke arguments in Bonn over whether housing, roads, or hospitals need more money, regardless of whether the money was originally granted for stabilization purposes. Since measures of multiplier effects are too time consuming and costly and work better for stimulus packages than stabilization cuts, the availability of stabilization funds is quickly translated into particular ministry programs.

Strict economic-management criteria also do not determine the level of stabilization expenditures. Policymakers agree only on the calculation of the direction of change but not the precise quantitative measure of it. This is because formal economic measures of the public budget's deficit do not agree with one another. Policymakers employed neither the full-employment surplus, the neutral-budget concept, nor any other formal measure. The kinds of criteria that did determine overall spending combined political, financial, and economic concerns in various and fluid ways.

In order to maintain the advantages of stable and incremental budgeting, policymakers also exploit the inability to accurately predict economic developments very far in advance. If economic management dictates that public spending should respond to fluctuations in private economic activity, not knowing what the fluctuations look like permits other priorities. The planning of the budget takes place one to two years prior to the actual spending of funds. At this stage, fine-tuning is not meaningfully possible, whereas rough-tuning, because it contains more slack, fits other purposes more readily. These prediction uncertainties thus allow the *Goal Projection* to serve the manifest function of setting government objectives in economic policy and the latent function of accommodating economic management to incremental budgeting.

A final way that decision makers exploit imprecise criteria is in the use of formal econometric models. Economic analyses and models should provide information that governmental decision makers want and need in their work. Economic management is concerned with aggregates including the governmental sector, which together with other undifferentiated economic sectors, produce the gross national product. The main feature of economic analysis, therefore, is the measurement of the aggregate impact of government action in relation to other sectors and the recommendation of appropriate changes in aggregate expenditure levels, debt volumes, and receipts. But governmental decision makers in Bonn do not directly employ aggregate economic measures of the public budget nor econometric models of the overall economy.

One explanation often given is their imprecision, and attempts to improve economic management have concentrated on the accuracy of formal measures of the deficit and behavioral interconnections of econometric models of the economy. German practice, however, suggests that, despite the usefulness of these improvements for economic theory, neither of them will necessarily insure a greater usage or acceptance of these analytic models in government because the emphasis on macroamounts and the tight interconnections among elements, common in formal economic analyses, does not account for nor easily permit the accommodation of incompatible budget purposes.

The Bonn government employs a form of National Accounts Model that allows for sequential and semi-independent construction of subsystems without subsuming conflict and contrary views into tightly specified coefficients. The government uses partial econometric models for particular sectors to support detailed information needs in these areas of energy, transportation, capital investment, and so forth; but adjustments among fields take place through a process of "successive approximation," in which judgment and negotiation determines the outcomes.

A degree of mutability and slippage between the participants' positions thus encourages compromise and exchange. The advantage of loosely coupled systems

Bureaucratic Politics

of this type is that they serve the strategic position of participants in bargaining by allowing for flexible and negotiable bilateral adjustment and meeting the detailed and specific information needs within particular policy fields. Loose coupling also reduces cognitive and bargaining requirements by permitting participants to concentrate on their own areas, limiting accommodation to just the aggregates of each area.

Tight interconnections, on the other hand, require that a change in one component produce appropriate changes in the other components. But if the model is based on one policy preference, for instance the economic function of the budget, it will not allow for adjustment to other budgetary preferences. In effect, the economic function becomes a nonnegotiable preference, thereby supplanting rather than supplementing the decision process. Undoubtedly, some fundamental values must remain nonnegotiable (such as the right to bargaining), but most values must remain negotiable or mutable to assure possibilities for adjustment and change. In the economic-budgetary area, for example, spending on national defense, health, the environment, or social welfare might each claim equal right to immunity from economic management, thus making these areas nonadjustable to other budget purposes. If nonnegotiable areas were allowed to proliferate in this fashion, eventually no change could occur.

In sum, there are two decision-making strategies that characterize economic policy: the emphasis on the direction of policy change rather than specific proposals; and the tendency to combine policy purposes in fluid and mutable ways rather than mutually exclusive alternatives. What is striking about these approaches to policymaking is that they are directly contrary to the prescription of public finance. Theories of public finance recommend keeping budget purposes separate; macroeconomic models of the economy build tight interconnections with little slippage.

These decision strategies are found, however, in other policy settings. Robert Axelrod describes decision making in the military assistance programs in the United States:

> The existence of a policy space in which agencies are positioned may also be useful in explaining the earlier finding that officials do not think in terms of mutually exclusive packaged alternatives. . . . Thus, the specific form in which a proposal gets packaged as an alternative may depend more on an estimate of bargaining strength than on the merits of that particular proposal. . . . If the researcher is looking for a stable aspect of this process he is more likely to find it in the general direction in which each agency is pulling rather than in the specific alternative each proposes.[10]

The presence of these strategies also fits into the typology of decision styles developed by Thompson and Tuden and elaborated by Landau (see chapter 1). An emphasis on the direction of policy is a form of trial-and-error problem solving under epistemic uncertainty. Not thinking in terms of mutually exclusive alternatives, but combining proposals in various and fluid ways, is a type of bargaining strategy under goal-based uncertainty. When decision makers do not know how severe a recession will be or how long it will last, they do not want to overcommit themselves to specific proposals that turn out to be wrong. Instead they spend a little and see how events unfold and then spend more if that is required. Likewise, proposals to determine how large an antirecession program should be are based on the bargaining positions of the Economics Ministry with the Finance Ministry, the spending ministries and the states and not just on the needs of the economy. In other words, decision makers gear their strategies to the context of the policy problem, which includes limited and uncertain knowledge and contrary political interests.

3. The third source of accommodation is the presence of informal norms. Some information must serve as common orientation points that create compatible expectations among policymakers. Types of information that serve integrative purposes are those that each participant group can recognize and at least partially understand and know how to use. The purpose of integrative information is to reduce calculational complexity and uncertainty and create mutual viewpoints and trust. Rules of thumb often aid the integrative purpose because they act as surrogates and indicators of more complex issues that each group internalizes and manipulates for its own strategic preferences. The main characteristics of integrative information, therefore, are familiarity, simplicity, wide applicability, and the capability to create common assumptions among each policymaker about what other participants will do.

The nominal growth rate in GNP, for example, despite its marginal interest for economic-management theory, receives great attention by officials in the Federal Republic as an orientation point in bargaining over public-employee union contracts, tax-revenue distribution among levels of government, and in negotiations with the spending ministries and outside interest groups. The figure serves to create common ground for bargaining that all sides can accept and use, including those groups with little or no formal economic background. Moreover, in the finance plans and the goals projections, the nominal growth in GNP assumes a regular, incremental growth trend, thereby further stabilizing and making more predictable bargaining positions.

There are also other important norms that guide fiscal policy in the Federal Republic. They range over grants in aid, the size of the public budget, what constitutes full employment, and so forth. Norms concerning the economy are

1. If unemployment approaches or exceeds one million workers, the government must take discretionary action to reduce it.
2. If the inflation rate goes above 5 percent, the government needs to control expenditures and emphasize monetary restraint.
3. Policymakers face a trade-off between structural changes in the economy

and anticyclical policy. Short-term measures may jeopardize long-term growth.
4. Policymakers should try for a steady 4 percent growth in GNP as the most desirable rate. Do not choose as a goal the extremes of what is possible.

Norms concerning the budget are

1. The public sector should grow at the same or a slightly increasing proportion of GNP.
2. The budget must be balanced in the longer-term, and deficit spending may only amount to the volume of investment expenditures.
3. In recessions, try for a 12 to 15 percent nominal budget growth; in inflationary periods, work for a 6 to 8 percent growth rate.
4. The relative shares of the tax yield must not change very much between levels of government.
5. The planning stage of the public budget is to be dominated by financial and political allocation concerns; stabilization policy enters only later, just prior to the execution stage.
6. The Cabinet does not like to entertain further budget changes once the budget has been approved by them.

Norms concerning antirecession programs and grants are

1. Antirecession programs must not exceed 1 percent of GNP (10 billion marks), for that is too alarming politically. In times of stagflation, they should be around 1 to 2 billion marks to emphasize action with restraint.
2. Antirecession programs have more political impact than the automatic stabilizers built into the budget because the public sees that the government is doing something to aid the economy.
3. With only a six-month lead time, an antirecession program must not exceed 2 to 3 billion marks because there is not enough time to prepare more meaningful projects of larger size. The government would have to resort to *digging ditches;* that is, meaningless expenditures just to stimulate the economy.
4. Anticyclical programs must consist of investment expenditures only; other expenditures only raise costs and are too rigid to vary in the short run.
5. Do not vary revenue sharing anticyclically because such a policy interferes too much with redistribution goals.

The state governments also have several informal norms that guide action, such as the belief that a balanced budget has a neutral impact on the economy (see chapter 5).

Do these norms make a difference for policy? Like more formal economic theories, they are guides to policy choice and common orientation points for policymakers to judge performance. Actual policy does not always conform to these standards, but the standards do influence how policy is formulated and evaluated. In his study of fiscal policy in the United States, Lawrence Pierce identifies similar norms and argues that they can simplify decision making and "act as guides to action, just as the rules derived from modern economic theory are guides to action.[11] In similar fashion, informal norms in the Federal Republic are a mixture of economics and politics and, while not held by everyone, do make a difference for public policy.

Turbulence and Federal-Fiscal Relations

Economic management produces uncertainty in expenditure policy. One means to reduce the uncertainty is to shift its negative effects onto other levels of government, thereby creating a form of turbulence in federal-fiscal relations.[12] But contrary to the position taken by the public-finance economists, the central government is not immune from shifting this uncertainty to other government levels, and in so doing sacrificing the collective macrobudget objective.

The central government of most federal systems competes with state and local governments over tax revenues and control over policy jurisdictions. Issues also arise increasingly not at the national level but internationally, saddling the central government with problems that are larger than its jurisdiction.[13] The central government, moreover, is not one unit but a collection of competing agencies and individuals that have different interests and perspectives. In addition, macropolicies have interconnections that are not well understood, thereby challenging the ability of the central government to know what to do.

The effect of expenditure uncertainty on federal-fiscal relations is well illustrated by the inability of the Finance Planning Council to maintain stable patterns of joint participation by the state and central governments during the recent boom-recession cycle. Bonn also increased domestic grants to the states and municipalities. But investment grants constitute a major engine for growth in state and local budgets, which takes sales-tax revenue away from the central government. With two leaks in the federal-budget bucket, Bonn turned from the problems of the economy to the deterioration of its financial position.

Certainty is thus not possible for everyone. The form that investment stimulus grants should take to satisfy economic management would be open-ended, general-purpose subsidies that allow the local units to choose the projects and how much to spend. In this way, the fiscal-policy intentions of the central government would conflict least with the allocation priorities of the municipalities. But Bonn rejected this approach because it did not guarantee the size of the programs nor the specifics of what would be done with the money.

But if the central government attempts to control detailed project selection through set ceilings and specified matching requirements, the result is to increase uncertainty for the municipalities and states which now have to adjust their own priorities and levels of spending to the wishes of the federal government. The same inability to avoid uncertainty is present in deciding how to distribute the funds among the states. If a population formula is used for matching grants, the poorer states will have to pay as much per capita as the wealthy states, even though the latter usually have larger reserves for stabilization purposes.

This policy dilemma is related to the policy-administration division of labor between the states and Bonn. The central government makes macroeconomic policy but has only indirect influence over its administration. To compensate for this deficiency, Bonn has tried to assure that its policy goals are implemented by regulating the details of how policy is administered. The state governments have reacted by hiring their own economic analysts to make projections and forecasts and by generally asserting their own control over policy. They also have withheld information, dragged their feet on projects that they did not prefer, and made cooperation difficult.

This tendency for administrators and policymakers to expand into each other's domain, according to Wildavsky, has a political rationale:

> Each one [administrators and policymakers] can reduce the bargaining powers of the other by taking unto himself some of his competitors advantages. Thus the administrators may recruit their own policy analysts to compete with the evaluators who, in turn, will seek their own contacts within the administrative apparatus in order to ensure a steady and reliable flow of information. If this feuding goes far enough, the result will be two organizations acting in much the same way as the single one they replaced but with additional problems of coordination.[14]

Not so surprisingly, Bonn shifted its policy emphasis from budget policy to tax and monetary policies. Both of these strategies short-circuit the need for administration by the states and thus give Bonn a more direct control over the policies' intent.

If saddling the central government with the risks of economic management does not work, what can the government do to avoid turbulence in federal-fiscal relations? Although no one right answer is possible because expenditure uncertainty will not disappear, a reasonable path to follow may be the attempt to share the uncertainty among levels as much as possible rather than the present option to leave it concentrated at one level or another.

The strategy of combining budget purposes has the effect of sharing the multiple uncertainties among the various participants. If allocation decisions take too long for fiscal-policy needs, paying attention to them creates uncertainty in managing the economy. But the short-term, macro-orientation of fiscal policies, in turn, creates uncertainty for state and federal budget planners in transportation, regional development, housing, and so forth. Zeroing in on the fiscal-policy goal by eradicating all uncertainties in its path overly threatens other interests. Hence a coalition develops against the macroeconomic objective.

Managing the economy is not the only policy area that must face multiple uncertainties that cut across political interests. Albert Hirshman, for example, in his studies of development projects in poor countries identifies similar kinds of contrary interests that trade-off redistribution of wealth, economic growth, political conflict, and efficiency. He concludes that:

> The attempt to eliminate totally one particular kind of uncertainty may not only be futile, but counter-productive. . . . It will often be impossible to mitigate some uncertainty judged excessive or particularly obnoxious, by increasing another one. . . . Planners should think in terms of an optimal mix or constellation of the various uncertainties.[15]

In economic management the problem takes the form of trying to reconcile the contrary uncertainties of demand (accurately predicting the needs of the economy) and supply (providing enough time to plan meaningful additional expenditures). Deciding where the two curves should intersect is the primary political issue facing policymakers.

How might this work? The last German grants-in-aid antirecession-stimulus package of September 1975 serves as a conceivable model of this approach to using grants in aid for fiscal-policy objectives. In this program, the central government set the overall size and determined the broad expenditure area (above-surface construction), but the selection of projects and monitoring of progress was left mostly to the state and local governments.

The only other alternative to a mixed strategy is the abandonment of investment grants-in-aid stimulus packages altogether and a shift in emphasis to the monetary instrument. But in the past monetary policy has not proved effective because of the openness of the German federal economy to interest-rate-induced capital flows. In addition, in the German federal system, the Bundesbank enjoys an independent status vis-à-vis the central government, and an emphasis on monetary policy would make political management of economic policy more a matter of negotiation than it is already. Over the past ten years, moreover, the local and state investment expenditure and credit assumption have shown a pronounced procyclical development. These cyclical swings in local expenditure cause disruption of local construction employment and the provision of local services. Consequently the monetary alternative solves the problem of expenditure uncertainty but does not necessarily adequately deal with the need for macrobudget policy.

To forego antirecession spending also deprives the government of the political symbolic rewards of discretionary economic management. Automatic measures generate little publicity and do not require special meetings and pronouncements of the Cabinet. Without the need to gain political support or take any special measures, automatic stabilizers have virtually no symbolic or psychological effect on the political or business communities.

If the government adheres to a grants-in-aid fiscal-policy strategy, it must decide on adequate distribution of the grants among the state and local governments. Ideally the distribution should not discriminate among the states, but that has been shown to be impossible no matter what distribution formula is employed. A possible way out of this dilemma is to trade-off autonomy for the wealthier states with equity for the poorer ones by having the central government attach more strings to a higher percentage subsidy. Presumably, the larger and wealthier states will choose fewer strings and more autonomy in exchange for smaller subsidies, while the poorer states will opt for more strings and less independence in exchange for larger subsidies. Although everything has its price, both rich and poor retain their right to choose.

A second possible strategy for dealing more adequately with the distribution problem is to include the municipalities in the system of mandatory stabilization reserves. The most likely municipal source of income that could serve this purpose is the local government's share of the income tax. Ideally the reserves would form one large fund that then could be distributed according to need. But more realistically a policy to create a municipal account at the Bundesbank would have to allow each individual contributor to regain his money given the appropriate economic circumstances. Even though the poorer cities' reserves would be less than the wealthy ones, the existence of any reserves at all is preferable to the present situation.

A final source of unavoidable uncertainty has been the type of decision making found in Bonn and in the intragovernmental arena. Bonn's decisions are characterized by informal, back-and-forth discussion. Prediction uncertainty and theoretical ambiguity actually aided agreement. Since the motivations of the participants were not challenged, ambiguity lubricated the negotiations. Analytical ambiguity, however, had the opposite effect on the formal, rigid relations among government levels. Here ambiguity created greater suspicion and conflict. Apparently the interaction effects between analysis and politics depend on the decision setting, especially its size, formality, and iterative aspects. The relation between politics and analysis, then, deserves closer scrutiny.

Analysis and Interactive Politics

The mixed purposes of the antirecession programs demonstrates the worth of not always clarifying objectives. Although trying to resolve analytical contraditions is desirable for academic theory, attempting to erase incompatibilities in policy goals is not always beneficial for government practice.[16] Favorable conditions in particular allow individuals as well as organizations to live with contradictory goals; only when difficult times arrive do circumstances force hard choices between objectives.[17] But the concern with clarifying contradictions has led some people to argue that mixed-purpose programs indicate a lack of planning between more or less beneficial policies. Yet clarifying goals entails real costs for some groups if the clarifications exclude or hinder them from further full participation in the program. Analysts must weigh these groups' opposition against the potential benefits (if any) to be derived from clarifying contradictory purposes.

Second, analysis attempts to separate components because allowing everything to vary at once overwhelms theory; politics tends to combine components and integrate functions to prevent independent variation from overturning agreement. For this reason, analytical ambiguity can serve a political purpose by allowing decision makers to combine elements in ways that do not overly jeopardize most groups' interests. It also suggests that technical improvements in partial analyses that assume other things to be equal, may initially increase conflict by making the political attempts to combine components more difficult.

In one way, however, both politics and analysis share common ground: both are hypotheses aimed at solving certain problems, either intellectual or actual. A particular analytical construct is not sacrosanct nor is a certain political configuration or organizational arrangement beyond criticism. Both are means to uncertain ends. The hypothetical and tentative character of politics and analysis makes them compatible. Their compatibility lies in the way they complement each other. Open, back-and-forth bargaining, for example, requires analysis for strategic purposes to convince others of the worth of one's preferences. Totalitarian dictatorships, in contrast, do not want analysis because the party's ideology and leader's utterances are not subject to factual dispute.

But analysis combined with politics sometimes produces policy that is unfamiliar to those concerned with strict analytic norms. To choose a more regular growth trend for GNP makes sense for incremental budgeting but has less plausibility for economic theory. To use National Accounts analyses instead of econometric models puzzles academic economists but not government forecasters who know what information better fits a political decision process. Likewise, the macrobudget serves as a useful theoretical idea, but attempts to draw one up do not work because no political or organizational constituency makes the macrobudget its primary responsibility. Drawing up special stabilization budgets in advance, while ostensibly directed at solving the problem of disrupting allocation preferences, ends up creating distrust and inflexibility in economic and budgetary policies.

Yet analysis and politics can complement each other in several ways. Politics can inform analysis by showing what is possible given the political and institutional forces and resources at hand; analysis can instruct politics by directing those forces and resources to useful policy ends. Trying something that does not work well, such as drawing up stabilization budgets in advance, may eventually alter original political agreements, costs, and risks. A policy that seemed a good political choice at one point may prove to contain a political cost later on because of wrong analysis. But analysis, if it does not account for political or institutional costs and benefits or makes unreasonable assumptions about the ability to manipulate the government and the society, may either end up on the shelf or in excessive conflict for those who try to implement it. The need is not to abandon analysis but to devise ways to provide information that policymakers can use to improve the outcomes of political decision making.

The policy environment is not constant, nor do other things usually remain equal. The assumption of harmony especially ignores the problem of uncertainty that may arise in other policy areas as a result of attempts to deal with the analytical problems of one particular policy priority. Uncertainty is an entity that is not easily captured by efforts within one area nor eradicated by efforts in many areas. The task of political analysis is to find ways to distribute its effects without jeopardizing policy benefits.

Although the major interconnections in the economy are not well understood, for example, the way government groups and institutions respond to each others' efforts to deal with these problems is even less well anticipated. Political analysis needs to worry not only about the correct policy for the economy but also the right policy for the government, including other policy goals.

Since conflict over many of these issues forced a shift in the Bonn government away from earlier macrobudget objectives, assuming other things to be equal may be the very avenue to ineffective policy. The task of political analysis is to point out the unstable character of uncertainty and the potential recoil effect that may result if one policy area bears its entire burden. Analysis should explore ways to distribute uncertainty so that top priority goals, which often entail the most risks, do not get sacrificed for conflict reduction efforts.

Another important role for analysis is to provide an intellectual understanding of the overall consequences of individual actions. At times, interactive bargaining among institutional and political actors produces outcomes that jeopardize the macroperspective. Budgeting priorities, for instance, do not always meet macroeconomic needs. Individual ministry preferences produce procyclical expenditure patterns, even though the spending in question may not be tied to a particular business-cycle tax. In a federal polity, the organizational interaction of various levels can also lead to conflicts and strategies that injure the overall, collective benefit.

The wrong way to deal with these problems analytically is to ignore selective interests in efforts to create collective goods. No matter how intellectually compelling the formation of a macrobudget is, decision makers will not form one if it runs counter to their own interests. The task of analysis is to bring selective and collective interests together by devising overall policies that either change the selective interests or fit them into broader schemes. For this purpose, it is necessary to understand these interests and determine how stable they are in relation to the collective undesirable consequences. The intellectual challenge of fitting selective interests into macropolicies is, of course, greater than developing macropolicies by themselves; but the potential rewards for analysts, in the way of possibly seeing their recommendations successfully adopted, should encourage the efforts.

Notes

1. Learned Hand, quoted in *Bartlett's Familiar Quotations* 14th ed., ed. John Bartlett, (Boston: Little, Brown and Co., 1968), p. 912.

2. Harvey Sapolsky, *The Polaris System Development: Bureaucratic and Programmatic Success in Government* (Cambridge: Harvard University Press, 1972), p. 230.

3. See, Joseph Scherer and James A. Papke, eds., *Public Finance and Fiscal Policy* (Boston: Houghton Mifflin Co., 1966), pp. 3–39 and 56–71, for a general discussion of the expenditure process and the role of fiscal policy.

4. See, Renate Mayntz and Fritz Scharpf, *Planungsorganization: Die Diskussion um die Reform von Regierung und Verwaltung des Bundes* (Munich: R. Piper, 1973), p. 50, who argue that the macroeconomic stopgap practice cuts out new reforms and programs rather than the established expenditures which are fixed as a consequence of legal or political ties.

5. For an analysis of the importance of trust for budgetary relations, see, Hugh Heclo and Aaron Wildavsky, *The Private Government of Public Money: Community and Policy Inside British Politics* (Berkeley: University of California Press, 1974), pp. 15–20, 61–63, and 120–123.

6. See, for instance, Edward M. Gramlich, "Measures of the Aggregate Demand Impact of the Federal Budget," in *Budget Concepts for Economic Analysis,* ed. Wilfred Lewis, Jr. (Washington, D.C.:The Brookings Institution, 1968), pp.110–126. Gramlich states that, "the crude measures that were so helpful in the early 1960s, when demand was well below its full employment potential, will no longer do now that the economy has entered a period when 'fine-tuning' is the word of the day" (p. 110).

7. The impact of crisis situations on the dominance of bureaucratic routines and processes over policy is explored in Graham T. Allison, *Essence of Decision: Explaining the Cuban Missile Crisis* (Boston: Little, Brown and Co., 1971); Robert Art, "Bureaucratic Politics and American Foreign Policy: A Critique," *Policy Sciences* 4(1973):467–490; Stephen D. Krasner, "Are Bureaucracies Important? (Or Allison Wonderland)," *Foreign Policy* (Summer 1972):159–179; and Francis Rourke, *Bureaucracy and Foreign Policy* (Baltimore: Johns Hopkins University Press, 1972).

8. Sapolsky, *The Polaris System Development,* p. 244.

9. See Arnold Meltsner, *The Politics of City Revenue* (Berkeley: University of California Press, 1971), p. 253, who argues that even unconditional grants usually have strings attached.

10. Robert Axelrod, "Bureaucratic Decision Making in the Military Assistance Program," in *Readings in American Foreign Policy,* ed. Morton Halperin and Arnold Kanter, (Boston: Little, Brown and Co., 1973), p. 165.

11. Lawrence Pierce, *The Politics of Fiscal Policy Formation* (Pacific Palisades, California: Goodyear Publishing Co., 1971), p. 33.

12. For discussions of the concept of turbulence, see, F. Emery and E. Trist, "The Causal Texture of Organizational Environments," *Human Relations* 18(1965):21–32; Ernst B. Haas, *The Obsolescence of Regional Integration Theory,* Research Monograph no. 25 (Berkeley: Institute for International Studies, University of California, 1975), pp. 3–20 and 40–63; and J.L. Metcalfe, "Systems Models, Economic Models and the Causal Texture of Organizational Environments: An Approach to Macro-Organization Theory," *Human Relations* 27(1974):639–663. Metcalfe in particular emphasizes that macroeconomic theory is a systems level approach: ". . . .what is individually rational may be collectively irrational and vice versa" (p. 649).

13. Haas, *The Obsolescence of Regional Integration Theory,* p. 9, who points out that one reason for turbulence in the environment of the European Community is that many major issues have their origin in world economic interdependencies. This seems also to be a main factor that forced the federal government in Germany to retreat from macroeconomic-budget objectives.

14. Aaron Wildavsky, "The Self-Evaluating Organization," *Public Administration Review* 32(September/October 1972):515.

15. Albert O. Hirschman, *Development Projects Observed* (Washington, D.C.: The Brookings Institution, 1967), p. 84.

16. See, for example, Harold Garfinkel, *Studies in Ethnomethodology* (Englewood Cliffs, New Jersey: Prentice Hall, 1967), p. 270; and Charles Lindblom, "Some Limitations on Rationality," in *Rational Decision* 7, ed. Carl J. Friedrichs (New York: Atherton Press, 1964), pp. 224–228. Lindblom states, "In collective decision making, do not try to clarify values if the parties concerned can agree on policies, as they often can, despite their disagreement on values" (p. 227).

17. Aaron Wildavsky, *Budgeting: A Comparative Theory of Budgetary Processes* (Boston: Little, Brown and Co., 1975), ch. 4 and 5.

Bibliography

"Aktuelle Beiträge zur Wirtschafts- und Finanzpolitik." 121 Bonn: Presse- und Informationsamt der Bundesregierung, 27 November 1974.

Allison, Graham T. *Essence of Decision: Explaining the Cuban Missile Crisis.* Boston: Little, Brown and Co., 1971.

Apel, Hans. "Massnahmen zur Verbesserung der Haushaltsstruktur und zur Verminderung der Kreditaufnahme." Bonn: Bundesministerium der Finanzen, Referat Presse- und Information, 8 September 1975.

Arndt, Hans-Joachim. *West Germany: The Politics of Non-Planning.* Syracuse, New York: Syracuse University Press, 1966.

Art, Robert. "Bureaucratic Politics and American Foreign Policy: A Critique." *Policy Sciences* 4(1973):467–490.

Baratz, Morton S., and Farr, Helen T. "Is Municipal Finance Fiscally Perverse?" *National Tax Journal* 12(September 1959):276–284.

"Bericht über die Konjunktur- und Sonderprogramme 1974–75." Bonn: Deutscher Bundestag, Bundestags-Drucksache, 7/4677, 1975.

Biehl, Dieter; Jüttemeier Karl-Heinz; and Legler, Harald. "Zu den konjunkturellen Wirkungen der Haushaltspolitik in der Bundesrepublik Deutschland 1960–70," *Die Weltwirtschaft.* Heft 2. Kiel: Institut für Weltwirtschaft, University of Kiel, 1971, pp. 142 ff.

———. "Zu den konjunkturellen Effekten der Länder- und Gemeindehaushalte in der Bundesrepublik Deutschland 1960–74," *Die Weltwirtschaft.* Heft 1. Kiel: Institute für Weltwirtschaft, University of Kiel, 1974.

Blinder, Alan S., and Solow, Robert M. *The Economics of Public Finance.* Washington, D.C.: The Brookings Institution, 1974.

Braybrooke, David, and Lindblom, Charles. *A Strategy of Decision.* New York: The Free Press, 1970.

Büchmann, Walter. "Planung, Kreditbeschränkung und kommunale Selbstverwaltung." *Archiv für Kommunalwissenschaften* 13, no. 2(1974):63–77.

Bundesministerium der Finanzen. *Finanzberichte.* Bonn: Bundesministerium der Finanzen, 1970–1980.

Bundesministerium für Wirtschaft. "Grundfragen der Stabilitätspolitik." Gutachten des Wissenschaftlichen Beirats beim Bundesministerium für Wirtschaft, Studienreihe 2(March 1973).

Bureau of the Census. "Guide to Recurrent and Special Governmental Statistics." Washington, D.C.: Superintendent of Documents, U.S. Government Printing Office, April 1976.

Caiden, Naomi, and Wildavsky, Aaron. *Planning and Budgeting in Poor Countries.* New York: John Wiley and Sons, 1974.

Campbell, John Creighton. *The Japanese Budgetary Process*. Berkeley: University of California Press, 1975.
Capron, William. "The Impact of Analysis on Bargaining in Government." In *The Politics of the Federal Bureaucracy*, ed. Alan Altshuler. New York: Dodd, Mead, and Co., 1975, pp. 196-211.
Chant, John F., and Acheson, Keith. "The Choice of Monetary Instruments and the Theory of Bureaucracy." *Public Choice* 12(Spring 1972).
Congressional Budget Office, U.S. Congress. *Temporary Measures to Stimulate Employment: An Evaluation of Some Alternatives*. Washington, D.C.: U.S. Government Printing Office, 2 September 1975.
Conradt, David P. *The German Polity*. New York: Longman, 1978.
Cowart, Andrew T. "Economic Policies of European Governments I: Monetary Policy," *British Journal of Political Science* 8(July 1978):285-311.
―――. "Economic Policies of European Governments II: Fiscal Policy," *British Journal of Political Science* 8(October 1978):425-439.
Cyert, Richard, and March, James. *A Behavioral Theory of the Firm*. Englewood Cliffs, New Jersey: Prentice-Hall, 1963.
Dawson, Richard, and Robinson, James A. "Inter-Party Competition, Economic Variables, and Welfare Policies in the American States." *The Journal of Politics* 25(1963):265-289.
Diesing, Paul. *Reason in Society: Five Types of Decisions and Their Social Conditions*. Urbana: University of Illinois Press, 1962.
Dye, Thomas R. *Politics, Economics, and the Public: Policy Outcomes in the States*. Chicago: Rand McNally, 1966.
Ecker-Racz, L.L. *The Politics and Economics of State and Local Finance*. Englewood Cliffs, New Jersey: Prentice-Hall, 1970.
Edelman, Murray. *The Symbolic Uses of Politics*. Chicago: University of Illinois Press, 1967.
Emery, F.E., and Trist, E.L. "The Causal Texture of Organizational Environments." *Human Relations* 18(1965):21-32.
Engerman, Stanley. "Regional Aspects of Stabilization Policy." In *Essays in Fiscal Federalism*, ed. Richard Musgrave. Washington, D.C.: The Brookings Institution, 1965.
Ernst, W. "Wozu Neugliederung?" *Die Oeffentliche Verwaltung* (1974):12ff.
Fried, Robert C. "Party and Policy in West German Cities." *The American Political Science Review* 70(March 1976):11-24.
Friedman, Milton, and Heller, Walter W. *Monetary vs. Fiscal Policy* New York: W.W. Norton, 1969.
Garfinkel, Harold. *Studies in Ethnomethodology*. Englewood Cliffs, New Jersey: Prentice-Hall, 1967.
Geske, Otto Erich. "Koordinierung der Finanzpolitiken von Bund, Ländern und Gemeinden: Möglichkeiten und Grenzen," *Wirtschaftsdienst*, Heft 7 (1955):372-373.

Giersch, Herbert. *Current Problems of the German Economy, 1976–1977.* Washington, D.C.: American Enterprise Institute for Public Policy Research, 1977, based on a discussion with Herbert Giersch on 9 November 1976.
Godwin, R. Kenneth, and Shepard, W. Bruce. "Political Process and Public Expenditures: A Re-examination Based on Theories of Representative Government." *The American Political Science Review* 70(December 1976):1127–1135.
Gramlich, Edward M. "Measures of the Aggregate Demand Impact of the Federal Budget," in *Budget Concepts for Economic Analysis.* ed. Wilfred Lewis, Jr. Washington, D.C.: The Brookings Institution, 1968.
Gross, Bertram. "The Managers of National Economic Change." In *Public Administration and Democracy,* ed. Roscoe Martin. Syracuse, New York: Syracuse University Press, 1965.
Haas, Ernst B. *The Obsolescence of Regional Integration Theory.* Research Series no. 25. Berkeley: Institute of International Studies, University of California, 1975.
Hahn, Thomas. "Förderung des Sozialen Wohnungsbaues: Dargestellt unter besonderer Berücksichtigung der Aufstellung und Durchführung der jährlichen Wohnungsbauprogramme in Baden-Württemberg." October 1974, paper.
Halperin, Morton H. *Bureaucratic Politics and Foreign Policy.* Washington, D.C.: The Brookings Institution, 1974.
Hammond, Thomas H., and Knott, Jack H. *A Zero-Based Look at Zero-Base Budgeting.* New Brunswick, New Jersey: Transaction Books, 1980.
Hansen, Alvin H., and Perloff, Harvey S. *State and Local Finance in the National Economy.* New York: W.W. Norton, 1944.
Hansen, Bent, and Snyder, Wayne. *Fiscal Policy in Seven Countries 1955–65.* United Kingdom: OECD Publications, 1969.
Hansmeyer, Karl-Heinz. *Staatswirtschaftliche Planungsinstrumente.* Tuebingen: J.C.B. Mohr, 1973.
Heclo, Hugh, and Wildavsky, Aaron. *The Private Government of Public Money: Community and Policy Inside British Politics.* Berkeley: University of California Press, 1974.
Hibbs, Douglas A., Jr. "Political Parties and Macroeconomic Policy." *American Political Science Review* 71(December 1977):1467–1487.
Hirschman, Albert O. *Development Projects Observed.* Washington, D.C.: The Brookings Institution, 1967.
Hosse, Dietrich. *Aufbau und Ablauf der Kommunikation im Arbeitsbereich des Finanzplanungsrates.* Opladen: Westdeutscher Verlag, 1975.
Institut Finanzen und Steuern, "Information über die Entwicklung der öffentlichen Finanzwirtschaft in der Bundesrepublik Deutschland von 1964 bis 1974." Bonn: Institut Finanzen und Steuern, 1974, working paper.
Johnson, Nevil. *Government in the Federal Republic of Germany: The Executive at Work.* Oxford: Pergamon Press, 1973.

Karstens, Karl. *Politische Führung: Erfahrungen im Dienst der Bundesregierung.* Stuttgart: Deutscher Verlag, 1971.
Klein, Richard. "Konjunkturbelebung und städtische Leistungskraft im Widerstreit." *Der Städtetag,* Heft 10 (October 1975).
Klein, R., and Gleitze, J.M. "Gemeindefinanzbericht," *Der Städtetag.* Stuttgart: W. Kohlhammer Verlag, January 1975.
Knott, Jack. "Conflict Behavior and Accommodation: The Case of Labor Relations in Weimar and the German Federal Republic." 1973, paper.
Koch, Heinz. *Stabilitätspolitik im Föderalistischen System der Bundesrepublik Deutschland.* Cologne: Bund Verlag, 1975.
Kommission für die Finanzreform, "Gutachten über die Finanzreform in der Bundesrepublik Deutschland." Stuttgart: Verlag W. Kohlhammer, 1966.
Korff, Hans Clausen. *Haushaltspoltik: Instrument öffentlicher Macht.* Stuttgart: Verlag W. Kohlhammer, 1975.
Kramer, Hans; Schuler, Manfred; Stümpfig, Gerhard; Weis, Dieter. *Gemeindehaushalt und Konjunktur.* Cologne and Opladen: Westdeutscher Verlag, 1966.
Landau, Martin. "Decision Theory and Comparative Public Administration," *Comparative Political Studies,* 1, no. 2 (July 1968) 175–195.
———. *Political Theory and Political Science.* New York: Macmillan Co., 1972.
Levy, Frank; Meltsner, Arnold; and Wildavsky, Aaron. *Urban Outcomes: Schools, Streets, and Libraries.* Berkeley: University of California Press, 1974.
Lindblom, Charles E. "Some Limitations on Rationality." In *Rational Decision,* ed. Carl J. Friedrichs. New York: Atherton Press, 1964, pp. 224–228.
———. *Politics and Markets: The World's Political-Economic Systems.* New York: Basic Books, 1977.
———. *The Intelligence of Democracy.* New York: The Free Press, 1965.
———. "The Science of Muddling Through." *Public Administration Review* 19 (Spring 1959) 79–88.
Lompe, Klaus. "The Role of Scientific Planning in the Governmental Process: The German Experience." *The American Journal of Economics and Sociology* 29, no. 4 (October 1970):369–387.
Markmann, Heinz, and Simmert, Diethard B., eds., *Krise der Wirtschaftspolitik.* Cologne: Bund-Verlag, 1978.
Maunz, Theodor; Dürig, Günter; and Herzog, Roman. *Grundgesetz Kommentar.* Munich: C.H. Beck'scher Verlag, 1973.
Mayntz, Renate, and Scharpf, Fritz. *Planungsorganisation: Die Diskussion um die Reform von Regierung und Verwaltung des Bundes.* Munich: R. Piper, 1973.
———. *Policy Making in the German Federal Bureaucracy.* New York: Elsevier, 1975.
Meltsner, Arnold J. *The Politics of City Revenue.* Berkeley: University of California Press, 1971.

Meltsner, Arnold, and Wildavsky, Aaron. "Leave City Budgeting Alone." In *Financing the Metropolis: Public Policy in Urban Economics,* ed. John P. Crecine, Beverly Hills: Sage Publications, 1970.

Metcalfe, J.L. "Systems Models, Economic Models and the Causal Texture or Organizational Environments: An Approach to Macro-Organization Theory." *Human Relations* 27, no. 7 (June–December 1974).

Musgrave, Richard. "Approaches to a Fiscal Theory of Political Federalism." In *Public Finances: Needs, Sources, and Utilization,* National Bureau of Economic Research. Princeton, New Jersey: Princeton University Press, 1961.

Musgrave, Richard, ed. *Essays in Fiscal Federalism.* Washington, D.C.: The Brookings Institution, 1965.

Musgrave, Richard. *The Theory of Public Finance.* New York: McGraw-Hill, 1959.

Naschold, Fritz. "Untersuchung zur Mehrjährigen Finanzplanung des Bundes." *Gutachten.* Bonn: Projektgruppe Regierungs- und Verwaltungs reform, 1971.

Neuman, M. "Zur ökonomischen Theorie des Föderalismus." *Kyklos* 24(1971):493 ff.

Olson, Mancur. *The Logic of Collective Action: Public Goods and the Theory of Groups.* Cambridge: Harvard University Press, 1965.

Perrow, Charles. *Complex Organizations: A Critical Essay.* Glenview, Illinois: Scott, Foresman, 1972.

Pierce, Lawrence C. *The Politics of Fiscal Policy Formation.* Pacific Palisades, California: Goodyear Publishing, 1971.

Porter, David O., with Warner, David C., and Porter, Teddie W. *The Politics of Budgeting Federal Aid: Resource Mobilization by Local School Districts.* Beverly Hills: A Sage Professional Publication, 1973.

"Programm der Bundesregierung zur Stärkung von Bau und anderen Investitionen." *Bulletin* 106. Bonn: Presse- und Informationsamt der Bundesregierung, 2 September 1975, pp. 1037–1043.

Quade, E.S. "Systems Analysis Techniques for Public Policy Problems," in *Perspectives on Public Bureaucracy,* 2nd ed., ed. Fred A. Kramer, Cambridge, Mass.: Winthrop Publishers, 1977.

Raabe, Karl-Heinz. "Gesamtwirtschaftliche Analysen, Prognosen, und Projektionen und ihre Rolle in der Wirtschaftspolitik." 12 December 1974, obtained directly from the Economics Ministry.

———. "Gesamtwirtschaftliche Prognosen und Projektionen als Hilfsmittel der Wirtschaftspolitik in der Bundesrepublik Deutschland." *Allgemeines Statistisches Archiv* (January 1974): 1–31.

———. "Prognosen und Projektionen der Kurzfristigen Wirtschaftsentwicklung in der Bundesrepublik Deutschland (Methode und Verfahren)." Bonn: Bundesministerium für Wirtschaft, 1969.

Rafuse, Robert W., Jr. "Cyclical Behavior of State-Local Finances." In *Essays in Fiscal Federalism,* ed. Richard Musgrave. Washington, D.C.: The Brookings Institution, 1965.

Rakoff, Stuart A., and Schaefer, Guenther F. "Policy Responsiveness of German and American Cities: A Times Series Analysis of Municipal Expenditures." Prepared for the 1973 Annual Meeting of American Political Science Association, New Orleans, 4–8 September 1973.

Reissert, Bernd. *Die finanzielle Beteiligung des Bundes an Aufgaben der Länder und das Postulat der "Einheitlichkeit der Lebensverhältnisse im Bundesgebiet."* Bonn-Bad Godesberg: Vorwärts-Druck, 1975.

———. "Politikverflechtung als Hindernis der staatlichen Aufgabenerfüllung." *Wirtschaftsdienst* 8(1976):413–415.

Reuss, Frederick G. *Fiscal Policy for Growth without Inflation: The German Experiment.* Baltimore: Johns Hopkins University Press, 1963.

Rein, Martin. *Social Science and Public Policy.* New York: Penguin Books, 1976.

Rolf, Earl, and Break, George. *Public Finance.* New York: Ronald Press Company, 1961.

Rothweiler, Robert L. "Revenue Sharing in the Federal Republic of Germany." *Publius* 2, no. 1 (Spring 1972):4–25.

Rourke, Francis. *Bureaucracy and Foreign Policy.* Baltimore: Johns Hopkins University Press, 1972.

Rowan, D.C., and Mayer, Thomas. *Intermediate Macro-Economics: Output, Inflation, and Growth.* New York: W.W. Norton and Company, 1972.

"Rückläufige Finanz- und Leistungskraft: Auszüge aus städtischen Haushaltsreden 1975," *Der Städtetag.* Stuttgart: W. Kohlhammer Verlag, January 1975, pp. 16–24.

Sachverständigenkommission für die Neugliederung des Bundesgebietes beim Bundesminister des Innern, Vorschläge zur Neugliederung des Bundesgebietes gemäss Artikel 296G. Bonn: Bundesministerium des Innern, 1973.

Sachverständigenrat zur Begutachtung der Gesamtwirtschaftlichen Entwicklung. "Zur konjunkturpolitischen Lage im Mai 1973." *Sondergutachten.* Stuttgart: W. Kohlhammer Verlag, 4 May 1973.

Sapolsky, Harvey M. *The Polaris System Development: Bureaucratic and Programmatic Success in Government.* Cambridge: Harvard University, 1972.

Scharpf, Fritz W. "Alternativen des Deutschen Föderalismus: Für ein handlungsfähiges Entwicklungssystem." West Berlin: International Institute of Management, 1974.

———. "Krisenpolitik" *Gesprächskreis: Wissenschaft und Politik.* Bonn-Bad Godesberg: Friedrich Ebert Stiftung, 1974.

———. *Planung als politischer Prozess: Aufsätze zur Theorie der Planenden Demoktratie.* Frankfurt am Main: Suhrkamp Verlag, 1973.

Scharpf, Fritz W.; Reissert, Bernd; and Schnabel, Fritz. *Politikverflechtung: Theorie und Empirie des kooperativen Föderalismus in der Bundesrepublik.* Kronberg/Ts.: Scriptor Verlag, 1976.

Schelling, Thomas. "On the Ecology of Micro-Motives." *The Public Interest* 25 (Fall 1971):59–98.
Scherer, Joseph, and Papke, James A. *Public Finance and Fiscal Policy.* Boston: Houghton-Mifflin, 1966.
Schick, Allen. *Budget Innovation in the States.* Washington, D.C.: The Brookings Institution, 1971.
———. "The Road to PPB: The Stages of Budget Reform," *Public Administration Review* 26 (December 1966):243–258.
Schmid, Günter, and Treiber, Hubert. *Bürokratie und Politik: Zur Struktur und Funktion der Ministerialbürokratie in der Bundesrepublik Deutschland.* Munich: Wilhelm Fink Verlag, 1975.
Schoeninger, Karl-Eugen. "Konjunkturstabilisierung als Koordinationsproblem zwischen den Trägern der Wirtschaftspolitik." *Schriften zur Wirtschaftswissenschaftlichen Forschung,* Band 54 (1972):19236.
Sharkansky, Ira, and Hofferbert, Richard I. "Dimensions of State Politics, Economics, and Public Policy." *The American Political Science Review* 63(September 1969):867–879.
Sharp, Ansel M. "The Behavior of Selected State and Local Government Fiscal Variables during the Phases of the Cycles 1949–61." In *Proceedings of the Fifty-Eighth Annual Conference,* ed. Walter Kress. Harrisburg, Pennsylvania: National Tax Association, 1965.
Shonfield, Andrew. *Modern Capitalism: The Changing Balance of Public and Private Power.* London: Oxford University Press, 1965.
Simon, Herbert A. *The Sciences of the Artificial.* Cambridge: The MIT Press, 1969.
———. *Administrative Behavior.* New York: The Free Press, 1965.
Smith, Warren L., and Culbertson, John M. *Public Finance and Stabilization Policy.* New York: Elsevier, 1974.
Starbatty, Joachim. *Stabilitätspolitik in der freiheitlich-sozialstaatlichen Demokratie.* Baden-Baden: Nomos, 1977.
Steinbrunner, John. *The Cybernetic Theory of Decision.* Princeton, N.J.: Princeton University Press, 1974.
Sturm, Friedrich. "Die Finanzverantwortung von Bund, Ländern und Gemeinden bei der Erfüllung staatlicher Aufgaben." *Die Oeffentliche Verwaltung,* 68(1971):466.
Thomas, Norman. "Political Science and the Study of Economic Stabilization." *Policy Studies Journal* 4, no. 1 (Autumn 1975).
Thompson, James. *Organizations in Action.* New York: McGraw-Hill, 1967.
Trimm, Herbert. "Gemeindefinanzpolitik in den Wachstumszyklen." *Finanzarchiv,* Band 28 (1969):442 ff.
Tufte, Edward. *Political Control of the Economy.* Princeton, N.J.: Princeton University Press, 1978.

Vesper, Dieter. "Die Personalausgaben der Gebietskörperschaften von 1961–72." *Vierteljahresheft,* vol. 2. West Berlin: Deutsches Institut für Wirtschaftsforschung, 1975.

———. "Vergleich der Ergebnisse des Neutralhaushalts mit anderen Konzepten." West Berlin: Deutsches Institut für Wirtschaftsforschung, Winter, 1975.

———. "Die mittelfristige Finanzplanung bei Bund und Ländern." *Vierteljahresheft.* West Berlin: Deutsches Institut für Wirtschaftsforschung, January 1974.

———. "Vortrag über Stabilitätspolitik." West Berlin: Deutsches Institut für Wirtscháftsforschung, 1974.

Vorstand der SPD. "Zweiter Entwürfines okonomisch-politischen Orientierungsrahmen für die Jahre 1975–85." Hamburg: Auerdruck, 1975.

Wahl, Rainer. "Die politische Planung in den Reformüberlegungen der Bundesregierung." *Die Oeffentliche Verwaltung* (January 1971).

Wildavsky, Aaron. *The Politics of the Budgetary Process.* Boston: Little, Brown and Co., 1964.

———. "The Self-Evaluating Organization," *Public Administration Review* (September-October 1972).

———. *Budgeting: A Comparative Theory of Budgetary Processes.* Boston: Little, Brown and Co., 1975.

———. *Speaking Truth to Power: The Art and Craft of Policy Analysis.* Boston: Little, Brown and Co., 1979.

Zentrale Datenstelle der Landesfinanzminister. "Mittelfristige Entwicklung der Finanzhilfen des Bundes an die Länder (1974–79)." 4 November 1975.

———. "Finanzhilfen des Bundes an die Länder (1970–75)." 21 August 1975.

Zimmerman, Horst, and Henke, Klaus-Dirk. "Stellungnahme zu dem Gutachten Untersuchung zur Mehrjährigen Finanzplanung des Bundes." Bonn: Projektgruppe beim Bundesministerium des Innern, 1971.

Zunker, Albrecht. *Finanzplanung und Bundeshaushalt: Zur Koordinierung und Kontrolle Durch den Bundesfinanzminister.* Frankfurt am Main: Alfred Metzner Verlag, 1972.

Index

Adenauer, Konrad: fiscal policy, 19
Allensbach Institute, 19
Anticyclical reserves, 20, 69, 98, 127, 171–174, 197; centerpiece of policy, 20, 130–131
Antirecession programs, 20, 24, 65, 66, 68, 69, 168; and anticyclical reserves, 130–131; and budget control, 168; demand and supply of, 78–79; determining the size of, 71–72; distribution of funds, 172–175; effect on financial aid, 150–152; objectives and content, 168–170; and allocation issues, 175–177; on state level, 94–95; in United States, 168
Apel, Hans, 31, 71, 74, 151, 157
Axelrod, Robert, 191

Baden-Württemberg, 85, 91, 130–140, 159, 173
Basic Law, 18, 21, 130, 167, 175
Bavaria, 115, 136–140, 159, 174
Brandt, Willy, 28
Bremen, 91, 174
Budget guidelines. See Budgeting
Budget uncontrollability. See Budgeting
Budgeting: balanced budget, 92–93; conflict, 51–57, 66–68; conflicting criteria, 40–43, 104–105, 149–152, 167, 183–187; contingency budgets, 63–64, 93; financial criteria, 56–57, 73, 94–95; judgment in antirecession programs, 69–71; and planning, 61, 91–92; execution of, 61–63; rationality in, 42–43; on state level, 90–92. See also Financial planning; Incremental budgeting
Bundesbank, 20, 48, 69, 76, 94, 98, 171, 173
Bundesrat, 20, 30, 69, 85, 129, 171, 173
Bundestag, 27, 30, 48, 68, 69, 73, 118, 170
Bureaucracy: autonomy versus leadership, 146–147; cabinet, 31, 74, 110, 112, 114, 158, 196; civil servants, 32; dispersion of power in, 31; generalists versus promotors, 153–154; loose coupling, 54–57, 190–191; policy-administration-dichotomy, 32–33, 87–88, 98–99; sections of, 32; tradeoff between inflation and recession, 76–77
Business-Cycle Council, 21, 170–171

Caiden, Naomi, 77–78
Christian Democratic Union, 25–28, 30, 71, 117–118, 119, 137–138, 171, 173, 177
Christian Social Union (CSU), 25, 137
Contingency budgets. See Antirecession programs; Budgeting
Council of Economic Experts, 19, 43
Cowart, Andrew T., 5
Cyert, Richard M., 77

Debt policy, 53–54; and debt ceilings 129–130; on state level, 88–89, 90–91, 97, 118–119
Deficit spending, 1, 19, 54, 92; in the 1960s, 19; Keynes, 23; on the state level, 97; surprise, 51
Diesing, Paul, 42

East Germany. See German Democratic Republic
Econometric Models. See Forecasting
Economic management: automatic stabilizers, 62, 74–75, 122; GNP growth, 53; conflict with budgeting, 41, 51–57, 66–68, 116, 184–187, 187–194; and debt policy, 53–54; difficulty of, 22; discretionary measures and, 62–63, 67, 75, 93–95, 122, 146–147; and federalism, 104–108, 119; forecasting, 45–50; glimmer of, 1; as level problem, 166; and macro-budget, 103–105, 106, 110–111; and public finance, 165–166, 183; stabilization policy, 67–68; and state budgeting, 83–102; state differences,

211

136–140, 158–161; structural deficiencies, 23, 70; and time lag, 70–71, 128. *See also* Fiscal policy; Macroeconomic policy
Economic stabilization. *See* Fiscal policy
Economics Ministry. *See* Federal Economics Ministry
Economy program, 150–151, 155
Electoral competition. *See* Partisanship
Erhard, Ludwig, 17, 25
Etzel, Fritz, 18
European Community (EC), 108, 113, 120–121, 151
Expenditure policy, 62–63, 66–68; accommodation with economic management, 187–191; conflict with macropolicy, 184–187; relation with economic management, 63–64; on state level, 120–121
Expert Commission for the Realignment of the Federal States, 135

Federal Constitutional Court, 175
Federal Economics Ministry, 33–35, 40, 44, 46–47, 49, 50, 52, 56, 65, 69, 71–72, 74, 76, 83
Federal Finance Ministry, 31–32, 33, 40, 43–44, 46–47, 52, 55–56, 65, 67, 69, 71–72, 76, 90, 114, 167, 171
Federal Ministry of Science and Technology, 23
Federal Transportation Ministry, 67
Federation of German Industry, 25
Federalism: centralization proposal over, 129; cooperative, 85; and economic management, 104–105, 117–118; effects of scarcity on, 113–114; federal political relations, 28–31; intergovernmental competition and, 107–109; intergovernmental lobby, 87–88; theories of public finance and, 104–106, 135–136, 165–166; and theory of public goods, 103–108, 152–153, 194–197; turbulence in, 105, 121–122, 194–197
Finance Ministry. *See* Federal Finance Ministry

Finance Planning Council, 21, 108–119, 153; and anticyclical reserves, 130; and antirecession programs, 170–171, 173; multiyear budget plans of, 21; and partisanship, 118–119; working group for expenditure development of, 107, 109, 111–112
Finance reform, 19–22, 27, 30, 85, 109–110, 127, 129, 147–148, 167
Financial aid, 20, 30, 127, 150–152, 167, 175, 177
Financial planning, 39–40, 63; conflict with economic management, 116–117; for contingencies, 63–64; financial criteria used in, 73–75; and flexibility, 73–74; intergovernmental budget guidelines under, 109–110, 114, 118, 120–121, 153; in joint tasks, 154. *See also* Budgeting
Fiscal policy, 3; definition of, 3; domain of applicability, 4; and German political economy, 15–38; programs, demand, and supply of, 78–79. *See also* Economic management; Macroeconomic policy
Forecasting: econometric models, 45–49, 190; effect of federalism, 113, 115–119; fine-tuning, 39, 62; goal projection, 39, 48–51, 56, 61, 90, 110, 111, 112, 119, 190; inaccuracy of, 49–50, 64–65, 90–91; interministerial working group on macroeconomic forecasts, 35; *Kreislauf* system, 46–47, 54; loose coupling and, 54–57, 190–191; National Accounts Model, 46–47, 190, 198. *See also* Macroeconomic policy; Economic management
Free Democratic Party, 25, 28, 71, 76, 118
Friedman, Milton, 3
Friedrichs, Hans, 31, 71

Galbraith, John Kenneth, 147
Garfinkel, Harold, 42
Gensher, Hans Dietrich, 31
German Democratic Republic, 18, 27

Index

German Economic Research Institute, West Berlin, 19, 46
Goal Projection. *See* Forecasting
Godesberger Program, 27
Godwin, Kenneth R., 146
Grants in aid, 29; anticyclical nature of, 130–131, 133–135; antirecession grants, 128; categorical grants, 28, 148; coercive power of, 128; and economic management, 166–167; effect on local public investment, 139–140; effect on service delivery, 128, 132–133; Financial Equalization Law, 29; follow-on costs of, 154–155; stabilization versus program purposes of, 147–152; state differences and, 136–140, 158–161; and state policy, 131–134. *See also* Federalism

Haas, Ernst B., 121
Hesse, 136–140, 159, 174
Hibbs, Douglas A., Jr., 5
Hirschman, Albert O., 196
Hitler, Adolf, 17

IFO Institute, Munich, 19, 46
Incremental budgeting: budget control, 94–95, 153, 167–168; budget cycle, 35–37, 66, 73–74; cuts, 95–96; and goal projection, 50–51, 198. *See also* Budgeting; Expenditure policy
Inflation: and antirecession programs, 70–71; and bureaucratic politics, 76–77; current economic controversy, 22–25; in German tradition, 15–16; in Keynesian theory, 3–5; in personnel costs, 85; as simplifying norm, 193
Institute of World Economics, Kiel, 19

Joint tasks, 20; planning commissions, 131, 148, 153–155, 170

Kennedy, John F., 146, 158
Keynes, John Maynard, 3
Keynesian theory: deficiencies of, 3; stagflation and, 23; theory of the state, 4; use in West Germany, 18–19, 72. *See also* Fiscal policy

Kiesinger, Kurt, 25
Kissinger, Henry, 147
Kreislauf system. *See* Forecasting

Labor unions, 87, 114–115
Lambsdorf, Otto Graf, 32
Landau, Martin, 8, 98, 191
Long, Norton E., 1
Loose coupling. *See* Political decision making
Low-cost housing program, 132–134, 147
Lower Saxony, 91, 136–140, 159, 174

Macroeconomic policy, 9, 43–44, 45, 149–150; antirecession programs for, 69–71; budget policy and, 44; conflict with budgeting, 66–68, 183–194; full employment surplus budget, 43, 93; neutral budget, 44, 92–93; nominal growth in GNP, 51–54; role of ambiguity in, 75, 96–97
Malabre, Alfred L., 61
March, James G., 77
Matthöffer, Hans, 32
Metcalfe, Les, 105
Monetary policy, 15–16, 24, 122, 179–180; international monetary system, 24; trade surplus, 25

National Accounts Model. *See* Forecasting
National Municipal Associations, 109, 157, 175
Nixon, Richard M., 147
North Rhine-Westphalia, 18, 68, 91, 115, 135, 136–140, 158–160, 174

Oates, Wallace E., 166

Partisanship: antirecession programs, 71–72; between parties, 25–26; effect on economic policy, 27–28; and electoral competition, 5; intergovernmental relations and, 117–118
Perversity hypothesis. *See* Federalism; Grants in aid

Political costs and benefits, 5, 62,
    145–146, 158–160, 177–178,
    197–200. *See also* Political decision
    making
Political decision making, 42; ambiguity
    and 7, 9, 48–50, 97, 198; and analysis, 197–200; coalition and power in,
    7; definition of, 6; econometric
    models and, 45–48; effects of complexity on, 6, 41; feasibility of, 8; interaction in, 42–43;
    intergovernmental, 116–120; loose
    coupling and, 54–56; and macroeconomic policy, 8–10; sequential approach to, 7, 41, 72; simplifying
    norms of, 6, 97, 169–170, 192–193;
    support and agreement in, 7,
    117–118; values and, 7
Political economy: analysis and politics,
    197–200; conservative philosophy of,
    17–18; corporatist, 15–16, 18; and
    federalism, 28–30, 103–126; in German bureaucracy, 31–37; and partisanship, 25–27; separating policy and
    administration, 17
Projections. *See* Forecasting
Public finance. *See* Federalism; Fiscal
    policy

Quade, E.S., 42

Redevelopment Bank, 23
Reissert, Bernd, 148
Rhineland-Palatinate, 136–140, 154, 156,
    174
Rourke, Francis E., 147

Saarland, 91, 135, 136–140, 158–159,
    174
Sapolsky, Harvey M., 74, 184, 188
Schäffer, Fritz, 17
Scharpf, Fritz, 152, 166–167, 172, 177
Shepard, Bruce W., 146
Schleswig-Holstein, 115, 136–140, 159,
    174
Schiller, Karl, 27
Schmidt, Helmut, 28, 31
Shonfield, Andrew, 18

Simon, Herbert A., 8
Social Market Doctrine, 17
Socialist Party, 25–28, 30, 34, 71, 76,
    118, 137–138, 171, 173, 177
Stability and Growth Law (8 June 1967)
    20, 91, 93, 112, 127
Stabilization Reserve Fund. *See* Anticyclical reserves
Stagflation, 1, 61; agreement, 72; economic theory and, 22–23; effect on
    service delivery, 128; grew worse,
    15–16; onslaught of, 4. *See also* Fiscal policy; Unemployment
State budgeting, 83–102; cuts in, 95; and
    macrobudget, 89–91; mandatory character of, 85–88; personnel costs of,
    85–86. *See also* Federalism; Grants in
    aid
Strauss, Franz Joseph, 118

Tax distribution, 30, 31, 107–108, 114,
    133, 148–149, 151–152, 157
Tax estimate committee, 35, 40; and estimated tax yield, 47, 56, 90, 116, 151
Tax Reform Bill (1974), 26, 72–73
Thompson, James D., 8, 191
Transportation Ministry. *See* Federal
    Transportation Ministry
Tuden, Arthur, 8, 191
Tufte, Edward R., 5

Unemployment, 70, 158–160; and anticyclical reserves, 20; and antirecession
    programs, 168–170; in the 1970s,
    15–16; and partisanship, 25–27;
    structural or business-cycle caused,
    22–24; as simplifying norm, 192. *See
    also* Antirecession programs; Fiscal
    policy; Stagflation
Uncertainty, 2, 74–80; agreement under,
    72–73, 74; avoidance of, 78,
    194–195; diagnostic, 75–76; of macroeconomics, 2; measurement of, 77;
    political, 40; political and cognitive,
    10; prediction inaccuracy under, 49,
    64–65, 74; resolving, 62; shifting organizational strategies under,
    156–157, 194–195

Wehner, Herbert, 32
Wildavsky, Aaron B., 43, 77, 195

Young Socialist Movement, 28

About the Author

Jack H. Knott is an assistant professor of political science at Michigan State University. He received the M.A. from Johns Hopkins University in 1971 and the Ph.D. from the University of California, Berkeley, in 1977. His publications include *A Zero-Based Look at Zero-Base Budgeting* (1980), with Thomas Hammond; "If Dissemination is the Solution, What is the Problem?" (1980), with Aaron Wildavsky, in *Knowledge: Creation, Utilization, Dissemination;* and "Jimmy Carter's Theory of Governing" (1977), with Aaron Wildavsky, in *The Wilson Quarterly*.

LIBRARY OF DAVIDSON COLLEGE